Carolyn Latteier

Breasts
The Women's Perspective on an American Obsession

*Pre-publication
REVIEWS,
COMMENTARIES,
EVALUATIONS . . .*

More pre-publication
REVIEWS, COMMENTARIES, EVALUATIONS . . .

"**W**ritten with a fine mix of intelligence, candor, and wry humor, this book has given me a whole new perspective on breasts. Latteier's sensitive antennae for what is important, fascinating, and just plain instructive about these visible signs of the feminine psyche have steered her through a complex and varied set of concerns, from adolescent anxieties about blooming breast buds to old wives' tales describing the magical properties of breast milk. Among subjects explored are the mythology and iconography of breasts; theories of why and how they evolved; men's and women's feelings about them; personal and cultural attitudes toward breastfeeding; historical and contemporary efforts to cover or uncover the breast or to alter its shape and size; breast sexuality; breast politics and activism; and the harm done by cultural stereotypes, exploitation, and what Latteier refers to as the Great American Breast Fetish.

I suspect that people with mammaries and those without will delight equally in this original, readable, and thought-provoking work."

Janet O. Dallett, PhD
Psychologist and Jungian Analyst;
Author, *When the Spirits Come Back* and *Saturday's Child: Encounters with the Dark Gods*

"**C**arolyn Latteier combines personal experiences with scholarly evidence to produce an insightful explanation for our . obsession with breasts. In an accessible, easy-to-read book, she weaves together the most recent research from fields as diverse as human evolution, fashion history, child development, and sexology to explore women's love/hate relationships with their breasts. Eating disorders, breast implants, and breastfeeding all have their place in a story that fascinates, yet reminds us how far we are from a healthy acceptance of our bodies and bodily processes."

Penny Van Esterik, PhD
Professor of Anthropology,
York University, Toronto,
Ontario, Canada

"**R**eading this fast-paced book was like watching my own development—not only my physical 'budding,' but the conversations I have had with my self and the flow of awareness I experienced entering, and living in, the outside breast-world. This book makes me feel more normal, in fact, relieved and filled with wonder. It explains and answers questions I had not formed but recognized as if they had always been present.

More pre-publication
REVIEWS, COMMENTARIES, EVALUATIONS . . .

Ms. Latteier presents her material with clarity and a thoroughness that makes sense of non-sense. She braces the reader with background information, giving a clear panorama of the landscape. With alacrity, the author picks through differing thoughts, philosophies, and actions and then paints a portrait of reality. Wit and compassion are the reader's constant companions while wandering through this grand forest of scintillating material."

Jacqueline Rickard
Family Mediator,
Jerome, AZ

"This courageous, well-researched, and vividly written book takes a sweeping look at the tragic vicissitudes of breasts in a masculine culture. Latteier's work takes one more bold step toward reclaiming woman's body, her honor, her beauty, and her necessary power."

Janine Canan, MD
Psychiatrist and Author,
She Rises Like the Sun:
Invocations of the Goddess
by Contemporary American
Women Poets

The Haworth Press, Inc.

Breasts

The Women's Perspective on an American Obsession

HAWORTH Innovations in Feminist Studies
Esther Rothblum, PhD and Ellen Cole, PhD
Senior Co-Editors

Breasts
The Women's Perspective on an American Obsession

Carolyn Latteier

The Haworth Press
New York • London

The Haworth Press, Inc., 10 Alice Street, Binghamton, NY 13904-1580

Cover design by Marylouise E. Doyle.

Library of Congress Cataloging-in-Publication Data

Latteier, Carolyn.
    Breasts : the women's perspective on an American obsession / Carolyn Latteier.
        p.   cm.
    Includes bibliographical references and index.
    ISBN 0-7890-0422-4 (alk. paper).
    1. Breast—Social aspects. 2. Body image in women. 3. Women—Psychology. 4. Self-esteem in women. I. Title.
GT498.B47L37   1998
391.6—dc21
                                        98-9556
                                        CIP

CONTENTS

ABOUT THE AUTHOR

Carolyn Latteier, MA, is a freelance journalist and recent graduate of Washington State University, where she obtained her degree in American Studies. Specializing in writing articles on health and psychology, her work has been published in such newspapers as the *Los Angeles Times,* the *Portland Oregonian,* and the magazine *Seattle.* For her work, Latteier has won five awards from the Western Washington Society of Professional Journalists for excellence in journalism. Latteier has shown her slide presentation, "The Social Construction of Breasts," to a number of audiences including the 1996 Lewis and Clark College Gender Studies Conference.

Preface

One night several years ago I had this dream:

I have discovered that women have long feelers growing out of their nipples. They use the feelers to test food. I am really happy about this extra function of breasts. I decide I will have to grow my feelers out. I had previously clipped them for cosmetic reasons.

It strikes me that this dream, with its strange and beautiful images of tentacled bosoms, is not just about breasts. It hints at people's capacity to test and verify the quality of things, to find out what might be nurturing or poisonous in the world around them. It presents an image of women in action, using their abilities to know and understand rather than keeping them clipped for cosmetic reasons. And it signals me that it is time to stop pruning back my own rhizomes and horizons.

In taking on this research about breasts and writing this book, I have let my feelers grow out, and it has, indeed, not always seemed very cosmetic. Last year, I presented a slide show called "The Social Construction of Breasts" to my colleagues in the American Studies Department at Washington State University. A number of my friends had graciously agreed to let me photograph their breasts, and for my presentation, I had added these to images from art, advertising, and soft-core pornography. The night before the show, I broke into a cold sweat. I was, I realized, going to be projecting large-screen images of "dirty pictures" in front of my entire department. That night I did not sleep well.

Despite my anxieties, my presentation was warmly received. But this feeling of working on a slightly off-color subject has continued to dog me. When I tell people what I am writing about, I have grown accustomed to seeing a peculiar ripple cross their faces. Sometimes people's eyes dart quickly to my chest and then away.

These ricocheting eye movements make me nervous. Nonetheless, there are reasons to take a good look at the things we usually turn away from—things that exist in the realm of what is "not very nice." The truth is, the "not very nice" is hopelessly interwoven with the "nice," and together the two form a fuller picture of who and what we are. People giggle, get embarrassed, and/or become overwhelmed by cleavage because breasts are the object of a cultural obsession. Examining our obsessions can be both enlightening and therapeutic. Here, it is not a question of gender. Both men and women are involved in fascinations and anxieties about breasts. Both sexes need to test the food our culture offers; both need to let their feelers grow.

Acknowledgments

I wish, first of all, to acknowledge the contribution of the women and men who shared their feelings and experiences openly and thoughtfully during interviews for this book. My work would not have been possible without their contributions.

I would also like to express my gratitude to the University of Washington, the Washington State, the Port Townsend, and the Jefferson County Libraries and their staffs. The research for this book required many specialized and obscure books, and the staffs of those libraries, especially Shery Hart, went all out to help me find them.

Thanks to Phyl Speser, Kathy Constantine, Liz Baldwin, and Gillian Bently, who read chapters and provided valuable criticism. Special thanks to my daughter, Pearl Latteier, for thorough, thoughtful readings and generous encouragement.

My agent, John Ware, was a good critic and a great champion of this project. In addition, warm encouragement from my father and mother, Eugene Klug and Clara Klug, my sister, Stephanie Rohloff, and my son, Amos Latteier, helped sustain my efforts.

It is difficult to imagine working without the writer's group: Janet Dallet, David Matthieson, Alex Fowler, Jacqueline Rickard, Marge Koch-Critichfield, and George Maynard, whose useful comments helped shape this book.

Finally, I wish to thank my husband, Richard Wojt, for enthusiastically supporting me in everything interesting and creative I have ever wanted to do.

PART ONE:
IMAGE AND ICON

Chapter 1

Love and Loathing

Sometimes I stand looking at my breasts in the mirror and I think: "Not bad. Not too saggy." They are more or less of equal size (the left one is slightly larger). They are small and round and the nipples and areolas are rosy brown. But then I look closer and think: "Not so good." There are tiny, jagged stretch marks on the upper hemispheres. The texture has gone soft, and the skin looks as if it has been stretched and not completely snapped back. These breasts are not going to make anybody say, "Wow!"

I have been looking at my breasts for a long time. I started watching as I was approaching puberty, and there was really nothing to see. While other girls were bursting out all over, my chest remained stubbornly quiescent. My breasts were still no more than little bumps when I reached eighth grade, and it had become absolutely unbearable not to be wearing a brassiere in the gym class locker room. After a good deal of private agonizing, I went to my mother. In a flood of tears, I begged her to get me a bra and, I added, better make it a padded one. I remember dreaming one night that I stood looking in my mother's bedroom mirror and, to my deep satisfaction, my breasts grew large, the way flowers bloom in a time-lapse film.

In my mid-twenties, I became pregnant and that dream more or less came true. I watched my breasts grow and grow and finally start to look like I had always thought they were supposed to. Then one morning I woke up and saw blue-lined stretch marks all over them. When the baby arrived, my breasts grew big as bowling balls and hard as rocks, and milk came out of them.

During my thirties and forties, my breasts went through monthly cycles, reaching a glamorous, firm fullness when my estrogen levels were cresting. "Boy, are they healthy-looking," my husband would say just before my period arrived, and then they shrank back down to normal. Since I have given up caffeine, they no longer swell and shrink, but I imagine they will keep on changing. If I live long enough, I will probably end up as an elderly woman with soft dugs hanging benignly against my chest.

It has taken me a long time to achieve this degree of acceptance of my breasts. There were many years when I despaired at the sight of my shirt lying practically flat against my chest. I would spend time searching for fluffy blouses to suggest there was something more underneath there. My discomfort with small breasts was more than just cosmetic. I felt the lack as a poverty of being, as if my very nature were somehow stark and bony. A hollow chest equaled a hollow heart. I was so used to this feeling that it puzzled me after I gave birth to my first child and began walking around in public with those big, lactating breasts on my same old skinny body. Suddenly, and unexpectedly, I was turning heads on the street. Later, when I saw my first copy of *Playboy,* I experienced a shock of recognition. My God, I thought, these women all look like nursing mothers.

Over the years, it was always those changeable breasts in the mirror—the little nubs with their pale, swollen nipples or the premenstrual pears and their deflated postmenstrual sisters or the swollen pregnant breasts with their dark nipples and blue veins lying on my swollen pregnant belly. All the time it was as if I could see them from two different perspectives. Personally, I was fascinated with the physical reality of each new incarnation. But the social me felt a critical, judgmental distress that they seldom looked much like I knew they should.

It was not hard to figure out what breasts were supposed to look like, though at first my ideas were pretty vague. I grew up in the late 1950s, the era of "mammary madness."[1] Breasts were practically the definition of femininity during those years. They had to, above all, be big. Brassieres of that era were highly engineered structures, with two conical cups stitched in precise spirals and carefully labeled from small to large: A, B, C, and D. The goal was to get as deep into the alphabet as possible. Size was everything. If you look at magazine ads or movies from that time, women have huge, bulky shapes projecting from their chests like the big fenders or hood ornaments on cars. This look could be faked, and often was, because the popular media were not yet plastering images of naked breasts everywhere you looked. Breasts were still mysterious masses. In the slang of the day, breasts were called "the shelf. "

I wish I had known, and I wish women today were aware that what seems like natural, universal beauty is really quite relative and transitory. Non-Western cultures have far different ideas of what a breast should be, if they care at all. Clellan Ford and Frank Beach, in *Patterns of Sexual Behavior* (1951), the only broad-scale cross-cultural survey of sexuality, came to the conclusion that the most universally admired feminine trait is plumpness. Less than a quarter of the tribal cultures surveyed, nine in all, preferred big breasts.

Just to put big breasts in perspective, please note that men in several cultures were turned on specifically by long and pendulous breasts. This preference is not at all unique in preliterate cultures. Margaret Mead claimed that women in New Guinea try to stretch their breasts to achieve this look.[2] Young women are annoyed with their perky breasts and long for the mature, plentiful look of the mother. The breast should be long enough so that it can be thrown over the shoulder to nurse the baby riding behind. Two cultures in the survey, the Manus, a tribe of Southwest Pacific islanders and the African Masai, shared our taste for the upright, hemispherical breasts.

In our own Western culture, even in recent history, the ideal breast has altered its form. From the nearly flat-chested look of the 1920s, the style in breasts slowly ballooned to the mammoth mammaries of the 1950s and 1960s, reached its zenith in the late 1960s, and then gradually leveled off. In the 1920s, the bust measurements of Miss America contestants averaged thirty-two inches. These vital statistics rose to thirty-five inches in the 1940s, and through the two decades following 1950, stayed at what was considered a "perfect thirty-six." Miss America contestants are supposed to represent the ideal nice girl next door. Meanwhile, incarnating the fantasy sex object, enter *Playboy* magazine in 1953 with its Playmate of the Month. The playmate's bust measurements usually ran a couple of inches bigger than Miss America contestants', but they also have gradually declined since 1960 (except for a quick, sharp second peak in the early 1970s).[3]

In the last twenty years, bulging breasts have given way to a smaller, more upright model, though the ongoing demand for silicone breast implants makes it clear that smaller does not mean less important.

Today media imagery communicates quite clearly that the best breast—the breast as it should be—is the adolescent breast. It is a firm, milky white globe. The nipple is smooth, not the lumpy, bumpy nipple of women who have nursed a baby or outlived their youth.

I believe that many women are aware that this image is a fantasy and that many of them intellectually reject it. They know better, but they cannot shake it off. Despite their disclaimers, at the moment of truth, when they look in the mirror at their naked breasts, they perceive that what they have, what they are, is not good enough. Their breasts are too long and pendulous or too flat or too saggy. The nipples are too big or too small or the wrong color. The two breasts are different sizes or different shapes. The reality is that breasts vary as widely as faces. But we see faces every day, and we know that. We do not see breasts, except mostly clothed and confined in a brassiere. It is every woman's secret that hers are different.

Maria is a dance instructor in her forties. In ordinary situations—driving a car or picking out a head of lettuce in the grocery store—she looks like someone's slightly ethnic-looking young aunt. But when she teaches in her leotards, she has the springy, well-toned sensuality of a healthy animal. She seems exceptionally relaxed about her body. I may be one of the few people who knows that she does not like her breasts. "I don't like the shape they are," she said. "They never stood up like I thought they were supposed to when you are young. I got old lady breasts right away. I didn't have those perfectly shaped cones. They were long and hung down. From the beginning, I was just self-conscious about my breasts. I knew from being in the locker room that other women had better breasts: round, pink-nippled ones were better than long, pointed, brown-nippled ones. I knew, underneath it all, that these were inferior breasts. To this day I still harbor that prejudice."

In her early thirties, Maria's anxiety about her breasts was validated when she took a new lover, a young, blond man ten years her junior. "Daryl freaked out when he saw them the first time," she said. "He gasped. He was really honest about the fact that seeing them startled him. He had never seen breasts like these. He admitted they felt very wild and womanly, and once he said that, I felt better. But he always felt a little devoured by dark women, and his reaction to my breasts was the first indication of that."

Some women have moments like that in their lives, when their vague anxieties about their breasts are suddenly confirmed in a clear and unmistakable way. However, most of the learning we do about how we are perceived takes place on a much more subtle level. It is nearly impossible to be objective about how wonderful or terrible our breasts look to others. I know that because for the last ten years my husband has been telling me that my breasts are beautiful, and I am starting to believe him, even though I knew full well before I married him that they were really pretty mediocre-looking. To a large degree, we believe the messages we receive from others. Seldom do they arrive in a neat bouquet of compliments such as those my husband so kindly hands me. More often, you cannot even see them coming.

A 1977 study conducted by the Psychology Department of the University of Minnesota provides an eerie demonstration of how the process can work.[4] The subjects of their experiments were fifty-one male and fifty-one female undergraduate students, who were to engage in a telephone conversation with a student of the opposite sex, someone whom they had never met. All the students filled out a questionnaire about themselves to be given to the phone partner as conversational fodder. The experimenters took Polaroid pictures of the men, then gave them information packets about the other member of their dyad, including a photograph.

Meanwhile, in the other room, the experimenters told the women nothing about the photographs, nor did they take their pictures. The pictures the men had received were of entirely different women, images which had been carefully scored and rated by a panel of men. The "stimulus" photos consisted of four "attractive" women and four "unattractive" ones.

Now that the groundwork had been laid, the students chatted for ten minutes on the phone. The experimenters recorded the conversations on two separate tapes—one with the woman's voice only, another that isolated the voice of the man. In the few cases in which the man mentioned the photo, the conversations were immediately terminated and the dyad excluded from the study.

Not surprisingly, the initial impressions the men jotted down after they had seen the photo and before they had spoken with the woman reflected cultural stereotypes. The men with attractive photos thought their partners would be suave, humorous, and friendly. The men with unattractive photos anticipated their partners would be awkward and serious.

What is more disturbing is that when naive observers, people who were not in on the deception and had not seen any photos, listened to the tapes of the women's voices, they rated the ones whose partners perceived them as attractive to be more charming, warm, friendly, likable and, yes, attractive. In the course of the ten-minute conversation, these women, whatever their past experiences, began to believe they were what their conversational partner expected them to be.

This experiment points out how quickly we pick up subtle messages from others, no matter how irrelevant they may be to who we really are. A ten-minute conversation is probably not going to change anybody's life, but a thousand ten-minute conversations will. She may hardly be aware of it, but a woman readily absorbs other people's versions of her reality. She is vulnerable to what society at large thinks about her breasts. Unfortunately for women, society at large has deeply conflicting feelings about them.

On the surface, it would seem that Americans love breasts. It is hard to imagine viewing a contemporary movie without catching at least a flash of breast, if not full exposure. In print media, advertisements show page after page of plunging cleavage. Women's magazines periodically run articles about exercises to "improve" the breast. A great media flap occurred a few years ago when a new, highly engineered bra guaranteed to create cleavage where there had been none before appeared on the market. Our nation seems to be engaged in a festival of breasts. Our fascination with them is insatiable, and the images are everywhere. Unfortunately, within this visual delight, runs a vein of hostility.

Large-breasted women take the brunt of it. Julie, who is in her early twenties, has been hearing remarks about her breasts since she was twelve. "It happens all the time," Julie told me. "Recently I went out to dinner with this guy. We got out of the car and some guys were standing on the street. They said, 'Hey man, you got a nice chick with you. She is stacked.'" There is no doubt that Julie's melon-sized breasts attract male admirers. She has more dinner invitations than she can handle. But her large breasts also invite disrespect. There is an old teenagers' tale that petting causes breasts to grow. You can tell who has been fooling around by the size of her breasts. The catcallers on the street acted as though they believed this were true. Julie has big breasts, so she must be hypersexual.

Another large-breasted woman told me she has twice had strangers squeeze her breasts in public places. "The first time, a man just walked by and grabbed my breast. It happened so fast I hardly knew what he had done. The second time, I was waiting in the subway. Just as a train was coming by, a man came up and grabbed my breast, opened his coat, and flashed. I remember feeling angry. I immediately began screaming at him, 'You bastard.' I was trying to draw attention to him. He quickly shut his coat, got on the train, and disappeared."

The uninvited squeeze of a woman's breast is so common that we have a term for it—copping a feel. Apparently, men are constantly counting coups on women's breasts because about half the women I interviewed had been groped by strangers, friends, brothers, or fathers. Once I was in a group of women who were talking about this phenomenon, and those who had not been groped by a stranger expressed, half-jokingly, feelings of disappointment. Even in such a context, the imperative to be desirable still runs strong in women, and I can bear witness to that from my own experience.

One warm, spring day I strode along a city sidewalk feeling pretty in my favorite white blouse with its delicate scoop neck. The city bustled with fresh energy; people crowded the streets soaking up the sweet weather. Suddenly, two young men rode past me on bicycles. Before I realized what was happening, one of them reached out and swept his hand across my breasts in a hasty caress. "Nice ones," he trumpeted, before disappearing down the street. I was astonished. I was mad as hell. And I was also distinctly flattered that this brute thought my small, unspectacular breasts were "nice ones." Looking back, I realize I have felt ambivalent about breasts for a long time.

During my early teenage years, I was constantly exposed to admonitions against letting boys "take advantage" of me. No one had ever tried, but I heard and read about it so often it seemed there must be a real threat out there. I distinctly remember thinking that maybe it was a good thing that my breasts were not getting very big because this way I was completely safe. No one could possibly want to take advantage of me. I think the ambivalence I experienced is also society's ambivalence about breasts and, underneath that, about sexuality. Breasts are attractive, and yet there is something disreputable or dangerous about them.

The few sociological studies that have been done about breast size preference did not produce consistent results, but they did tend to agree on how breasts are interpreted.[5] Research shows that women with large breasts are typed as incompetent, immoral, immodest, and not very smart. "The more bosom, the less brain. That's the law of nature; that's why the poor miserable females are the way they are," says a character in Isabelle Allende's *The Infinite Plan*.[6] It is hard to miss the archetypes and stereotypes swimming like sharks below these waters. Woman is "the other" and somehow less than human. She is nature with all its unpredictable, untamed power. She is flesh with all its temptations. When she has large breasts, she is even more so. Surprisingly, the positive side of the archetype does not seem to appear in these studies. People do not describe large breasts as comforting or nurturing. Breasts have become so sexualized that people no longer think of them as motherly.

Small-breasted women, on the other hand, are seen as competent, intelligent, moral, polite, and modest. They tend to be stereotyped as tame and asexual or masculine. Their passions are supposedly neutralized, and thus they can cope in a world of masculine values.

These contemporary stereotypes have their roots buried deep in Western civilization's long tradition of devaluing the fleshy and the sexual. Socially and politically, this metaphysical malaise has played itself out on the bodies of women. Under a historically male-controlled power structure, the qualities of fleshy sexiness are projected onto women's bodies. Those fleshy objects must be ruled, regulated, and owned. In America today, women's bodies are owned, not in the old way of slavery and marital rights, but they are mastered by the demand that their bodies be attractive and by the cultural stereotypes that determine what those bodies should look like. Yet, when it comes to breasts, the territory is land-mined. If a woman has small breasts, she falls short of being desirable. If she has large breasts, she is treated like a slut.

Though human beings may not be as communally driven as bees or ants, we are herd animals. We experience a very private, personal sense of being alone, and yet, our realities interlock tightly with those of other people. We take in messages from others and plow them under to the deep layers of our selves. When one part of our bodies, such as our breasts, is subject to so much attention, it creates a disturbance in our personal subsoil. Breasts can no longer be part of our integrity—a functioning, feeling organ of our physical selves. They become, instead, icons in the social fabric. We become self-conscious about them, and they begin playing complex roles in our lives.

In 1986, sociologist Raymond L. Schmitt presented a paper at the annual meeting of the American Sociological Association on the subject of breast identities. Quoting Gregory Stone, he defined identity as something that "establishes *what* and *where* the person is in social terms."[7] Based on a sample of forty case histories of American women, he distinguished eight different breast identities. The identities involved age, health, motherhood, occupation, physical appearance, sexuality, womanhood, and what he calls deviance, but I would call rebellion. In a lifetime, women typically live out and experience more than one (and as many as eight) breast identities.

My friend Maya is a good example of someone whose small breasts are important to her identity as a tomboy and her rejection of grown-up womanhood. Maya is married to a professional man and has two children. At thirty-eight, she is youthful, athletic, and thin as a rail. She dresses comfortably in jeans and a shirt and never wears makeup or jewelry.

"I associate womanhood with voluptuous bodies," she told me. "I feel like I could never be a part of that. It's hard for me to put on a dress, though I am concerned about my appearance. In my mind—and I think my husband would agree—I resist being more feminine. It definitely ties to having small breasts. Breasts are the definer for me. I'm kind of curious about womanhood. But I feel like I've always stayed on the other side of the fence. I keep thinking about this frau and fraulein thing. I don't like the idea of being a frau. I think it probably has more to do with breasts than anything else. If I had a voluptuous body, would I have been different? Maybe. I've found my little comfort zone in how I am and how I define myself." Maya has had other breast identities. At the time her children were babies, she strongly identified herself as a breast-feeding mother. For now, her most important breast identity is as someone who is separated from socially recognized womanhood and who prefers it that way—a fraulein, not a frau.

Schmitt (1986) found the most frequent breast identities were related to physical appearance and sexuality. Sometimes it is difficult to make a clear distinction between the two. For the large-breasted woman, constantly greeted by, "Hey, baby, you got nice tits," sexuality and appearance slide together. In other cases, they can be quite distinct. My daughter told me about attending the birthday party of a lesbian acquaintance. When the woman's friends brought out her birthday cake, it consisted of two enormous, white mounds with an icing inscription that read, "Happy Birthday to a Real Breast Woman."

"In what way was she a breast woman?" I asked my daughter.

"I don't know," she said. "I was afraid to ask." Consequently, I don't know either, but it seems likely that hers must have been a sexual breast identity, clearly recognized and celebrated among her social group.

Sometimes two different breast identities come together and reinforce each other, and that was the case for me when I was breast-feeding. My primary breast identity at that time was as a mother, but a rebellious or political breast identity came along for the ride. I made a big deal about breast-feeding. You would never see me hiding in a corner with a baby blanket discreetly draped over my cleavage. I breastfed openly, brazenly, and wherever I happened to be. I breastfed each baby for a year, which was, at that time, longer than anybody I knew and which provoked friends to ask, didn't I think I was carrying this a little far? I was an in-your-face breast-feeder, and I enjoyed every minute of it.

Sometimes, however, breast identities eat away at one another. Leah was always proud of her breasts. They are firm, medium-sized, and pink nippled. When she was in her late forties, suspicious calcifications were discovered on a mammogram and an immediate biopsy recommended. In a matter of minutes, she was living a new, frightening breast identity. She had the biopsy, with negative results, much to her relief. But it left her with a little less breast and what she considers an ugly scar. Now she feels wounded in the breast and haunted by the possibility of breast cancer.

Schmitt (1986) found that many of the breast identities contain a built-in ambivalence. For instance, a woman might be proud of her beautiful breasts but nervous that the status they give her is vulnerable to aging or disease. A woman might find it flattering or convenient that her breasts attract sexual attention, yet be distressed that she is categorized as fair game for rude comments. A woman might be glad her prominent breasts make her more employable but upset that they attract unwanted attention. These unresolved ambivalences, Schmitt pointed out, form a divided self. Breast identities are soaked in values absorbed from the media and from other people—friends, family, employers, lovers, and complete strangers. Psychologically, a woman's breasts become split off from her personal being. Emotionally, they belong more to other people than to herself.

In 1986, the psychiatric journal *Psychosomatics* published a brief article about a woman who acted out this split in a disturbingly graphic way.[8] The subject of the article, a thirty-one-year-old pregnant woman, amputated her own right breast. Her parents discovered her shortly afterward, lying naked in her bloody bed, nonchalantly smoking a cigarette. The daughter at first claimed an unknown intruder, a man, had attacked her. Soon she confessed she had done it herself, explaining, "It didn't seem like me." Though she was a long-time alcoholic, she had been sober at the time of the incident.

Still, her state of mind was far from ordinary. She could not remember undressing or cutting off her breast, nor could she say why she did it. Later, under sodium amobarbital, she remembered the details but not her feelings or motives. She had tried to initiate sex with her landlord just before the incident but did not link his rejection to her self-mutilation.

Though she grew up in a successful, upper middle-class family, her personal life had been a patchwork of misery. She had been raped, had abused alcohol and drugs, had undergone two abortions, suffered through the suicide of her boyfriend, and at the time of the incident, was pregnant, unmarried, and without a permanent partner.

She would not talk about her feelings, but psychological tests showed that she had intense conflicts with her mother and sister and negative feelings about sex. She had a deep mistrust of the idea of femininity and of herself. Family members said that she had always been unfavorably compared with her mother and sister.

Surgeons successfully reattached the breast, but the woman was unable to bond with her baby when it was born. The child was put in foster care. Eventually the woman committed suicide.

It is a sad story, and I feel sick to think how desperately miserable this woman must have been to do such a thing to herself. I do not know what could have brought her to this extreme—the final splitting off into a state of depersonalization that allowed her to complete the act. I do know that there are forces at work in our culture that can drive a wedge between a woman and her breasts. Sometimes the deeply disturbed, or the unusual, or the marginal people play out the cultural conflicts that most of us suffer in smaller ways.

At one time, I photographed some of my friends' and acquaintances' breasts for a slideshow I would present at an academic conference. The women's ages ranged from thirty to fifty-six. Some of them were shy about taking off their shirts or sweaters; others pulled them off with abandon. But they all had one thing in common: every woman I photographed apologized for her breasts. One said hers had been "wrecked" by nursing. Another regretted that her nipples did not stand out from their areolas. Several pointed to biopsy scars.

These minor apologies and disappointments have none of the bizarre drama of a psychotic woman who cuts off her breast, but they still represent a poignant reality of women's lives. Breasts are so private that they stay pale year-round, hidden from the sun. Yet breasts do not remain personal. They become what sociologists such as Raymond Schmitt call "the enacted body for the other" or "the they-self":[9] infused with social importance, myself and yet not mine.

When do I begin losing parts of myself? Some would say from the day I was born. But for me, at least, body consciousness remained dormant during childhood. My body troubled me when it fell down and got scabs on its knees, but otherwise, it was invisible. Body consciousness came about the same time as this girl's small nipples began to swell. Breast consciousness arrived, at adolescence, feeling like a small fall from grace.

Chapter 2

Initiation

For a growing girl, the advent of body consciousness often comes with the first appearance of breasts. Sometimes a girl's self-awareness arrives quite innocently and gradually. One woman described how, when she first noticed her nipples were puffing out and gently poked at them to understand what was happening, she discovered what felt like little square boxes hidden inside. She secretly monitored the little boxes as they grew into breasts. Other women remember feeling mortified when they suddenly realized they had full-grown women's breasts. It is not the breasts themselves, but the consciousness of them, that precipitates the crisis.

The body is no longer the me of childhood—that bundle of amorphous pleasures and pains, the me that loves to run and jump and eat ice cream. The body becomes my equipment, my display, and something I own, something for which I'm responsible. My body is a quantity to be judged by others who draw conclusions about me based on what they see. After a while, I come to agree with their conclusions. I learn to feel hostile toward or vain about my body, depending on what kind of attention it gets me. I may want to change it, to alter it. If I want to keep it in shape, I should stop eating ice cream.

Helen is a seventy-six-year-old woman with enormous breasts. She calls them her "watermelon boobs." She often jokes about them, pats them, and sticks her chest out in funny, suggestive ways. I have spoken with many women about their breasts, but she is the only one who ever flashed me during an interview. As we were talking, she suddenly pulled up her sweatshirt to reveal the breasts of a Paleolithic fertility goddess encased in an large white brassiere with lots of extra elastic tape she had sewn on to increase support.

She did this to show me how awful she thought they were and what she had to put up with every day of her life.

In the beginning, she liked them. "In high school, I was the first one in gym to get a bra," she said. "At first I was proud. I would stand up on the bench and lean over the lockers so the other girls could see my straps. I'd love to be that size again. I'd be just right if they stopped there."

But they did not stop. Soon she was a little girl with 36-D breasts, which she thought were ugly and embarrassing. She did her best to hide them. "I was just devastated," she said. "I could never walk around. I just sat on the bench." Big breasts were not fashionable in the thirties, when Helen was growing up, but they were considered sexy. A classmate of Helen's, the only other girl in school with equally large breasts, took advantage of their erotic appeal. "A gal built like me in school didn't wear a bra. She was one of the fast girls. We used to love to talk about her. 'Did you hear about Edith? She made out with one of the teachers in the gym.'"

Helen, however, was a good girl and did not want to be associated with that blatant sexuality. "Men saw my boobs and thought I was horny," she said. She did have sexual feelings, but they were not located in her breasts. First her husband and, after she was widowed, her boyfriends liked her breasts, but she did not derive any pleasure from breast attention. "If they're so big, you don't feel a thing," she said.

Interestingly enough, over the years Helen has developed a bawdy personality to go with her figure. She is a big, warm, loud, hard-drinking woman, like a flamboyant madam in an old-fashioned house of ill repute. In this persona, her "watermelon boobs" have become her trademark, kind of a standing joke. But she still does not like them. "It's isn't fun," she insisted. "It would have been fun at half the size."

Adolescence is a developmental crisis. The body is changing, and at the same time, social demands are altering radically. The physical transformation stimulates both a heightened awareness of and a confusion about the body. Although both sexes share tremendous self-consciousness, boys and girls react differently to these changes, partly because of their social roles. Despite recent changes in gender expectations, boys are still judged by what they can achieve, and girls, by their appearance. For instance, early-maturing boys tend to be stereotyped as powerful and early-maturing girls, as promiscuous.

Both sexes tend to be preoccupied with the earliest and what they see as the most important signs of maturation. In boys, genitals mature before the growth spurt. Girls tend to get their growth first, followed by breast budding. A study of how adolescents perceive their bodies began by photographing nude bodies of late adolescent boys and girls from several different positions.[1] A month later, the subjects were shown pictures of their own and similar bodies, unidentified and with faces cropped from the pictures. In general, girls took a longer time than boys to recognize their bodies, though it is not certain whether that was because they were more preoccupied with comparing bodies or because they have less knowledge of and perspective on their bodies. In general, girls were better at recognizing the whole body, while boys were better at recognizing parts. Boys were particularly quick at recognizing their own genitals, which are so often the focus of their attention during those years. Girls, on the other hand, were most preoccupied and best at recognizing their breasts. Everybody, of course, recognized the pictures of their own faces. But there were moments of confusion, trying to recognize a newly changed and changing body.

While the body changes, the adolescent's developmental task is to draw apart from the family and create an adult identity, to become a man or woman. Some psychoanalytic thinkers believe the earlier separation from the mother, the one that takes place around age two, tends to be less complete for boys than for girls.[2] Unlike boys, girls do not have to make a gender adjustment from their first identification with the mother. If that is true, then the job of wrenching away must be done at adolescence. Identification with and dependence on the mother must begin to give way.

It can be a harsh separation for both, a kind of changing of the guard. Since our culture puts a high value on young feminine beauty and perky breasts, on one level the mother is losing out to the daughter. Now the daughter is growing into her fresh, young beauty; now she has the breasts and often does not know what to do with them. Adolescent girls' feelings about their breasts encompass the gamut of emotions from pride and a sense of power to rebelliousness and fear. Some girls wear baggy clothes and coats everywhere they go or bind their chests in a vain attempt to slow breast growth. Other girls challenge their mother by flaunting their breasts. According to psychoanalyst Joseph Rheingold, in *Fear of Being a Woman* (1964), these behaviors are different ways of acting out the same conflict. The fundamental ambivalence in the antagonism is expressed by opposite tendencies—"the tendency to yield and to inhibit, and the tendency to defy and to exhibit."[3]

The psychiatrist Maj-Britt Rosenbaum (1979), working with "normal" middle-class girls, discovered that, of all their body parts, their hair provided the best and most harmless way of working through their desires for independence. Interviewing a group of thirty girls between the ages of eleven and seventeen, she found their preoccupations with the body to be intense. They underrated their attractiveness; even the girls she thought were most beautiful saw themselves as only about average. But of all their body parts, the girls felt most satisfied with their hair; two-thirds of them said it was their best feature. It is significant that hair is far from the bodily core. Rosenbaum writes that in styling their hair, girls were able to externalize their conflicts, to cut, color, curl, spike, bleach, shave, to exercise control. Here girls could successfully play out the ongoing struggle for separation from their parents. When it came to hair, they could clearly demonstrate: This body belongs to me.

With breasts, the story is far different. From a fairly early age, girls desire breasts. A study of female body image found that girls in sixth, seventh, and eighth grade show a marked preoccupation with the breast by drawing pictures of naked breasts or cleavage.[4] Young girls are fascinated with breasts because breasts symbolize the new identity they are trying to forge. One woman I interviewed had strong memories of that longing.

Maria desperately wanted breasts. "I couldn't get them soon enough," she said. "In fifth or sixth grade I had this little plaid dress with a trainer bra. Between being taken to school in a car and getting to class, I'd dash into the girl's room and stuff the bra with tissue. I went snooping through my mother's drawers and found falsies, those conical rubber things. I used to steal those from her. I knew everyone knew I didn't have breasts, but I still felt better with those things on.

"The big style was a one-piece bathing suit, which I would stuff. It was traumatic to go into the water, because the tissues would float out and the cups would become hollow.

"I have no idea why I wanted breasts. I wanted to look like a woman. It was the late 1950s and early 1960s. Elizabeth Taylor awed me with her breasts. She had those throaty breasts and she was about my mother's age. I did an emotional transfer to Elizabeth Taylor."

However much little girls yearn for them, when they arrive, breasts can be difficult to live with. Unlike hair, breasts are not distinct from the body's core, but snuggle close to the heart. Hair is dead to feeling; breasts are not. They get sore. They get excited. While hair can be brought under control, breasts cannot. They grow—or refuse to grow—at a speed that has nothing to do with the girl's wishes. Breasts take shape according to some invisible plan, and nipples, susceptible to every passing gust of wind, have a life of their own. Rosenbaum (1979) found that girls have difficulty incorporating breasts into their images of themselves; ". . . breasts are often disassociated from the rest of the body for quite some time, experienced as 'not-me,' as appendages that don't quite belong—yet."[5] They are new body parts, built on existing structures to be sure, but something new that wasn't there before.

That something commands a lot of attention. Breasts are public—visible. They exist "out there," as a sign, a password. They define and determine other people's perceptions of a girl's femininity. They express what kind of person she is without her will or consent.

It is interesting to compare the growth of breasts to the first crinkles of pubic hair. These are the earliest visible signs of puberty, and both developments occur at about the same time. For most girls, breast buds emerge between the ages of nine and eleven and then take two to five years to develop fully. It is sill considered normal to start as early as eight years old and to delay as long as eighteen. Yet, although girls agonize about their breasts, they breeze through growing pubic hair. What is the difference? Unlike breasts, pubic hair is not public. Nor is it expected to attain a specific, idealized look. True, some girls whose abundance spills down their legs or grows up toward their navel feel troubled and anxious about their femininity. Now that men's magazines have begun showing models sheared of all but a small, central patch, that look may eventually find legitimacy. But for the present, pubic hair is largely private.

Breasts, on the contrary, are public edifices. They are visible, noticed, and commented upon. One study showed 50 percent of girls with intermediate breast development had been teased by mothers, fathers, and female peers.[6] And a girl's emotional environment is made up not only of spoken taunts, but also of glances and gestures that lead her to guess and imagine what other people are thinking. She is self-consciously aware that her breasts are available for all to see. They become public property and the catalyst for confusing interactions with others.

For me, adolescence came as a huge surprise. In seventh grade, I was still rushing out to the playground after lunch, perfecting my ability to leap over the bike stand. Eventually, someone dragged me to the gym and introduced me to noontime dance hall, and when I saw those mature-looking kids swaying in close embrace to music throbbing out of the P.A. system, I knew had totally missed the boat. I started to assess myself. It was 1956, and curves were in. Being skinny and flat-chested became for me the symbol for my immaturity, my cloddish inability to be "in." I felt the lack of breasts was an impoverishment of my own nature—a deep failure that was my fault.

Years later, I talked to Beth, who spent her adolescence believing her large breasts were her fault. "My breasts were too big," she said. "I thought maybe I was to blame. Maybe I should be ashamed." At thirty-eight, Beth has a pretty, youthful face, devoid of makeup. She is wearing a baggy sweater and has a matter-of-fact, tomboyish way of talking that makes me suspect she's spent her life trying to be something different than a sexy woman. Beth and her twin sister quite suddenly grew large breasts in the eighth grade. She was just as shocked to discover she had breasts as I was to discover that I did not. "I just remember being alarmed, feeling I wasn't ready for this. It seemed like it happened really quickly. All of a sudden I was wearing a bra." Beth and her twin were promptly named "the Tit Sisters" and teased unmercifully. They obtained some comfort from sharing the affliction. Both wore bulky clothes to armor themselves against prying eyes. If any boy stared at their chests, they would secretly mock him and name him a "boob-looker."

"I've always associated big breasts with someone sexy," said Beth. "I've never wanted to be that. I don't want people to give me attention because of my body. I want them to like me for other reasons. If a man stares at my breasts, I just don't give him a chance," she said. "I wish just once a man would look into my eyes with the same interest that he looks at my breasts." She believes men's admiration is false in the deepest sense because it is not centered on her as a person. She is playing second fiddle to her breasts.

Despite the traumas so many adolescent girls experience as their breasts begin to grow, it would be misleading to suggest that the development of breasts is, on the whole, a negative experience. Most adolescents have at least moments of glowing self-assurance, of glorying in their newly acquired curves. Who can claim that the sense of attracting men of all types and ages—that constant background hum of male attention—does not have its pleasurable moments?

One reason the shaky adolescent transition can be so difficult for girls (and for boys too) is that we do not organize around it. Psychologists used to believe a girl's pubertal identity crisis is resolved when her period arrives,[7] but our culture holds no initiation rites to help solidify the new identity. The Native Americans who lived in what is now San Diego County, California, dug pits for young girls at menarche.[8] The girl would lie naked in the pit, which had been lined with fragrant sage and warm rocks. For five days, the women sang and danced around the pits, placing warm rocks between the girl's legs and teaching her women's lore.

Most North American girls suffer their cramps alone with maybe a hug and a few tears from mother. We have no rituals to help them. On the contrary, North Americans as a whole distinguish themselves by an unusual squeamishness about sexual maturation. A West German pamphlet published by Johnson & Johnson shows photographs of girls in various stages of pubertal development, but the North American version does not. Such images are considered too graphic for North American readers.[9]

We do have a small exception to the general barrenness of ritual. It cannot compare with warm rocks and sweet-smelling sage, but most women remember it as an important moment in their coming of age. That is the purchase of the first brassiere, an occasion on which a girl acquires the trappings of womanhood.

A study by Jeanne Brooks-Gunn and colleagues (1994) at Columbia University explored the meaning of the event by having eighty different girls make up stories about the same picture. The picture showed a man, a woman, and an adolescent girl together in a living room. The woman is holding a bra up over a shopping bag. Virtually all the girls in the study identified the picture as the purchase of the first bra. Here is a typical story:

> Okay. This girl is about thirteen years old and she just went shopping with her mother cause her mother thought it was time she got a bra. And she comes home and her mother is unpacking all this stuff that they bought for shopping because her mother wanted to show the father everything they bought and the mother just took it. The girl was laying back because she didn't want her mother to show her father the bra, but the mother couldn't understand because the mother was, ah, just didn't understand her generation and didn't understand what the girl was thinking. And the father had seen the bra, was also very embarrassed about the situation and at the end of the story the father doesn't say anything to the little girl and the girl just goes to her room with her shopping bag very annoyed with her mother.[10]

The girls in the stories feel joy and shame. They feel the kind of strong emotions that might be expected from an initiation ritual but, usually, without a sense of clear meaning and completion. This is potentially a moment for closeness between mother and daughter. But the mother/daughter alliance can be an uneasy one, coming out in jests, as Nora Ephron recalls in her essay, "A Few Words About Breasts: Shaping up Absurd." "My mother was really hateful about bras, and by the time my third sister had gotten to the point where she was ready to want one, my mother had worked the whole business into a comedy routine. 'Why not use a Band-Aid instead?' she would say."[11]

While the storytelling girls had mixed feelings about the mother figure, they quite clearly gave the father a negative role. Symbolically representing the dominant culture, the father seems to disapprove of what is happening. He is embarrassed and angry; he wishes he hadn't seen the womanly item. At the end of the story, the daughter usually retreats alone to her room.

Skye retreated further than that; she ended up running away from home when her parents tried to initiate her into wearing a bra. Today, Skye is thirty-three years old, has three children, wears a nose ring, and loves herbs and magic. "Now they call me a hippie," she said. "Then, they used to call me a tomboy."

Back in Illinois, before she had changed her name to Skye, she was called Sarah. "I didn't want to grow up," she said. "I didn't want to become a woman. All the women I knew were Pentecostals and they had breasts.

"When I was eleven, I got my mom to promise I'd never have to wear a bra. It felt like slavery to me. I had a little doll named Scooter. I loved her; she didn't have breasts. Then they got me a Barbie doll and I hated her. I hated Barbie dolls. They had big tits."

When she was thirteen, Sarah's mother took her to Kmart and bought her several bras. "I couldn't even stand to touch them," Skye recalled. "I couldn't talk about it. My throat hurt." Sarah left them in her drawer and refused to wear them. Finally her mother could stand it no longer. She came up, laid Sarah on her bed, and fastened on a bra. When she left, Sarah tore off the bra, cut it in little pieces, and sewed them inside the baggy T-shirts she loved to wear, so she would not have to lie about whether she was wearing her bra.

"When my mother found out I'd cut the bras, my dad came up and spanked me," she remembered. "I was humiliated. I decided to run away. I only stayed out over night. They sent the police out, but they didn't get me. I came back on my own. But it was the only day of freedom that I had for years and years."

Instead of ritualizing pubertal events, our society organizes its children by grade levels. The hope and expectation is that children will advance with their class. The structure is geared toward the norm. And true to our organizing principles, psychologists find girls who develop medium-sized breasts and whose development coincides with the herd are less traumatized than the early or late developers; they suffer less than the big-breasted and small-breasted girls.[12]

The crisis of adolescence demands that a girl reassess who she is. This is not the same body; this is not the same social environment;

these are not the same feelings that she has always had. Her child identity no longer serves her. This change can be exhilarating; it can also seem frighteningly out of control. Sometimes adolescents have a sense of their physical maturation as a random draw—as a throw of the dice that profoundly determines who they are.

However, the story is different for girls and boys. Adolescent boys are often perceived (and perceive themselves) in terms of their growing physical power and their potential for useful work or for physical violence. More often, girls are assessed (and judge themselves) in terms of their new sexual allure. During this transition, they are like animals in molt; they are extremely vulnerable to influence and interference. Messages about how their breasts should look, and about what kind of girl their breasts make them, find fertile ground in the adolescent psyche. Even though many adolescents assume a critical, questioning, rebellious stance, this does not protect them from the powerful reach of these suggestions.

When grown women talk about their breasts, many of them are still gripped by strong memories from their adolescence. These recollections are personal origin stories. Out of the mists of childhood something is forming. Starting with little swollen buds, breasts are forming. Unlike in most origin stories, these new breasts do not emerge into a fresh universe still damp from its first soft rain. They come to life in a world full of silicone-enhanced super models and Barbie dolls, a world impatient for perfection, ready to judge and declare what they are before they have decided who they want to be.

Chapter 3

Dressing the Part

For over a thousand years there lived on the island of Crete a civilization who revered the breast. The Minoans, highly developed by 2800 B.C., thrived until around 1450 B.C. Homer called Crete "a rich and lovely land, washed by waves on every side/And boasting ninety cities."[1] The Minoans left no decipherable written history, but based on the joyful frescoes, sophisticated pottery, metalcraft and architecture that remain, scholars have pieced together a picture of prelapsarian splendor.[2] While other Bronze Age peoples carved images of angry warrior gods severing heads and trampling their enemies, the Minoans painted frescos of flying fish, springing deer, and women dancing with dark hair swirling about their shoulders. Evidently they possessed sophisticated technology but had little interest in war. Apparently they worshipped the elemental forces and lived a life of gaiety and innocent sensual pleasure.

The Minoans are recorded in history as the people whose costume completely bared and emphasized the breast. In paintings and sculpture, Minoan women wear bell-shaped dresses that reach to the floor while above their cinched waists, tightly laced, short-sleeved bodices support and display their bare breasts. The breasts are generous and round, like the full breasts of a nursing mother. Never in the annals of fashion have women shown off the breast with quite the same exuberance as the Minoans.

As the focus of women's clothing, breasts must have been a key cultural symbol. All truly evocative symbols reach out in more than one direction, and the enthusiastic display of breasts among the Minoans must have expressed many parts of their culture. Breasts could have represented material abundance and political power and sacred authority as well.

Minoan women probably held high social positions. Minoan art indicates they were priestesses and athletes; possibly they were also artists, landowners, and rulers. Their exposed breasts may have been a statement of power, just as images of masculine power pervaded other cultures. Their breast exposure is not a sly, nipple-tease décolletage. It is frank, open, and proud.

Among the Minoans, breasts almost certainly had a sacred meaning. Sacred images provide some of the best examples of the costume. A small statuette of a goddess holds two writhing snakes while her breasts protrude in dynamic fullness. Gold seals show large-breasted goddesses receiving adulation. The open-breasted costume may have originated as an image of the goddess, then become priestess' garb and eventually dress for all women.

As with most early agricultural people, the Minoans worshiped some incarnation of the Great Goddess. Just as the sacred heart of Jesus has profound meaning for Christians, so the sacred breasts of the Goddess would have signified much to the people of Crete. "The Great Goddess as a whole is a symbol of creative life and the parts of her body are not physical organs but numinous symbolic centers of whole spheres of life," wrote Erich Neumann.[3] Her breasts embodied the nourishing life stream, the compassionate side of nature.

As providers of nourishment, breasts also symbolized material abundance. The Minoans sailed all over the Mediterranean and traded wine, textiles, oil, and an exquisite purple dye. They left clay tablets that enumerate immense stores of provisions. Other peoples who worshiped the Great Goddess emphasized the bulging belly or the pubic triangle, but the Minoans' preoccupation with the breast may reflect a belief that their riches were Her gifts. Full breasts demonstrated the Goddess' generosity in granting them a successful agriculture and a flourishing trade.

The Minoan civilization ended when violent earthquakes destroyed the great palaces around 1450. Scholars believe that the culture's weakened state allowed the warlike Myceans from the mainland to take over Crete.[4] The Myceans not only captured the palaces but adopted Minoan ways, including the woman's costume. In examining the images they left, you can almost see a page of history turning. Unlike the slender Minoans with their feathers and loincloths, the Mycean men wore leather, fringes, horns, and heavy metal. The women still openly revealed their breasts, but already the meaning must have been changing. Minoan women carried weight and authority. The most celebrated Mycean woman was the beautiful Helen of Troy, history's most famous bone of contention and warrior's prize.

The meanings that hover like a nimbus around those proud Minoan breasts would reappear in the clothing of later periods in Western culture. Over and over again breasts have evoked the themes of eroticism, nurturance, abundance, hunger, feminine power, and feminine subservience. But each time breasts come back into fashion, the context has changed, the emphasis is new, and the old themes are played to a different tune.

Scholars disagree about where fashions in clothing come from and what or whom they express.[5] According to one common notion, influential people set the fashions, and the rest of us follow.[6] The classic example is a favorite mistress of Louis XIV whose hat was ripped off by a branch while she was riding through the woods. She pulled up her golden tresses and fastened them with a garter. Within days the new style had swept through the court and lasted many years. In modern times, a movie star or couturier can cause the same flurry. But the truth is, these popular innovations only take if they really speak to what people are feeling.

There are a number of theories that describe fashion as a self-contained organism that follows it own cycles and rules. One claims that fashions go as far as they can in one direction and then start swinging back in another, like a pendulum.[7] Skirts will grow as wide as they can, with massive crinolines and hoops, then start getting narrower, until they are skintight.

Other kinds of cycles have been suggested. J. C. Flugel (1950) wrote about an erotic cycle in women's clothing. Fashion will emphasize one part of the body for a while until people get sated and lose interest. Then, that body part recedes in importance, going into a kind of dormancy that allows it to build up erotic capital and emerge again much later as something freshly exciting.

Anybody over thirty has experienced fashion cycles and knows that we are constantly cannibalizing looks from the past. However, most of these cycle theories have their limitations. It's true that during the twentieth century, erotic interest seems to have jumped skittishly from bosom to legs to buttocks and around again. But in the long view, clothing has gone through some major, dramatic changes over and above the shorter cycles. For instance, women wore long skirts through most of the Christian era, up until the twentieth century, when suddenly the area below the waist bifurcated and appeared in pants. Women in pants was a huge innovation in Western fashion, with connections to profound changes in gender equality, education, occupation, and sexual freedom.

Restless cycles and important people influence fashion, but clothing also represents the voice of a culture, as surely as pottery and painting, furniture and food, and literature and film. Clothing is an aesthetic expression of human beings, at once very personal and very public. As one voice of a people's identity, it gathers together many different threads of experience and meaning.

Throughout most of human history, breasts were not hidden. It wouldn't make sense to cover them when they were needed for frequently suckling babies. Even in the sophisticated culture of dynastic Egypt, women did not cover their breasts as a matter of course. They wore sheath-like skirts that wrapped around and fastened below the bosom.[8] As the culture matured, shoulder straps appeared, and heavily beaded collars obscured the breasts somewhat, but often breasts were bare or covered only by a diaphanous robe. The ideal Egyptian woman, with her slender body and high, firm breasts, would fit well into the pages of today's fashion magazines. The Egyptians must have valued breasts, because mummies of elderly women have been found in which the breasts are filled with wax and sawdust. The Egyptians loved bold makeup. Sometimes the women accented the veins showing through the skin of their breasts with blue pigment and painted their nipples and areolas gold.

At various times in history, women have painted and padded their breasts, flattened and bound them, supported them and puffed them out, presented them as one huge shelf or two aggressive points. Over the centuries, breasts have been shaped and controlled to fit the prevailing ideal. But after the days of Egyptian breast painting and the open-breasted bodices of the Minoans and Myceans, it would be many centuries before the breast would again be celebrated with such élan in Western costume.

During the thousand years that separated the destruction of the palaces on Crete and the flowering of classical Greek culture, philosophy, religion, politics, and clothing all had dramatically changed. Both men and women wore rectangles of woven wool, pinned at the shoulders and draped with exquisite simplicity. The human body was free to move, unconstricted, among the soft folds. Classical Greek art expresses a harmony, a graceful interplay between anatomy and drapery. Some Greek sculpture depicts the breast showing sensuously among the folds as if the drapery were damp, but it's questionable whether these images give a realistic picture of how women actually looked. What we see in the sculptures are idealized forms. Modern-day scholars have tried and failed to reproduce the effect; the woven wool always seems to bunch rather than drape in form-revealing shapes.[9]

Classical Greek culture tended to repress women.[10] The Greek matron stayed home and attended to the running of the household. Only the Hetaerae, a special class of well-educated companion/lovers, participated in the intellectual and social life of men. The hetaerae wore supporting undergarments to improve the drape of their chitons. A girdle, called a zone, controlled the waist and hips. The apodemos, made of linen or kid, supported the breasts and could be considered the earliest brassiere. But the apodemos did not push the breasts out or in any way make them more prominent. Indeed, it was sometimes used to flatten them. However, one tale leads us to believe that the Greeks were vulnerable to the charms of the breast. Phryne, a hetaera famous for her gorgeous body, was judged guilty of a crime and about to be sentenced to death in a court of law.[11] Her lawyer Hypereide, who was also her lover, rushed up before the sentence could be pronounced and tore off her chiton, revealing her lovely, round breasts. Once everyone could see the perfection of her form, she was pardoned. She is said to have served as a model for Praxiteles' Venus of Cnidos, so those terrific breasts can still be seen.

Scholars say that Greek art shows a marvelous dialectic between fabric and figure.[12] With Christianity, the dialectic turned into an argument, one that the body lost. Christianity brought with it the belief that flesh is sinful and should be covered up.

The draped effect lingered in the folds of Europeans' gowns for many centuries, but the human figure was muffled under fabric that covered everything but their hands and heads. This enrobement faced down a number of challenges. Barbarian warriors invaded Christian enclaves. Their women wore loose tunics, exposing their arms and part of their breasts. But the dominant culture absorbed these people, and they learned to cover themselves. Art historian Kenneth Clark said that the Greeks created nudity and the Christians created nakedness.[13] The Dark Ages cast a shadow on the body. This cloaking permitted the development of exaggerated and idealized notions about the body. When the body finally reemerged, it would be in a newly contrived form.

During those centuries when the breast hid under layers of fabric, changes were stirring that would begin to uncover it. The Crusades brought Europeans in contact with different customs and whetted their appetites for the riches of the east. Merchant and trades classes grew in the towns and began to acquire wealth equal to or greater than the nobility. By the end of the thirteenth century, the unity of the divine and the secular began to fall apart.

Fashions tend to change rapidly during times of instability and disruption. The fourteenth century was such a time. It saw that great explosion of artistic and creative energy we call the Renaissance. It also experienced widespread crop failure and famine, the bitter Hundred Years War between England and France, the papal schism, and the peak of the Black Plague. People responded to these hardships not with sackcloth and widows weeds but with frivolity and celebration. When a plant suffers harsh conditions, it hurriedly puts out buds in a last-gasp effort to reproduce. Perhaps a similar dynamic makes people turn toward the erotic in the presence of war and pestilence. During the fourteenth century, the human form began to emerge from the folds of drapery. Men's legs and eventually their crotches appeared, clothed in parti-colored tights as the hemlines of their tunics rose. Women's dresses tightened to reveal the torso, necklines lowered, and the first décolletage appeared. "Décolletage is as much a sign of the first dawn of the Renaissance as the novels of Boccaccio," wrote James Laver. "Life was opening like a flower and clothes were responding with a symbolic gesture, as they always do."[14]

Underneath the gesture, a huge, slow shift was taking place in the way people thought and felt about women's bodies. For centuries during the Middle Ages and the Renaissance, a woman's stomach had been the central symbol of her sexuality. It is hard to imagine now that a rounded belly was once considered attractive, but it is true. The fashionable posture, as Europe emerged from the Middle Ages, was a sinuous S-shape. Women drew their upper torso back in inward-turning modesty and let their stomachs extend out under a swell of skirt. The shift of erotic focus from belly to breast did not happen all at once. Décolletage first emerged in the fourteenth century, then rose and fell during the next 300 years while the stomach still retained its importance. However, in the first quarter of the seventeenth century, a rather sudden postural shift took place. With the help of the corset, women began sucking in their stomachs, pulling back their shoulders, and throwing out their chests. Necklines curved lower and stayed that way for more than 200 years. The age of the breast had arrived.

It's interesting to speculate about why the European consciousness shifted its attention from women's stomachs to their breasts. A swelling belly says that a woman is fruitful; it suggests pregnancy. The ideal woman during the Middle Ages and Renaissance would be patterned after the Virgin Mary, who contained in her belly the mystery of salvation. The swelling belly hides an inner miracle, a token of faith. It symbolizes constant renewal, the enigma that supported the stable, hierarchial world of the Middle Ages. With the Renaissance and Reformation, changes occurred that ate away at that security. The discovery of the Western Hemisphere radically altered people's concepts of the world; the rise of the middle class undermined old hierarchies, and the reformation destabilized religious faith. While the old world of faith was crumbling, a new one was bursting through. Europe was undergoing an expansion, a movement away from the interior and the mysterious to the outward and the visible. In the Western imagination, the world had changed from a flat plate in the center of the heavenly spheres to a planet circling the sun. Socially, mobility replaced stasis. Economically, wealth poured into the nations, supporting material extravagances. The center did not hold. Women's bellies flattened and their breasts expanded.

Why did breasts fill the symbolic needs of the seventeenth century? Because they are both erotic and productive. This century was an age of sensuality. After the ascetic rigidities of the Roundhead reformers, the Catholic monarchies relaxed into a sensuous, celebratory life. Breasts signified that luscious sensuality. While the belly is fruitful, the breast is tantalizing. While the belly symbolizes fulfillment, cleavage appeals to the drama of seduction and the thrill of anticipation.

This sensuality was also a celebration of wealth and power. The clothes people wore, their hats and wigs, were profuse and overflowing. Large breasts fit in with these tastes and feelings. Since time immemorial, full breasts have symbolized an abundance of food. During this era, when Europe was flush with wealth pouring in from the new world and the products of the growing trade, full breasts were a satisfying echo of that abundance. Symbolically, they converted wealth into the erotic through the luxury of sexual display.

The shift from belly to breast could not have taken place without the technical assistance of the corset. What was to become women's most infamous undergarment began its existence in the fourteenth century as a stiffened linen bodice. It was constructed like a sandwich, a layer of paste between two layers of linen. In the sixteenth century, the corset was fortified with whalebone, and the busk became an institution. A long, flat piece of wood, ivory, or whalebone, the busk slid into the front of the corset to give it added strength and stability. The busk soon became a toy for flirtation. Women pulled it out, warm, from the front of their low necklines and used it to rap the knuckles of importunate suitors. Busks were sometimes carved with erotic verse and presented as a token of the lady's favor. "To both ends of the busk," was the drinking man's ribald toast.[15]

Much has been written about the corset as erotic armor;[16] how it both protected and attracted; how it layered a masculine hardness over feminine swells; how it represented a soft woman symbolically putting on a hard man and at the same time a man's fantasy of a woman; how, ultimately, it defined and controlled women.

While the corset shaped women's torsos, it also sculpted their breasts according to the demands of the age. During the sixteenth century, the corset covered the breasts and mashed them down to completely eliminate the curve, emphasizing the hips and stomach rather than the breasts. During the seventeenth century, the corset was used to restructure women's posture, eliminating the S-curve and holding the body up straight. It cinched the waist in tight and pushed up the bosom to create the desired full décolletage. One seventeenth-century wit wrote that women "commite their Body to a close imprisonment, and pinch it in so narrow to a compass, that the best part of its plumpness is forced to rise toward the neck."[17]

Décolletage reached an institutionalized pinnacle in the court of Louis XIV. Royal courts were the theaters of fashion in this century, and just as the Sun King's imperialism dominated European politics, his personal taste influenced fashion. These were the days when men wore cascading curled periwigs, silken coats, and blousey breeches; women put on huge flouncey dresses made of gold and silver brocades, costly velvets, satins, and laces. Clothes cost a fortune, and Louis insisted that his courtiers dress exquisitely and appear in entirely new outfits for important events. In fact, fashion dictates became a conduit for power. Poor courtiers were reduced to begging for lucrative sinecures from the king, which put them under his thumb.

Women used rich fabrics, jewels, and décolletage to compete for the interest of a perennially seduceable King.[18] Louis hopped from one bed to the next, often maintaining several mistresses and always ready to succumb to someone more beautiful. Athénaïs, the Marquise de Montespan, was so ambitious for his attentions that she became best friends with his current favorite so she would come in contact with him every day. When that failed, she looked for supernatural help. She could not pray to God to aid her in consummating a double adultery (both were married), so she made a pact with Satan, with the help of a corruptible priest who performed a rite using pigeons' hearts and a consecrated chalice. Apparently it worked, because Athénaïs won a place in his majesty's bed. A portrait shows her under a canopy of cupids reclining with a gown open to her navel, showing one bare foot and one bare breast.

In the court of Louis XIV, good décolletage could be a road to preferment. Being the Sun King's mistress was the ultimate in worldly success. For a time, Louis demanded décolletage of all the court women. He would personally expel any woman who showed up at mass in other than a low-cut gown. James Laver wrote, "Louis obviously considered that a décolleté gown was a mark of respect not only for himself, but to the Deity."[19] How strange that in a seventeenth-century Catholic mass the breast would hold a sacred or ceremonial significance, a faint echo of its meaning in the time of the Minoans.

After Louis' death, fashion changed from the rich, sumptuous baroque of the Sun King's court to the high, frivolous rococo of the eighteenth century, but deep décolletage, tiny waists, and huge skirts stayed in style until the French Revolution.

*   *   *

It was 1794. Josephine de Beauharnais had narrowly escaped the guillotine and now everybody was looking at her breasts. Actually, Josephine's breasts were not the only ones in view. Fashionable women were walking around with their breasts barely covered, a style that expressed the spirit of this new, postrevolutionary world. Josephine, the future empress of a soon-to-be-established empire, wore thin, white gowns, classically draped and tied with a wisp of a sash under the bust, a style that came be called the empire waistline. Her deep décolletage revealed the upper hemispheres of her plump breasts.

For more than a decade following the French Revolution, after the bloody chaos and during the ascendancy of Napoleon, the French upper class incarnated in their dress the Romanticism that had been brewing for half a century. A fresh wind was blowing across Europe and America. Rousseau's plea for a return to nature mingled with democratic ideas of intellectuals such as Voltaire. People sensed the need to break out of old molds, to achieve a new equality, a new voice for the "common man." At the same time, the rediscovery of Pompeii and Herculaneum ignited a widespread nostalgia for classical antiquity. The hunger to relive the golden age blended with the Romantic dream of natural, unfettered man.

Through most of the eighteenth century, noblewomen had dressed like ornate tea cozies. They wore towering hairdos, stuffed with padding, held together with paste, and topped with fruit. So much flour was used to paste and powder their hair that bread shortages were blamed on the aristocracy, a claim used to heat up the killing frenzy of hungry revolutionaries. During these chaotic years, people could be arrested on the streets for powdered hair and other symbols of the old order. Since the fifteenth century, women had altered their shapes with corsets and bustles. Revolutionary Romanticism cut through these customs like an assassin's knife. Women threw away the whalebone and laces that had held them together for the last 400 years. For a short period after the Revolution, artificiality was out, and breasts were in.

The breast was a perfect symbol for Romanticism. It provided a visible connection with the instinctual and the mysterious gifts of nature. Following the advice of Rousseau's *Emile*, a landmark book that defined the new child rearing, breastfeeding became a fad. Once again fashionable among ladies of leisure, breastfeeding was seen as a natural act, a democratic act, independent of social hierarchies. What's more, the Romantics revered emotions, the flow of tears and tenderness. The breast had traditionally been the site of emotional stirrings and compassion. During this period, breasts embodied a kind of sacred, tender naturalness.

Breast worship also took on a political meaning. In the iconography of the Revolution, the Republic is portrayed as a huge, sphinx-like goddess with milk spouting from her breasts. The idea was that the mother breast of the Republic could be trusted to provide unendingly for people of all classes.

The artist Jacques-Louis David, who designed the regalia of the revolutionary government, wanted to create an effect of simple Greek nobility. Wicker, an enthusiastic pupil of David, proposed that women go native and wear nothing above the waist.[20] Some daring socialites are reputed to have done exactly that. Many women dressed as the one in David's *Portrait of a Young Woman*. Cut in a deep V, the top of her nearly transparent bodice reveals the dark shadows of her nipples. Dresses were made of fabrics so fine a lady was supposed to be able to draw the entire dress through her wedding ring. Some women dampened the fabric to achieve the look of marble drapery clinging to a Greek statue. On several occasions, wetted-down women were said to have caught cold and died after leaving a hot ballroom for the chilly streets of Paris.[21]

It was a wonderful, terrible, free-swinging time, but it didn't last long. Soon ruffles and frills started appearing on the Grecian gowns.

Then corsets came back, and within a dozen years, women had once again become creatures who were artificially padded and squeezed. Throughout the nineteenth century, women wore décolletage at night, though rarely during the daytime. A huge separation between men's and women's fashions took place as men switched from velvets and satins to the somber business suit, showing that earning money now had more prestige than nobility of birth. Women continued to wear the long-skirted fripperies of leisured nobility. The corset pinched their waists tighter and tighter. It's painful to see the photos of ladies with their hourglass figures, squeezed in the middle to an eighteen-inch waist, a little armored channel of flesh encircled by a dainty ribbon. Falsies made of pink rubber, which had been invented during the Revolutionary breast craze, became more popular. An 1860 patent described "an improved inflated undulating artificial bust."[22] Another type of bust improver was a boned bodice with wire springs that could be adjusted to produce the desired swell. Photographic images of women divide them into two types. One was the strumpet lounging in her frilly corset or lifting her dress to expose an ample bottom. Paralleling her was the formidable matron with an imposing monobosom.

Around the turn of the century, things started to fall apart, and corsets loosened and lowered from the nipple line eventually down to just a couple of inches above the waist. One of those odd, postural shifts took place, completely reversing the medieval S-shaped stance. Now women stood with their tops swaying forward and their buttocks sticking out. The bosoms still looked like a single bolster pillow without a hint of division, but as the corset softened, the bosom sagged downward and hung just above the waist. It was as if under all the rigidities of the Victorian century, women had slumped into a final maternal posture. This would be the last gasp of gentility and the old-fashioned woman. Neither the kangaroo posture nor the low-slung monobosom would stay in style. But remnants of it survived in my own lifetime. I remember as a child seeing women of my grandmother's era who were oddly flat in their upper chest but had a bosom that swelled just above their belts. That look was not repeated by my mother's generation.

Gentility disappeared to the sounds of celebration: the Roaring Twenties—what a time for women. They threw off their corsets, smoked cigarettes in public, cut their hair, and danced all night in gin joints. Feminism was one of the great movements of our century, almost from the beginning. Ironically, women's new freedom bound their breasts.

The twentieth century has been the age of the brassiere. Socialite Mary Phelps Jacob, also known as Caresse Crosby, claimed to have invented it in 1913, in an act of revolt against the boned bodice.[23] Jacob, a New York debutante, grabbed two handkerchiefs and a few snippets of baby ribbon and, with the help of her French maid, made a brassiere. Her creation was a soft, wispy little item which she later patented and sold to Warner. Actually, the word brassiere appeared in *Vogue* magazine as early as 1907, so Jacob probably does not deserve the full credit. And nobody wants credit for inventing its name. The English claim the Americans originated the word brassiere, which appears to be a bit of bungled French. The French call the garment in question a *soutien-gorge*, a euphemism meaning, literally, something to hold up the throat. In French, the word brassiere means an infant's T-shirt.

The brassiere has gone through many changes in its eighty-year existence. Women got the vote in 1919, and soon after, the brassiere became a strong cotton band wrapped around the chest to flatten the breasts. During the decade that followed, women rebelled against the traditional feminine signs and symbols—long hair, long shirts, and boned underwear—that had defined and confined their bodies. The look they sought was boyish and youthful. Say goodbye to the old maternal bosom and hello to legs. Their dresses had a waistless, tubular shape, and their legs emerged as their main allure. How interesting that legs, which first emerged in the fourteenth century as men's erotic charm, would finally, after all those centuries, become the property of women. The great age of partying ended abruptly with the stock market crash of 1929. The Great Depression followed. People sobered up, and women put on girdles and bras with cups. The breast still did not return. The erotic interest shifted to the back, and women's back décolletage got so deep in some cases it revealed their entire dorsal geography.

It took the shock of World War II and the horror of the bombing of Hiroshima and Nagasaki to frighten the Western world into a conservative retrenchment that brought back the breast. The longing for security and a return to normalcy spurred a nostalgia in women's dress. The war ended in 1945. In 1947, Christian Dior unveiled his "new look." The new look, which was wholeheartedly embraced, had a haunting familiarity. It was a return of the hourglass figure— large breasts, a pinched waist and long, flaring skirt. This was the era of mammary madness, when a woman's charm depended largely on the sweetness of her face and the amplitude of her bosom.

Large breasts offered security value and also stood as emblems of plenty during this era of greatly expanding prosperity. During this time, brassiere manufacturers developed the whirlpool stitch brassiere that made breasts stick out in perpendicular cones. It gave them a kind of phallic, man-over-nature look as well as a sense of being modern and machined. The machine image has been one of the motifs of twentieth-century clothing. It started in the flapper era when tubular-shaped clothing and sleek, oiled hair called up images of machine parts. It would reemerge in the late 1960s in plastic, helmet-like shapes and later in the 1980s as sleek, spandex-covered, well-honed limbs.

All during the 1950s, while men dressed in gray flannel and women wore heavily-built brassieres, there simmered underground a bohemian urge to break out of the ordered mediocrity of our ways. It emerged in the social revolution of the 1960s, the age of radical politics, free sex, and free breasts. Women threw away their bras; they let their swaying bosoms galumpf along as they walked; they allowed their nipples to perk insolently under the fabric of their T-shirts. In extremely radical settings such as rock concerts or great family camp-outs, shirts were discarded entirely, and bare breasts signified acceptance of the natural and love of the human body. I am fascinated by how the braless breast worked as a cultural symbol. During the late 1960s and early 1970s, there was a great surge of feminist scholarship and philosophical writing for which the unbound breast is a wonderful symbol. Yet, having lived through that era, I know that there was a deeply chauvinistic strain among the breast-baring flower children. The stereotypical hippie chick was barefoot, pregnant, and good at embroidery. Like me, many of those young braless women were not yet aware of the changes in thought for which their unbound breasts served as an excellent symbol. Yet, it seems the culture was a whole organism that found the appropriate expression on the streets for what was happening in academia, or maybe vice versa.

At any rate, bra burning emerged as a symbol of woman's liberation, one that ran in two different directions. The image fueled the prejudice against feminists stereotyped as unkempt drabs who didn't have what it took to be loved by men—bra-burning radicals in their shapeless sweaters. But bra burning also served as a poignant symbol of women's refusal to be bound and their unwillingness to get their power through beauty and sex or subjection to male erotic fantasies. The concept of bra burning originated when feminist protesters of the 1968 Miss America Pageant planned to stage a burning of "woman garbage" in a "freedom trash can." Because they could not get a permit from the Atlantic City fire department, the burning never took place. Journalist Lindsey Van Gelder claims to have invented the turn "bra-burner" for her *New York Post* coverage of the event.[24]

One final image of the breast haunts us as the century nears its end. After the natural shagginess and sagginess of the1960s revolution, the machinelike body returned. In the subsequent years, the ideal female shape was created on a workout machine. It was slender and honed to perfection—masculine in its muscular thighs and tight little buttocks but feminine in the large, firm breasts that completed the look. Almost anyone who works hard enough can achieve that tight, slender body, but breasts do not always conform. They take their own odd shape and can't be exercised into obedience. That's why many women in search of the right body have found perfection in manufactured silicone breasts.

I'm sorry to end the story of breast fashions on such a note, but of course, the story is not over. I do not think most women are ready to go unaffectedly topless as we did in the pre-Christian era, and no doubt we will continue to change our minds about how breasts should be displayed and decorated. Happily, we have a rich cultural tradition to draw upon as we work through the variations on naturalness and artificiality, sensuality and discipline, and power and dependency. Surrounded by our history, we are like city dwellers living cozily in an old apartment. The many coats of paint that soften the angles of the walls remind us we are not the first people to act out a drama on this stage.

Chapter 4

A Matter of Life and Death

Elizabeth had thought about it for a year before she went for breast implant surgery in 1982. For her it was like going back to something missed in childhood. Pretty Elizabeth with her violet eyes and dark curls. By the time she was twelve, Elizabeth's mother was enrolling her in beauty contests and stuffing falsies down the front of her bathing suits. "I wonder why you're not developing," her mother would say. "Everyone in our family is large. Why would you be so small?"

Here she was at thirty-nine, with beauty contests well in the past. Married and divorced, a single mother of three children, she is owner of her own beauty shop. She has a hard time saying why, after all those years, she decided to have breast implants. "It was that deep inside yearning," she said. "It was going to do something for me. It was that void in me that I was trying to fill."

When she woke from the anesthesia, her breasts felt painfully stretched. She had told the surgeon, "Just make me normal," and now, where there had been just a suggestion of mounds, she had visible fleshy breasts that fit solidly into a brassiere. When the pain went away, she loved her new breasts. Postoperative elation is not unusual for women with new breast implants. Psychiatrists report that women often weep for joy when they first see their augmented breasts. One woman told me, "It was like a miracle."

When I spoke with Elizabeth, it was fourteen years after her surgery, and she had been marching back and forth in front of a San Francisco television station whose syndicated TV doctor tells women that implants are perfectly safe. She carried a picket sign and passed out leaflets filled with damning statistics about implants and showing photos, torso shots, of women whose breasts have been deformed by complications.

For the first six years, Elizabeth's implants were wonderful. In fact, they looked and felt better as her skin stretched and loosened. She remarried; her business thrived. But slowly her breasts became stiff and uncomfortable. "For years I felt like I had bowling balls sitting on my chest," she said. Then she began developing allergies, fatigue, and bronchial asthma. Her health got worse and worse. She became prone to chronic bladder infections, joint pain, memory loss, and numbness in her arms. She developed an angry, inflamed mastitis. It took her a long time to connect the mysterious ailments with her breast implants, and of the many specialists who treated her, only two agreed that silicone in her system might be responsible.

Elizabeth is one of 440,000 American women who are involved in lawsuits against silicone breast implant manufacturers.[1] Her list of symptoms is pretty typical of those reported by the other women. Elizabeth is actually one of the lucky ones because her implants did not rupture and because she has money. Too fatigued and disoriented to continue working, she sold her business to pay for her recovery. She could afford to go out of town to have the implants removed by the most skilled surgeon. She has been able to pay for extensive tests and detoxification treatments. She is gradually getting better.

The silicone breast implant controversy has simmered and flared through the 1990s, producing millions of printed words but very little clarity. Are implants safe? Or are they time bombs waiting to go off? Are they a case of an oppressive patriarchal beauty standard? Or an example of women exercising free choice? Are the legal cases about callous manufacturers making millions on a defective product? Or are they about greedy lawyers and hysterical women getting on the lawsuit bandwagon?

The Food and Drug Administration estimates up to two million women have had breast implant surgery. Twenty percent of the implants replaced a breast lost to cancer; the other 80 percent were done for cosmetic reasons. In 1992, the FDA banned the use of implants for cosmetic surgery, reserving them for cancer patients only. The FDA stated that not enough was known about the product's safety. Despite the research that has followed, the safety of breast implants remains controversial. Although they banned silicone implants, the FDA allowed saline implants to remain in use while manufacturers complete studies to prove their safety. These implants are constructed of a silicone rubber envelope filled with salt water. In 1996, some 87,000 women were implanted for augmentation and 42,000 for reconstruction, mostly with saline implants.[2] The FDA has received almost 23,000 complaints of adverse reactions to saline implants and over 100,000 to the silicone ones.[3]

Efforts to augment breasts have been taking place for more than fifty years. The earliest attempts were crude by today's standards. Breast enlargements, similar to back-alley abortions, were often performed by unskilled practitioners under unsanitary conditions. Often women received a series of injections of paraffin or beeswax. The results were sometimes disastrous. In some cases, women died of fat embolism; in others, doctors treated the women's inflamed and deformed breasts with bilateral mastectomies. In 1968, a surgeon reported in the *British Medical Journal* on thirty-one unpublished cases of women disfigured by foreign materials injected or stuffed into their breasts. The material included: "paraffin waxes, beeswax, silicone wax, silicone fluid, shellac, shredded oiled-silk fabric, silk tangle, glazier's putty, spun glass, and epoxy resin."[4] As the materials drifted, the women's breasts had become puckered and asymmetrical with indrawn nipples and masses of nodules. Sometimes injected substances migrated and built up in the abdomen or labia.

Silicone was developed in the 1940s. It is said that Japanese prostitutes had industrial-grade silicone injected directly into their breasts to satisfy the tastes of American soldiers during the post-World War II occupation.[5] In the United States, surgeons also injected women with liquid silicone. The FDA never approved liquid silicone injections and, in fact, seized supplies of it from California doctors. Nonetheless, the practice continued through the mid-1960s, when a San Francisco topless dancer named Carol Doda gained her fifteen minutes of fame by achieving and displaying a surrealistically large bust. Using the injections, she ballooned from 36-24-36 to 44-26-36. *Newsweek* quoted her as saying, "Science has invented all these wonderful things. Why shouldn't we use them?"[6]

Meanwhile, as early as the 1940s and 1950s, American and European physicians experimented with various polyvinyl sponges inserted behind the mammary glands to increase breast size. No doubt the postwar fashion for large breasts influenced this development. Also, the war-driven enthusiasm for technology, so well expressed by Carol Doda, supported this kind of experimenting. There was a growing vision of a new prosperity replete with dishwashers, ovens, and automobiles. If Jane Russell's bras were to be engineered by Howard Hughes, why not engineer a better body? Perhaps these were the early beginnings of what would become a cyborg vision—a perfect body, part flesh and part machine.

By 1962, silicone gel breast implants had been invented. In conjunction with the Dow Corning Corporation, a Houston plastic surgeon, Thomas Cronin, and his protégé Frank Gerow developed the first silicone implants. Originally, they were made of a sturdy silicone rubber envelope filled with silicone gel. Women who had a professional stake, such as actresses and dancers, were among the first to have the surgery, but also white, upper-middle-class housewives were getting implants from the start. In 1959, an article in *Vogue* magazine urged that "Prejudice need not deter women from cosmetic surgery—and that includes cosmetic surgery for the breast . . ."[7] Through the 1960s and 1970s, the number of women getting implants quickly rose. Cronin's clinic performed sixteen augmentations in 1966; that number rose to 192 in 1976.[8] In 1975, Dow Corning began making implants with thinner envelopes that gave a more natural look and feel.

By the 1980s, cosmetic surgery of all kinds really took off, and breast implants became the most common procedure. The major expansion of plastic surgery came about for several reasons. First, plastic surgeons as a group embarked on a major ad campaign to beef up their practices. Medical schools had overproduced plastic surgeons, and there just were not enough patients to go around. Along with the ads, plastic surgeons began offering no-money down, easy-credit terms. As a result, the number of plastic surgery patients doubled in the five years between 1983 and 1988. The patients were no longer just the wealthy and the pampered but included women earning under $25,000 a year.

The plastic surgeons' ad campaign worked, however, because breast implants fit well with the zeitgeist of the 1980s. After the social revolution of the 1960s and 1970s, people in the 1980s turned their energies to personal accomplishment and the business of making money. Popular media idealized the "yuppie" who flaunted achievement by buying beautiful merchandise and displaying a trim body. The newly popular hard body replaced the willowy shape that had been "in." Large breasts and a sleek, firm body, a nearly impossible body type, could be had with the aid of breast implants. To young professionals who worked eighteen-hour days for their wealth, a great body was seen as an achievement, part of "having it all." In the 1970s, second-wave feminists had created a vocabulary of choice. Now that vocabulary was applied to breast implants and other cosmetic surgery. Getting breast implants could be understood as going after and getting what one deserved. The great body could be bought.

Sylvia is a forty-year-old single mother of two children. She has an excellent career in financial services; she also has implanted breasts that, in her words, "look better than any I've ever seen."

When Sylvia got her implants in 1986, she wasn't trying to fill the kind of void that Elizabeth talks about. She made her decision very much in the spirit of choosing to take good care of herself. "I've been in really good shape all my life," she told me. "I've always been into exercising; I eat right, and I've kept myself in good shape. I always looked great, and then after nursing, you go from having nice breasts to having fried eggs. I thought, I don't really have to accept this, because I'm body conscious."

Sylvia's breasts were small and firm, until she had children. After nursing, she didn't like the way they sagged. "There was all this skin," she said, "and they just sagged, and there was nothing to them." Her husband didn't care, but after two children, she decided to undertake surgery for herself.

Sylvia's story, as she tells it, is very much about making an excellent purchase. A friend told her the name of the plastic surgeon who did all the *Playboy* bunnies. "He does all the stars," she said. "He was more expensive, but I thought: This is something for my body." Even though it was six years before the FDA ban, the surgeon put in saline implants; he'd heard some bad things about silicone and didn't want to take any chances. At the time, saline implants were advanced technology.

Sylvia didn't lose any sensitivity in her nipples, and her breasts looked very natural. One of the breast implants did become hard after several years, but the surgeon operated again, and she hasn't had any problems since. She continues to be delighted with her implants. "I definitely look better in a bathing suit," she said. "And hey, I'm forty years old and still have a good body."

At the time Sylvia had her implant surgery, women had already begun claiming that silicone breast implants caused toxic reactions in their bodies. They were suing implant manufacturers and winning court cases. The FDA had only gained authority over medical devices in 1976 after the Dalkon Shield problems, and breast implants were "grandfathered" at that time. As media attention grew in the early 1990s and implant manufacturers failed to produce evidence of their products' safety, the FDA placed the moratorium. Since that time much more research has come to light. The research findings have been contradictory, but when two major epidemiological studies found no connection between silicone implants and immune system disease, public opinion began to change. Although reliable studies linking silicone to immune disorders continued to emerge, the pro-implant forces effectively articulated the idea that implants are perfectly safe. The furor, they claimed, was caused by greedy lawyers, hysterical women, and "junk" science. Meanwhile, an estimated 100,000 women were sick with atypical autoimmune disease;[9] 440,000 had joined class action suits against the manufacturers,[10] and a growing but unpopular silicone survivors' resistance movement claimed that pro-implant rhetoric was bought and sold by implant manufacturers.

Breast implants have emerged as yet another women's health issue that is covered with ambiguities caused by insufficient information, strongly held interests, and conflicting opinions. Here is what is actually known: The most common negative side effect of breast implants is capsular contracture, the formation of tough scar tissue around the implants. This process represents the body's basic foreign-body response, the organism's attempt to protect itself from an unknown nonliving intruder by walling it off. Capsular contracture happens to some degree in virtually all women, though not all women experience it as tightness and hardening. Originally the standard treatment for capsular contracture was for the surgeon to grab the breast and abruptly twist. Because this manual popping method has been implicated in implant rupture, it is no longer recommended.

Other common side effects are scarring, loss of nipple sensation, and shifting of the implant. Again, there are no good statistics on how often these mishaps occur. Implants can also mask breast cancer, either during a manual exam or a mammogram. There is no evidence, however, that, as once suspected, silicone implants actually cause cancer.

Implants rupture, though there is no consensus on how often they do. The FDA says the rupture rate for silicone implants is somewhere between 5 and 51 percent.[11] It may well be higher for saline implants. Older implants have a greater tendency to rupture; the rate seems to go up after ten years. Sometimes women have a good indication when their implants have ruptured. One woman told me she reached up to get a pan off a high shelf and "felt something give." Other women report particularly painful mammograms that may have caused ruptures. Sometimes one implant will start to go down, a sure indication of a problem. It is not always easy to tell, though. Implants can also develop slow leaks. Mammograms will not detect a ruptured implant, but a much more expensive test, magnetic resonance imaging (MRI), will. In addition, virtually all implants "bleed" through the silicone membrane, and the membrane itself releases silicone molecules. Silicone may migrate through the body using the lymph system, but conclusive research on this has yet to be done.

Medical science has assumed that silicone is inert; the body does not react to it. That assumption is now under question. An uncertain number, possibly somewhere between 100,000 and 400,000, of women with silicone implants suffer from a host of symptoms including chronic fatigue, inflammation and pain in muscles and joints, swollen lymph nodes, abdominal pain, low-grade fever, night sweats, memory loss, dry eyes and mouth, headache, rashes, bladder problems, numbness, lung problems, and depression. Dr. Frank Vasey, a rheumatologist at the University of Southern Florida, maintains that this atypical silicone-related autoimmune disease is not well understood and difficult to diagnose.[12]

For over thirty years medical journals have contained case studies of silicone-related autoimmune disorders. Research shows that women with ruptured implants exhibit more symptoms and more severe disease than women whose implants are intact. But most of this research did not include a control group. It doesn't mean much to say that 100,000 implanted women have autoimmune disease unless it can be shown that the percentage of implanted women with the disease exceeds the percentage of nonimplanted women (the control population) who have similar symptoms. Two recent major epidemiological studies with controls failed to find that proof.[13] But those studies have been criticized as too small to be statistically significant and because they did not trace the specific atypical silicone-related syndrome.

Clearly we need more studies to be sure. But based on incomplete evidence, it seems reasonable to think that silicone (and even saline) implants may pose a risk of immune disorders, that probably some women are more susceptible than others, and that a ruptured implant poses a greater risk than one which is intact.

Many women who suffer from the syndrome end up having their implants extracted. Colleen finally came to that decision after suffering for many years. The forty-nine-year-old bank teller got her implants in 1981 because, in her words, "I just never had any breasts." She was divorced with two children. She went to the doctor who had given her brother a nose job, and assumed he was qualified, though she did not check on his credentials. Plastic surgery is not well regulated; any doctor can perform it, and it sounds as if Colleen's doctor was not one of the best. The original operation had complications; she had to be reoperated on within hours of her first surgery and again two weeks later when her breasts began to hemorrhage.

Her breasts encapsulated at once. "That seemed to happen pretty much right way," she said. "They were just never that soft. They felt like little softballs. You can't lie on your stomach or anything. If somebody touches them, they don't feel like a real breast. I mean, they're hard."

Her surgeon manually popped the capsular contracture. That procedure was, said Colleen, "the most painful thing you can go through. He just pressed it between his hands and popped it. Then it would just get encapsulated again. Not as bad. I think the popping helped, but it may have damaged them."

In spite of the problems, she liked having bigger breasts. She found she attracted more men. Although the surgery had decreased her nipple sensation, men paid more attention to her breasts and that seemed to build her own passion.

But three or four years after her implants went in, Colleen's health began to deteriorate. It started with irritable bowel syndrome, and then her immune system seemed to weaken. She was sick seven days out of every month with long-lasting colds and influenza. "I just didn't seem to have any resistance at all," she said. Colleen was always contracting sinus, bladder, and vaginal infections. When the silicone implant crisis hit the news, she went to her doctor and asked for an MRI. Her doctor did not believe there was any connection between her symptoms and her implants, and he refused to authorize the test. But Colleen felt something was really wrong, so she began arguing with her HMO, filing appeals over a period of three months until the HMO finally agreed to send her to a specialist. The specialist ordered an MRI, which confirmed that Colleen had one leaking implant and a second that had fully ruptured.

Six months before we spoke, Colleen had the implants taken out. She was devastated by the results. She had so little breast tissue left on the right side that the breast was folded over upon itself and the nipple tucked inside. The left side looked just like a mastectomy scar, with an inverted nipple. After seeing pictures of this, her HMO made no argument about paying for reconstruction. This time the surgeon performed a latissimus dorsi flap. In this procedure, the surgeon transfers a block of fat, muscle, and supporting blood vessels from the back to the breast by tunneling it inside the body. Because blood vessels and nerves retain part of their original attachment, the fat and muscle stay alive, though the back sometimes suffers scarring and weakness. A similar procedure called the transvers rectus abdominus muscle, or TRAM flap, transfers fat, muscle, and blood vessels from the abdomen to the chest.

Colleen is happy with the look and feel of her reconstruction, and she says she is no longer getting sick as often, though she still experiences a good deal of fatigue. The explantation and reconstruction have been too recent to tell how fully she will recover. What bothers Colleen most is not her lingering fatigue but what is happening with her daughter. Colleen's daughter liked her mother's implants and had the surgery herself when she was twenty. Now at twenty-seven she too has developed irritable bowel syndrome and a painful vaginal condition. The daughter's doctor thinks her problems are related to the implants, but the daughter refuses to part with them. "This really horrifies me," said Colleen. "I feel like it's my fault."

Could the daughter's implants seriously be her mother's fault? It is an interesting question—the matter of who should take the blame or the credit, who is responsible for this breast implant phenomenon. Currently most of the voices speaking out against breast implants—the silicone implant activists, consumer organizations, and various journalists—put the blame largely on the manufacturers. The actions of implant manufacturers do deserve scrutiny. But instead of placing blame, I would like to look for ways of understanding the breast implant phenomenon: why women get them and what they tell us about how people experience their world.

Plastic surgeons have frequently taken up the subject of patient psychology. Their interest is, at least in part, a matter of their own survival. Unbalanced patients who are not satisfied with their plastic surgery have been known to cause their surgeons big problems—from lawsuits to gunning them down in their offices. As a result, plastic surgeons often work with psychiatrists to study the mental state of patients. Judicious plastic surgeons eliminate potentially volatile patients from their practices. Right alongside the earliest legitimate experiments with breast implants appeared psychological studies of implant patients. The analyses they produced tended to view the desire for implants as a personal rather than a social phenomenon and to consider implant patients as neurotic.

From a psychoanalytic perspective, these women were supposed to be suffering from a negative mother complex. They had had bad relationships with their mothers and were unconsciously seeking to heal this wound. Since the breast symbolizes the mother, getting breast implants would be an unconscious way of reuniting with the mother. Although not all of the existing psychological studies of breast implant patients spell out this negative mother complex theory, they consistently claim breast implant patients are depressive people who had unhappy childhoods.

No doubt some breast implant patients have had unhappy childhoods (unhappy childhoods are not that unusual). Though psychological studies from the 1950s through the 1980s wrote about implant patients in these terms, this kind of analysis does not strike me as very useful to understanding why women get breast implants.

The numbers of women are too large. It just does not seem reasonable to speculate that two million women are neurotic. Is it possible that this vast quantity of people were all poorly nurtured in childhood? Is it fair to blame two million mothers? It seems to me that these claims are not only unreasonable but are also misogynistic—another round of the old habit of putting down women. That is not to say that insensitive parents never drive their daughters closer to implant surgery. Elizabeth, whose story began this chapter, believes that all her mother's comments about her small breasts contributed to her wanting augmentation. After Elizabeth had her implants taken out, her mother dealt the final blow by asking, "How does it feel to be flat-chested again?"

Colleen also connects her feelings about her breasts to childhood, but the important influence was her father. "My earliest memories of breasts are of my father always coming up when my mother was doing the dishes and grabbing her breasts." She told me. "My father was an alcoholic, so I saw things I probably shouldn't have. He was pretty uninhibited. He was a real tit man. He was very attracted to my mother's breasts. So I thought you needed breasts to attract men. Later he made fun of my small breasts. He said I had a body like a boy."

Of course the remarks and actions of parents, siblings, and friends are formative, but today analysts and commentators are much more likely to point to social pressures to be beautiful than to personal neuroses as the reason women get breast implants. Western culture has many subtle and effective ways to control women's feelings about their breasts. They all affect the choice for breast augmentation, but on top of that, the dynamics described by Susan Faludi in *Backlash* (1991) and by Naomi Wolf in *The Beauty Myth* (1991) have been especially important. Both writers describe a contemporary culture that has responded to women's liberation by imposing increasingly rigid body standards. Once women began making their way into well-paying, traditionally male professions, the culture began producing media imagery, what Wolf calls "beauty pornography,"[14] with renewed vigor. In the 1980s, the images appeared with a new clarity and specificity. Failing to live up to the new hard body, big-breast beauty standards, even professionally successful women felt weak. Big, firm breasts became a power symbol. They are, as one commentator remarked, "a dick for women."[15] Although I would not want to carry this analogy too far, I think it brings to light certain contradicting yet coexisting facets of the silicone breast situation. Women were feeling weakened, insufficient, and unwomanly because their breasts were not right. Buying a pair of implants could thus be not just a boost for the self-esteem but a move for more social power. Ironically, getting a symbolic "bigger dick" made women feel more feminine. Such are the contradictions and complexities of human desire.

Another way to get a perspective on breast implants is by comparing them to beauty practices in other cultures. We know that all cultures mold and form their citizens' yearnings in deep and personal ways. Many societies ruthlessly favor one type of person over another; many hold up specific beauty standards, and some require their members to go under knife or tattoo needle to meet those standards. Some cultures inscribe their members' bodies with all kinds of messages and meanings. Aren't breast implants just another form of such inscription? The answer is both yes and no; there are similarities but also significant differences.

It is always a little bit iffy to make cross-cultural comparisons because you risk running roughshod over subtle cultural differences. Keeping in mind that such comparisons tend toward oversimplification and that there are many exceptions to general cultural rules, comparisons can still throw light on a subject. Breast implant surgery resembles body inscription rituals in other societies in being based on gender, in causing pain, and in changing the shape of the body. In many non-Western cultures, body rituals mark important transitions (such as puberty or marriage) in a person's life. In Western society, breast implant surgery does not mark socially recognized life transitions, though it sometimes takes place at moments when the person feels a need for a change. One woman I spoke with got breast implants during a major shift in her life, when she left her husband and came out as a lesbian. She had been thinking about augmenting her breasts, breaking with her husband, and being honest about her sexuality for a long time. To her, they all signified fixing something that was not right, and she built the momentum to accomplish it all in the same period of several months.

Pain usually figures in non-Western rituals as part of a transformative process. In Western countries, though some women feel pain after the implant surgery, it is usually not embraced and experienced as transformative. In fact, plastic surgeons advertise freedom from pain; all parties in the process desire to avoid it.

Non-Western, flesh-altering rituals are often symbolic events that not only mark transitions, but define status or affiliation. Scarification or tattooing, for instance, can show that a woman is married. Although breast implants may increase a woman's personal power, they are no longer only accessible to affluent women, and thus, probably cannot be viewed as a status symbol. Nor do they show affiliations, either marital or otherwise.

In non-Western cultures, flesh rituals are almost always community centered, involving participation of groups. Western breast implant surgery, by contrast, takes place in a world apart—in the plastic surgeon's office operating room. Far from being a community-based ritual, breast implants are most often done in utter privacy. Most of the women I interviewed told me that only their closest friends knew about their surgery; sometimes they hid it from even their own parents and children. Like flesh rituals in non-Western cultures, breast implant surgery is often experienced as transformative, but the transformation is personal, private, and often hidden.

Take the case of Stacey, a married woman in her thirties who lives in a small, conservative town. She and her husband run a high-profile local business. When Stacey told her husband she was considering breast augmentation, he was quite concerned about social repercussions. People had known Stacey since high school. What would they think? When she described these anxieties to me, Stacey talked a lot about not wanting to be a "freak show." Far from being part of a community ritual, Stacey secretly broke with community standards in having her breasts augmented.

Breast implant surgery, then, helps a woman fulfill a social stereotype of the good body, but it is not a flesh-changing ritual that serves to deepen and cement community ties as some non-Western body rituals do. For women who have problems with their implants, it is just the opposite. In general, their suffering is not credited by the medical establishment, which tends to view them as vain, hysterical women or hypochondriacs. Although a few women have won major monetary awards, today legal opinion seems to be changing. Those in the huge, class-action lawsuits are mostly either waiting for the outcome or have received an insignificantly small award. Many of them feel alienated, cut-off from the greater community, and sustained only by their support groups. "A lot of times the most important thing is to find someone to talk to," one woman told me. "No one believes that we're really sick. The media has portrayed us as greedy women looking for money." Just as these women are not believed, many of them have ceased to trust their doctors, the media, and the manufacturers. To their illness, add disillusionment.

Having breast implants, then, puts women in a subtly contradictory relationship with society. An implanted woman makes herself more acceptable, maybe even more powerful, by augmenting her breasts, and yet, the flesh-changing ritual must remain a secret, something apart. If she has problems and wants to talk about them, then she risks becoming a social pariah. She lives in a state of social cohesion that contains deep fault lines.

In Chapter 1, I contended that our society's obsession with breasts can lead to a kind of splitting or fragmentation within a woman. Breast implant surgery may deepen that fragmentation. It does this in several ways.

First, some of the concepts and technologies of breast implant surgery have a fragmenting influence. Even before implants went on the market, plastic surgeons had invented a term to diagnose small breasts as disease. In the 1950s, doctors were already using the term micromastia for, as one journal put it, "flat discoid breasts which are almost male in character except for somewhat enlarged nipples."[16] By defining a woman's breasts as diseased or deformed, medical nomenclature gives the official stamp of approval to the self-doubts already laid by social standards. Second, the practice in the plastic surgeons' office of scrutiny by the doctor and confronting the patient with the evidence in a well-lighted mirror reinforces the idea of breasts as objects apart from the rest of the body—objects in need of repair.

The other side of the coin is the existence of objective standards for breasts. In the 1950s, plastic surgeons were trying to develop the perfect breast geometry. Several systems were proposed: Penn (1954-1955) devised one involving an equilateral triangle, each side six and one-half inches long, its points lying on the two nipples and sternal notch. Malinac's (1950) system was based on six inches and Da Silva's (1964) on eight centimeters. Each system proposed to isolate ideal measurements that could work for every woman. [17] Today, plastic surgeons have gotten away from these mathematically rigid systems but still hold to preconceived aesthetic standards. Decisions about how the breast will be reshaped begin with a browse through a book with torso shots of breasts different size and shape. "It was like looking through a Christmas catalogue," one woman told me.

All these practices have the effect of disembodying a woman, of perpetuating a body-as-spare-parts mentality. Breast augmentation also favors form over function. By filling out breasts with a prosthesis, we are saying how they look is more important than how they work or how they feel. True, some women retain nipple sensitivity, but diminution of feeling is not uncommon, nor is uncomfortable hardening of the breasts. Breast-feeding with implants is another matter. If they retain nipple sensitivity, women can and do breast-feed, but some of their babies have developed problems that resemble autoimmune disease. The safety of breast-feeding with implants remains controversial.

If augmentation objectifies breasts by favoring form over function and looks over feeling, it also does so by making them, quite literally, into objects. We are talking about inflated and filled plastic bags here. These objects are manufactured; you pay money for them. Spiritually, metaphysically, and physically, they are not the same thing as body, not the same thing as self. Now it's true that we are late-twentieth-century creatures who dye our hair, wear contacts, and have fillings in our teeth. Some of us even have knee and hip replacements, pacemakers, and other medical devices implanted in our bodies. We're not cavewomen any more; we're not Eve in the Garden. We cannot claim to live a wholly natural existence. Still, this body that is me has the power to amaze me. Every time I heal from a nasty flu or a cut finger, or just feel good moving my body through the world, I am impressed by what a gift this body is—a real gift, not a free introductory offer. And even though hardly a day goes by that I do not lament some imperfection of my face and form, once in a while I catch a glimpse of my physical self and see an animal beauty that defies cultural norms.

The whole issue of breast implants is difficult and complex. It is hard to get good information, hard to absorb all the information that is available, and hard to sort it out. There are a lot of trust issues with the medical establishment, the courts, the manufacturers, and the activists. As a woman who cares about what happens to women, as a feminist, I am deeply troubled by breast implants. I question their safety and I fear that, while seeming to build self-esteem, they undermine a woman's sense of wholeness. Still, I understand and sympathize with the women who get implant surgery, and not just the women who desire to put their lives back together after breast cancer by having breast reconstruction. Given the messages women receive from society, breast implant surgery for augmentation can be a rational, understandable choice.

Many women with breast implants are extremely happy with the results. When asked by an acquaintance, Stacey out and out denied having implants, but she says she wished she could go public because the implants have been so wonderful for her. When Stacey was an adolescent, classmates frequently teased and humiliated her about being flat-chested. Once in eighth grade, she said, "I walked into my math class, and a boy had written on the board 'Stacey is a pirate's delight. She has sunken chests.' That was pretty tough when the whole class was there, and they were laughing, and I had to laugh along. I think that I have a fair sense of humor, and if anything, it was like a shield."

Stacey tells her story without any self-pity. She finds humor in everything, and her remarks show a good deal of self-knowledge. After high school she married a man she loves, had two children, and built a comfortable and loving family. During her pregnancies and nursing, it felt so good to have bigger breasts, that she started thinking about implants. Despite his qualms, her husband supported her decision. After she finished nursing her second baby, her breasts were, in her eyes, deformed. When the milk was gone, they looked misshapen and irregular. With the discrete aid of her gynecologists, she located a good plastic surgeon.

"The surgery wasn't a problem," she said. "It didn't feel invasive. It was so easy; it was like it was meant to be. I think it's really important to have a settled life. I think it could be kind of tumultuous otherwise. I feel like it really enhanced my life."

She explained in great detail the ways her implants have improved her life. "I think that in my work I have more confidence," she said. "Because of the ridicule I suffered when I was younger, I would always wonder if people were thinking, gee, she's flat. That's too bad, but I think that's how I'd feel. Now I don't think they're thinking, 'Boy, she's got good knockers,' but to me it's just an inner confidence that all the parts are there. Before I did not feel all the parts were there."

Implants have also improved her sex life. Breast play had always been an important part of her erotic menu, but she had shied away because she felt as if she didn't have much to offer. She knew that implant surgery might cause loss of nipple sensitivity. "That was a very big concern when I went in initially," she said. "That's not something I really chose to lose, but I was willing to, I guess." She did lose sensitivity on one side for about a month, but it came back. Now she feels that she has enough breast to enjoy and deserve breast attention when she makes love.

One unexpected satisfaction that Stacey talked about is more maternal than erotic. She loves comforting her children against her breasts. "It feels just like the maternal mommy chest," she said. "I can tell that it's comforting to my children to have a cushion. It just feels great for some reason. I really can't explain it."

Stacey has not had any problems with her implants; she thinks of them as part of her. "We have mirrors all over the wall, and when I get out of the shower in the morning, I see them and they're mine. It doesn't run through my mind that I have implants, that these are silicone or a foreign body. I don't feel that way at all unless I think about it. They're mine. It's still me. The implants feel very, very natural to me.

Stacey does not lack perspective on her situation. She told me that she wished she could have accepted the breasts she was born with and that maybe self-acceptance is better than surgery, but she felt that, for her, augmentation had been a positive good.

By ending with Stacey's story, I do not mean to indicate that I think breast augmentation is a good thing or that I recommend it to women. Instead, I am saying that the breast implant issue is not easy, and we need to understand why women get them. Stacey is not a vain woman caught in a narcissistic web. She is a decent person trying to do a good job with her life. Maybe she made the right choice for her. But I am sorry that women have such choices to make.

Stacey said, "When we found out about the silicone implant situation, I actually made the statement to my husband: if it shortens my life by just a couple of years, it has been worth it because it enhanced my life so much. That's a really big statement, but it really has helped me a lot." That shocks me. I once saw a woman who had a hole in her face where her nose should have been. It was hard to look at her; she was truly deformed. I could understand if she were willing to give up a couple of years of life for a normal face. It shocks me that flabby, or uneven, or small breasts have become a deformity. It troubles me that the appearance of breasts has become a matter of life and death.

PART TWO:
WE TWO ARE THE UNIVERSE

Chapter 5

Garden of Paradise

A baby emerges from the birth canal looking like a small, wrinkled alien. Its skin, so long protected in a glove of amniotic fluid, is impossibly fine-textured and soft. A net of blue veins shows through the transparent derma. The infant's slate-gray eyes shine but do not give up their secrets. Its face has not yet learned to show emotions, and sometimes a series of expressions will flit across, as though it were trying them out for future use then discarding them after a few second's preview. An angry wrinkling of the brow, a mouth-stretching grimace, a sheepish wobble of the lips—all pass in reflex over this tiny human face.

Although helpless, the infant has fierce survival instincts that draw it toward its mother, that bind the infant to her in a mutuality of we two are the universe. It is attracted to the human face and can recognize the sound of its mother's voice and the smell of her milk. Tiny infants in the laboratory will turn their heads toward a breast pad taken from their mother's brassiere, ignoring a breast pad that soaked up the molecules of another woman.[1] The infant has a strong, sucking reflex. Brush it lightly on the cheek, and it will turn its head rapidly in that direction, mouth agape, rooting for the breast. It will latch onto anything. If it finds its hand in its mouth, it will suck on the entire fist with great energy. It will affix itself to your cheek and leave you with a purple hickey. Science does not know where human souls come from or what they go through in the womb, but one thing is clear: this creature was born to suck.

There are different ways of talking about the primal sucking urge. Some psychologists say it is the first expression of the instinctual erotic drive that propels us through life. Some see it as a reflex action hardwired in babies to keep them alive. Some say it is just one mechanism in a series that cements the infant and the caretaker into an interactive unit. No matter how you explain it, sucking is one of the original great passions.

An experiment done in 1977 with infants with blocked esophageal tubes points to some of the less tangible benefits of suckling.[2] The infants were divided into two groups. One group was fed through a stomach bypass without any mouth stimulation. The second group of infants were given sham feedings by their mother at the same time as the bypass feedings. Mothers were encouraged to ignore the mess and just hold and feed the infant. If the sham feedings were started early enough, these infants turned into strong sucklers and healthy babies. The infants who did not receive sham feedings did not develop normal hunger-satiation patterns. Moreover, according to report, "these infants' attachment to their mothers was tenuous, and their overall functioning lacked motivation, vitality, intentionality . . ."[3]

The infant's mouth is a lifeline to the mother. The mouth is not the only faculty by which it knows her. It has fingers that grip her hair; it has ears and a nose and skin to hear her and smell her and touch her. But the mouth is a special center of energy, serving as the main channel for satisfaction and for love. And the first object of desire and of love is the breast.

During the first year or so of life, impressions of the breast are tucked away in our psyches, creating some of the buried feelings that linger through our lives. Of course, not every baby is breast-fed. Those who are bottle-fed form a strong attachment to the bottle. But because a mammal is born with a mouth that seeks the breast, whatever infant feeding and loving experience it has is tied forever in its deepest mind to the breast.

One school of psychology, object relations theory, takes as its foundation the relationship between the infant and the breast. While Freudian psychology calls the penis the primal object of desire, envy, and fear, object relations theory gives this role to the breast. Freudian psychology emphasizes the father and puts the crucial developmental moment around age three, with the phallocentric crises of castration fears and the oedipal complex. Object relations pushes the crucial period back to the first year or so of life—the time of the mother. Object relations theory, which branched off from Freudian psychology, says humans are not impelled by drives so much as by the desire for objects; they are not pushed but pulled. Objects, in this sense, mean people, real or imagined, or things that symbolize people. The primal object—which all other objects echo and imitate—is the mother's breast.

Object relations theory began with Melanie Klein, who was born in Vienna in 1882 and was influenced by the early Freudians Sandor Ferenczi in Budapest and Karl Abraham in Berlin. Later she settled in Britain where she became a pioneer of child analysis. She developed a method of play analysis that allowed her to work with preverbal and autistic children. Stocking her consulting room with paper and pencils, figurines, and little cars and trucks, she observed children's play and interpreted its symbolic meanings. Her theories came out of these observations and also from her work with older children and adults. She found working with children particularly valuable because their unconscious is so close to the surface. She writes about Ruth, a four-year-old from a wealthy family who complained that she did not have enough to eat or clothes to wear. Where did this unrealistic sense of poverty come from? Ruth gave the answer symbolically as she turned on the taps in the washbasin and watched the water run down the little holes in the drain cover. The faucets are milk taps, she said, and the holes are mouths, but not very much milk gets into the mouths. Klein traced the sense of poverty back to infant nursing trauma.[4]

Reading Klein's theoretical writing can be a shocking experience. She had a wholly unsentimental vision of infants, whom she portrays as endowed with two inborn instincts: a life wish and a death wish. The life wish expresses itself in a passion for the breast. The death wish comes out in a destructive fury when the breast fails to meet the infant's every desire. When an infant, denied the breast, lies in bed screaming and flailing, Klein says it is playing out an enraged fantasy of attacking the breast. When an infant fights the breast, refusing to nurse, Klein says it has projected its own anger onto the breast and is afraid the breast has turned bad.[5] When an infant bites the breast, it is acting out an oral, sadistic desire to eat up the breast, to take the mother in and make her its own.

According to Klein (1984), in order to tolerate ambiguous feelings about the breast, the infant's imagination splits the breast into two: the good, nourishing breast and the bad, poisonous one. Take the case of Baby L, observed by a child psychologist.[6] Baby L was fed by a bottle, which became the symbolic good breast. Her desire for the bottle was constantly at odds with her mother's wish to feed her solid food. Her mother probably had been told that it is good to start solid foods early. Maybe she wanted her daughter to "do well" by moving on to the next developmental step. By three months, Baby L had formed the habit of stuffing her thumb into her mouth to block solid food, the symbolic "bad breast" force-fed by her mother. However, the thumb was never in evidence when Baby L sucked the bottle, which she was usually given while lying on the floor, propped with a pillow. When Baby L resisted solid food by spitting it out or stuffing her thumb in her mouth, her mother would prepare the bottle in front of her. Baby L would watch transfixed then hurriedly gulp down as much as she could before her mother yanked the bottle away, telling the baby it was just a drink between courses of solid food.

From our adult perspective, we can see this drama as a power struggle between Baby L and her mother. At three months, Baby L cannot claim what she needs or explain what she wants to a mother who believes she is doing what is best for her infant. In order for Baby L to survive emotionally, her imagination creates a split between the loving and disciplining aspects of her mother breast. The food becomes the bad breast, upon which she projects her anger and frustration. Meanwhile, she craves and savors the good-breast bottle, her solitary comfort.

Out of these first interactions grow lifetime habits of relating. Baby L projects what feels brutal and unacceptable about her mother unto the solid food—in Klein's terms, the bad breast. Later, she may tend to use the same defense to protect herself from other bad feelings and project them onto a specific person or perhaps a racial group or a class of people.

As the infant grows, though, the breast turns out to be only one part of the mother, who is a real, whole person. The infant must learn to broaden its heart, to go beyond its greedy hungers and sensuality, and to love the mother as person, not just her nourishing breast. This, as most of us know, can take many years. And this movement from part to whole is repeated again and again in future relationships as we must move from infatuation for the part of a new friend or lover that gratifies us to embracing the whole person, "warts and all." Maturity means moving from part objects to whole objects.

The Kleinian system resembles a theology. The death wish is a kind of original sin—a built-in anger and envy that can poison the breast and infect the sinner. God is the nurturing mother breast. The infant is a small Job, being tested in an impossible situation. The stakes are its very fate—its satisfaction or misery for the rest of its life.

After Klein, other object relations psychologists softened and broadened her position into something less scary and more reasonable. It is the kernel of her thought that lives on and throws light on infant psychology and on breasts. This nugget is that our earliest relationship with breasts marks us for life and echoes through many of our future relationships. Humans are born with potentiality, with temperament, talents, strong urges, and inclinations, but become who they are as these inclinations take on the imprint of culture—as translated to them by their parents' actions. This cultural indoctrination begins with fantasies that take shape in the infant's unconscious as it suckles or longs for the breast. The infant lies in its bed desiring the breast for comfort and for food, and it cries. Say the mother lives in a culture that believes people should be independent; the ideal human being is a rugged individualist. She has been told that she will spoil the infant if she picks it up too often. Left alone, an infant may suck on its thumb and fantasize the breast in its mouth, deriving comfort from the image. Through many such incidents, it learns it must take care of its own desires with its thumb. Another infant, left to cry, becomes distraught, imagines the breast as cold and withholding, and weeps in great despair as it takes this rejection into itself. Through many such incidents, it learns that it is not lovable, that it drives love away.

How do we know babies have unconscious fantasies about breasts? And if they do, why would these experiences continue to affect the person throughout life?

The truth is we do not know for sure, but infant research provides some intriguing hints. The newborn infant's brain is a surprisingly smooth and knobby white globe. As it develops, the brain becomes wrinkled and crinkled. It appears that knowledge and habits and attitudes may etch themselves physically into the convolutions as the person grows. "The infant brain—a product of heredity, chance, and circumstance—molds and remolds itself as the days merge into weeks then into months, " writes Dr. Richard Restak (1986).[7] The infant does a tremendous amount of learning in the first year: how to coordinate its hands and touch the mobile hanging from its crib, how to roll over, lift its head, smile. What it learns at the breast becomes almost instinctual, so deeply imbedded is it in the brain and the imagination.

Research tells us that the infant lying in its crib is not capable of symbolic thought or of memory as we know it. It does not rationally think the concepts "good breast," "bad breast," "comforting breast," "withholding breast," but can only experience them as images and feelings. There are, after all, two worlds—the external world of which we adults are conscious most of the time—the world that contains friends, trees, dogs, the Empire State Building. Then there is the unconscious world—the world of dreams, where black panthers stalk through your old high school halls, where you can fly high over buildings by an act of will, where large snakes pursue you, or where a stranger glimpsed on the street shows up and enfolds you in the most tender embrace.

Object relations psychology holds that the infant's fantasies about the breast take place in this realm of inner images. The infant experiences the breast giving and the breast receding, the taste of milk and the taste of hunger. These pictures in the imagination do peculiar things; they act out dramas as scary as the panther and as tender as the stranger's arms. As the infant grows into cognition, these images do not become conscious but live on in the hidden world. For a long time, the conscious and unconscious mingle. Infant researchers believe that our first weeks and months are spent in a state of perpetual semi-consciousness, never quite sleeping or waking but fluttering someplace in between.[8] Slowly the conscious world separates from the unconscious, but it takes a while. Young children are still close enough to the unconscious that they fear snakes and bears under their beds. By the time we grow up, most of us have learned to dismiss the imaginary grizzlies and fantasy cobras glimpsed out of the corner of our eyes.

Almost all adults have forgotten their early intimacy with their first caretaker. Some people, however, believe they remember. Psychological literature contains a number of references to adults lapsing into trace memories of nursing at the breast. First described in 1936 by the psychoanalyst Otto Isakower,[9] these occurrences are now known as the Isakower phenomenon. The memories typically come unbidden when a person is falling asleep or is ill. Often, the person remembers a large, dark object approaching closer and closer, can sense that the object is lumpy or doughy, and he is aware of the round, purplish shape of the areola. All this is perceived in a fuzzy and indistinct way. The person often has difficulty distinguishing between what is inside and what is outside the body, as the huge mass seems to wrap itself around the body. A firm sensation is felt in and around the mouth and lips. Sometimes there is a salty or milky taste. The individual merges with this large object, loosing boundaries, feeling open and fluid. Some people who experienced the phenomenon reported waves of emotions and inexpressible feelings associated with childhood or with sex. Many people have said the experience is strangely all encompassing; they couldn't tell if the sensations were inside or outside the body. It seemed to be the famous "oceanic feeling" described by Freud.[10]

Not all psychologists credit the authenticity of these phenomena; they could be just hallucinations. And not all authorities agree that there is anything to remember. Some infant researchers conclude that babies are not even aware of their mother until they are about eight months old. Some say that the brain is not sufficiently developed to lay down memories in the early months of life. But object relations theory maintains that people are deeply affected by their first love, that they imbibe a sense of self, of who they are, and what kind of world this is along with their mother's milk.

People tend to slip into these memories of breast-feeding as a defensive posture, literally a going back to the breast for comfort. A number of recorded occurrences have taken place on the analyst's couch. Patients are just encountering some horrific truth about their personality, and they suddenly zone off into the delicious, passive feeling of being cared for by a larger force. These cases are rare. The drama of retreating to the breast out of fear and frustration shows up much more commonly in eating disorders. Eating disorders, which affect over half of American women between the ages of fifteen and forty-five, include compulsive eating, anorexia, and bulimia.[11] For the infant, the breast is the object of desire and also the symbol of the mother. For the compulsive eater, food is the object of desire and also a symbol for emotional fullness and containment. Food is forever linked with mother; why else do people get that overwhelming urge to eat (or that feeling of nausea) when they enter their mother's house? Eat, darling, eat. Food is the center of family life. Family parties are typically feasts. Food has psychological meanings for everybody; in eating disorders, the psychological meanings overwhelm the physical responses of hunger and satiation. The emotional hunger comes out of a well of fear: fear that you will not get what you need, fear that you do not have enough, fear that nobody will give to you. Food symbolizes the comfort and containment we knew in our mother's arms; eating temporarily allays the gnawing. But it is a losing game. Food does not really satisfy the craving for caring or the fear of being alone or not good enough. And the craving is complicated by society's demand that women be thin. Thin is seen as healthy, strong, and disciplined; fat symbolizes weakness, sadness, and isolation. The more the compulsive eater engulfs, the more she confirms her fears.

Anorexia, seemingly the opposite, is really part of the same continuum. In *Starving to Death in a Sea of Objects* (1989), John Sours describes the classic anorectic as a person such as Catherine who has love/hate feelings for her mother. Catherine's mother is an efficient, well-educated, charming woman. She breast-fed Catherine for two months but did not particularly enjoy having the little creature tugging at her breast. It was a relief to wean her to the bottle and get her on a regular schedule. A good baby and an uncomplaining child, Catherine took to the new regimen without protest. At first a quiet toddler, later an excellent student, Catherine pleased her parents over and over again. The year she started junior high, Catherine began fleshing out; hips and breasts swelled on her body. Near the end of seventh grade, her periods arrived. That summer, Catherine had her first romance, a summer camp flirtation with hurried caresses in the bushes. But the boy dropped her after a week and moved on to someone else.

Catherine showed no pain and did not talk about the incident to anybody, but she began fussing about her figure and started taking early morning runs around the neighborhood. Her plate often remained half full at the end of dinner; she complained the servings were too large. Catherine lost weight quickly, and by November, her periods stopped. In a cheerful conspiracy of silence, her family ignored the increasingly gaunt appearance of the daughter who continued to get good grades and keep her room tidy. She was not diagnosed as anorexic until a school counselor demanded that something be done.

Some psychologists say that eating disorders grow out of a woman's desire for, and fear of, fusion with her mother.[12] Catherine needed to get away from her parent's perfectionist expectations that held her in their stainless steel grip. At the same time, the infant in her had never been properly nourished, and she still unconsciously longed for her mother's breasts. By starving herself, Catherine expressed a deep rejection of the breast. She was refusing to let womanly fat grow upon her body. She was refusing to mature, to become like her mother, or to have breasts herself. At the same time, she was repeating the drama of the breast that withheld love and nourishment from her when she was an infant.

Anorexia is a serous disorder that does not always yield to therapy. In the worst cases, the girl continues to turn cadaverous, all the while complaining about pockets of fat on her thighs. Her skin gets a strange, downy growth of fuzz; her hair takes on an orange hue. She dies looking like a skeleton—starving in a land of plenty.

Hunger for the symbolic breast of childhood can take many forms. In infancy we are bound to our mother in a symbiotic unit, connected to the life stream that we draw out of her breasts or the surrogate bottle. It may be that some internal homing force scans for ways to recapture that feeling of being wholly loved and cared for. It is not uncommon, at least in our culture, to hear people speak about a sense of being incomplete, of needing something or some one to make oneself whole. Often people seek that missing piece in romantic love or in religion. At their best, either ecstatic prayer or passionate lovemaking can lead to that eye of the hurricane, that place of well-being that may be replicating our contentment at the breast.

In the 1960s and 1970s, psychiatrist Lloyd Silverman conducted a series of experiments aimed at better understanding this sense of wholeness that is so deeply sought by human beings.[13] He was working with schizophrenics at the Veterans Administration and New York University laboratories. Schizophrenics tend to fluctuate between periods of craziness and periods of rationality. What causes the fluctuations? What therapy could keep a schizophrenic balanced and stable? One schizophrenic man said when he felt a bad spell coming on he often could stop it by visiting a brothel and paying a prostitute to lie naked with him in a long, quiet embrace. He would feel himself melting into her; a calmness would seep into him and the crazy feelings would subside. Silverman was fascinated by the curative powers in this sense of being fully accepted and loved by another—what he called the feeling of oneness.

Silverman wanted to apply the rigors of science to the concept of oneness and to see how it affected his schizophrenic patients. It wasn't practical to bring in a platoon of prostitutes to hug his subjects, but he could trigger what he called a oneness fantasy through subliminal suggestion. He had his subjects, male schizophrenics, look through the eyepiece of a tachistoscope, an apparatus that exposes visual stimuli for controlled amounts of time. The subjects received a series of four millisecond-long blasts, subliminal messages that appeared to the conscious mind as flashes of light. The message was "mommy and I are one." This communication, Silverman hoped, would stimulate an unconscious fantasy of unity with a good mother, giving the subject a sense of security and ease. It worked. After receiving the subliminal message, many of the subjects felt and acted more sane and stable and tended to feel good for an extended period of time (Silverman, Lachmann, and Milich, 1982).

Other researchers replicated these experiments with schizophrenics. The word "mommy" proved important because of its affectionate tone, calling up the image of the beloved mother of early childhood, the nurturing breast of infancy. Let it be noted, however, that the wording of the "mommy and I are one" message had some limitations. In one instance, a psychiatric hospital in Virginia tried to replicate Silverman's work but failed. Then the experimenters realized that the word "mommy" didn't pluck the right cord for southerners, who typically call their mothers mama. Nor did "mommy" work for Puerto-Rican subjects, but it did work for blacks, who do call their mothers mommy. The message "mommy and I are one" was not helpful for schizophrenics whose sense of their personal boundaries were too blurred; it made them feel engulfed in a great, devouring oneness. The subject had to have a reasonable sense of separate identity for the oneness fantasy to help. The message "mommy and I are one" worked less reliably with women than with men. Some women responded well; some didn't. Often, other messages, such as, "daddy and I are one, "My lover and I are one," and "mommy and I are two" helped women. Why don't women respond well to the mommy fantasy? Probably because women are less differentiated from their mothers than men are. Although women desire oneness, the fantasy of merging with mommy threatens their sense of self.

As the research expanded beyond the schizophrenic population, experimenters found the subliminal oneness message helped smokers break their addiction, boosted the reading skills of adolescents with behavior disorders, helped alcoholics stay off the bottle, improved grades for American and Israeli college students, and helped obese women to lose weight.

It seems, then, that the mothering breast is terribly important for emotional health. There's evidence that a subconscious feeling of oneness with a caring mother gives people the sense of security they need to feel better and do better. And it seems that a bad experience at the mother's breast can plant the seeds for later emotional dysfunctions such as eating disorders.

Here is where object relations theory enters the political arena. It would be easy—though wrong-headed—to draw the conclusion from all this that mothers have been ripping us off of our god-given right to be happy and that they should quit being so selfish and put their breasts at the service of humanity. Some feminist thinkers have objected to this breast-centered psychology because it seems to put this terrible burden on mothers, blaming them for our neuroses and insisting that they do better.

But that conclusion really does not follow. Child rearing is a function of cultures. Parents do not just invent how to care for children. They read magazine articles and baby books, get advice from friends and parents and professionals, and pick up hints from television and movies. Cultures provide formulas for the right way to feed and love an infant. These routines have long-term effects. "Culture and personality theory has shown that early experiences common to members of a particular society contribute to the formation of typical personalities organized around and preoccupied with certain relational issues," writes Nancy Chodorow in *The Reproduction of Mothering*.[14] It may be that some of our national neuroses—our preoccupation with money and consumer goods, for instance—are related to an infancy spent sucking on a pacifier alone in our cribs, instead of sleeping in a warm valley of flesh in our parents' bed. If that is so, it is a shared burden of responsibility belonging to our culture, not the fault of an individual woman—mother.

Breast-centered object relations theory has also been criticized because it seems to limit women to motherhood, to lock them into a demanding, unpaid, and largely unappreciated job. One of the first thrusts of modern feminism has been to seek equality for women by claiming they have few or no intellectual or temperamental differences from men and no need to stay in traditional roles. Today, more women seem willing to honor their differences from men instead of trying to deny them, but they still are seeking to define themselves apart from their reproductive functions. Women are fairly certain that true gender identity does not consist of being "as soft and pink as a nursery."[15] But how to define the feminine gender is by no means clear. Meanwhile the job of mothering gets little real respect, and mother is still pictured as a cheerful but impotent martyr of women. Like the breast of early infancy, she is a part object, limited to nourishing and giving, not expected to expand into a whole person. No wonder many women see it as a trap.

The fact that infants need the breast and that women are the ones who have breasts has not changed. What must change is the way we define and treat motherhood. Of course, women who choose to stay home and be mothers should be respected and seen as people who are doing real, meaningful work. It makes me angry that the welfare system no longer recognizes mothering as real work; now, single mothers are pressured to get jobs and place their children in day care. But the fact is, our culture respects work that earns money so systems must be developed that allow women to work and also nurture and breast-feed their babies. Some women are already doing it; the final chapter of this book provides some examples of women who have combined professional careers and extended breast-feeding, either by working at home or by taking the infant to work. But these women work in privileged occupations—one is a lawyer, the other a writer and college teacher. It is much more difficult for women working in a factory assembly line. Still, as business moves increasingly into formats that include flex-time and outsourcing, and as more businesses install on-site day care centers, nurturing at the breast should become more workable.

We are not there yet. Meanwhile, human beings continue to grow up bearing the imprint of the breast they knew in infancy—whatever that breast or surrogate breast was. And the breast they peek at or yearn for in adolescence, the breast they encounter in lovemaking, the breast they see in the movies or on individuals walking by on the streets—all these breasts will be entwined with feelings so deep they are felt as fact. On some level, our feelings about the breast will always mingle with our sense of how we are fed, how we are nourished by life, and whether the world is a place we can trust.

Chapter 6

When Instinct Meets Culture

In 1991, a young mother in Syracuse, New York, called a local information hotline. She was worried, she said, about feeling sexually aroused when she nursed her three-year-old daughter. That call launched a police investigation, the removal of the child by social services, and a national media furor.[1] This was not the first example of American discomfort about breast-feeding. In 1977, Barbara Damon was evicted from a swimming pool for refusing to go to the changing room to nurse her infant.[2] A few years later, a police officer surveying a parking lot for shoplifters asked Marlene Pennekamp to stop nursing her eight-month-old baby in her car.[3] More recently, in 1994, a shopping mall guard made Liza Habiby leave because she was nursing her baby in the food court. "The mall said I was exposing myself," she reported.[4]

The Syracuse case was particularly shocking because most media left out the fact that the woman had felt arousal; it appeared that mothers could lose their children merely for breast-feeding beyond the customary allotted time. Even if it had been better known, the fact of arousal should not have been so threatening. Though unusual, sexual arousal while breast-feeding is perfectly normal. In fact, given our culture's sexual attitudes toward breasts, it is quite understandable. But it frightened and confused the young mother, and it upset the person who answered the hotline. None of the parties handled the situation very well.

The Syracuse incident and another dozen or so arrests for public breast-feeding illustrate a social embarrassment that would be incomprehensible elsewhere in the world. In many non-Western cultures, women breast-feed casually, with open sensuality, and no one gives it a second thought. Here, for instance, is anthropologist Penny Van Esterik's (1985) description of breast-feeding in rural Thailand:

Chat sat breast-feeding her two-year-old son, absently tweaking his genitals, and reflecting on the fact that she might be breast-feeding for the last time. Now in her forties, Chat richly deserved her reputation as a woman who nurtures well (*liang di*). Each of her eleven living children which she delivered herself was breast-fed until she confirmed her subsequent pregnancy. By giving of herself in this manner, she creates a reciprocal obligation in her children which she expects her sons to repay by ordaining as Buddhist monks, and her daughters by attendance at sermons and merit-making activities. Both activities would increase her merit store, guaranteeing her a better rebirth. She was particularly anxious to draw her youngest daughter to her in this manner so that she would feel obligated to care for her parents in their old age.[5]

America and Thailand represent two radically different ways of viewing breast-feeding. Western science recognizes that baby boys (even infants) frequently get erections when nursing. Anthropologists have observed breast-feeding mothers in many cultures playing with the baby's genitals. This act, which would be totally unacceptable in the Western world, does not have a sexual meaning in these cultures; it is simply a way of soothing a baby. Chat sees her behavior as entirely honorable.

Western medical science has also known for decades that a baby's suckling produces hormones that stimulate sensuous feelings in the mother. But North Americans—queasy about the body and nervous about the specter of child abuse—tend to be embarrassed by observing a contented nursing couple and upset to think this could be a sensual, let alone arousing, act.

Breast-feeding is one of those biological acts (such as lovemaking and using language) that is very much culturally determined. We learn how to feel about these instinctual behaviors, the techniques, the ethics, and the commitments involved. Humans are born with the ability to nurse, to make love, and to speak, but how they do these things varies widely. Without the proper support, people may not even be able to do them at all.

Lactation is an ancient animal function. From an evolutionary standpoint, it predates most of our complex, reproductive dance.

Three hundred million years ago, when today's mammals were just a gleam in Mother Nature's eye, mammal-like reptiles laid eggs and nursed their hatchlings on milk from their bodies. Eventually, a whole class of animals, the mammals, came to be named for their ability to nurse their offspring.

It is widely accepted that breast milk is the best possible food for human infants. Each animal species makes its own unique kind of milk. The kangaroo has two teats; from one, she secretes a pink-colored, highly concentrated milk to feed the hairless embryo in her pouch; from the other, she releases a thinner milk for her yearling who hops along beside her but retreats to the pouch for a quick drink when it becomes frightened. A 2,000-pound baby whale nuzzles up to its mother's mammary slits, stimulating her to pump out a creamy substance that contains 50 percent fat.

Human milk specially suits the needs of human babies. For the first three days, the human breast produces colostrum, a yellowish substance rich in antibodies that protects the infant from infection. Colostrum acts as a laxative; it helps flush out the black, sticky meconium that accumulates in the infant's bowels during its time in the womb. When mature milk comes in after a few days, it contains substances that have a long-term effect on the infant's future. Amino acids aid rapid development of the infant's brain and central nervous system. This function may explain why some studies report that the IQs of children who were breast-fed test, on average, ten points higher than those of bottle-fed children. Breast milk contains substances that block absorption of large protein molecules, preventing food allergies. And, to fight the ongoing daily battle for survival, human milk contains a large number of white blood cells that protect the infant against whatever microorganisms the mother's system is encountering at the moment.

All this magic can only happen if the milk flows, and the milk will not flow unless a mother feels good about what is going on. Milk letdown is very much psychologically determined; it depends on an intriguing hormone called oxytocin. Oxytocin predates humans on the evolutionary ladder. Birds, amphibians, and fish all have oxytocin operating in their bodies. This hormone's functions are not all known. In humans, oxytocin has been called the happiness hormone or the sex hormone. It is stimulated by an infant suckling but can also be released almost as dramatically by an infant's cry or even by a mother thinking about her baby. When either happens, there is a rush of blood and a rise in temperature in the breasts. The woman feels the warm, tingling sensation of the "letdown" reflex. Inside the breasts, "basket" cells surrounding the alveoli contract to squeeze the milk. Infants cannot drain the breast the way they can draw milk out of a bottle. Without a flood of oxytocin, only the milk in the sinuses closest to the nipple will come out; the richer "hind" milk stays in the breast.

Experimenters have successfully stopped the flow of milk by immersing a nursing woman's feet in ice water and applying other stresses in the experimental lab.[6] They have pulled her toes and required her to solve complex mathematical problems, giving her a mild electric shock if she did not respond quickly enough. Under pressure, mothers cannot let down much milk. After stopping the flow of milk, experimenters can release it again with an injection of oxytocin.

People who have lived through trials and disasters do not need scientific proof to tell them the obvious. I once knew an elderly Dutch farmer who had harbored Jewish escapees during World War II. He told me he would shelter as many as fifty Jewish refugees at a time, moving the furniture out of his large farmhouse and filling the place with hay for people to sleep on. One night, a Jewish woman gave birth, but she was so frightened by the pursuit of Nazi soldiers that she could not let down her milk. The farmer had to go out in the middle of the night and find another woman to nurse the baby.

Oxytocin's functioning depends very much upon feelings. A woman who is nervous or upset may not be able to produce the hormone, and it does not take a war to stop the flow. Helene Deutsch, in her classic *Psychology of Women* (1945), tells of a young Polish wet nurse, poor and illiterate, who particularly enjoyed one advantage of her job—the quart of beer she drank each day to maintain her milk supply. When her employer cut back on her beer rations, her milk immediately stopped. The employer relented, and as soon as the wet nurse regained the pleasure of her favorite treat, her milk returned. Everybody around was impressed by the miraculous qualities of beer, though the real magic factor was the wet nurse's state of mind.

In some cultures, a woman's milk will dry up if an enemy gives her the evil eye. In Western society, many women have trouble with milk letdown, probably related to deep-seated attitudes toward the body. "I tried breast-feeding," one woman told me, "but I could not stand it. It just seemed so weird." She was not sure why she felt so ill at ease about breast-feeding, but there are plenty of possibilities. If, for instance, a woman believes that substances that come out of her body are unclean, chances are good that breast-feeding will make her uncomfortable. She could have problems if she feels her breasts are ugly or bad in some way. She may feel tense if she thinks sucking on a breast is a sexual thing to do.

The fact is that breast-feeding can be understood as one aspect of women's reproductive sexuality. Niles Newton, a psychologist at Northwestern University Medical School, conducted research to support this idea back in the 1950s, when respect for breast-feeding was at its historic low point in America. Her work delineated multiple connections among the three elements of woman's sexuality: lovemaking, childbirth, and breast-feeding.[7] She pointed out that, in both breast-feeding and lovemaking, marked vascular changes occur in the skin of the breasts and the nipples become erect. Breast stroking and stimulation play a part in both experiences. The uterus contracts during both. It is common for milk to leak from a lactating woman's breasts while she is making love. And women occasionally have orgasms while they are nursing, though it is more typical for them to experience a diffuse, tender sensuality. "The survival of the human race," writes Newton, "long before the concept of 'duty' evolved, depended upon the satisfactions gained from the two voluntary acts of reproduction—coitus and breast-feeding."[8]

The hormone oxytocin provides a concrete, measurable link between all three reproductive activities. In a classic experiment conducted in Ghent, Belgium, researchers connected the circulatory systems of two sheep, a ram and a lactating ewe.[9] They joined the two at the jugular veins with plastic tubing. The researchers then massaged the ram's sexual organs to the point of emission, and within seconds, they measured a sharp rise in pressure in the ewe's udder. Oxytocin released by the ram's sexual response stimulated the ewe to begin letting down milk. In a second experiment, two ewes were joined by tubes. Using a balloon, experimenters distended the vagina of one ewe, mimicking the sensation of intercourse and childbirth. Milk immediately began leaking from the udder of the connected ewe.

A final connection Newton found is that all three reproductive acts seem to trigger caretaking behavior.[10] If things are going as they should, lovers treat one another tenderly, and mothers dote on their babies. Anyone who has observed farm animals has seen the caring and intense interest mothers lavish on newborns. Sheep, cattle, and horses lick their newborn infants, which soon rise on shaky legs and begin to nurse. If something goes wrong, and the initial bonding does not take place, mother animals sometimes reject their young. It seems as though, without these early intimacies, they do not recognize the babies as their own.

It may be that, in a state of nature, humans also bond directly after birth and that breast-feeding can play an important role in that bonding. In an experiment in Sweden, newborns were placed on their mothers' bellies and the mothers were instructed not to move the infants. Within the first hour, healthy babies, making what looked to be random movements, managed to wiggle up to their mothers' breasts and begin to suck. Although the concept is controversial, some researchers believe that humans, when not hindered by hospital routine, go through an instinctual, clearly patterned, species-specific bonding behavior.[11] This instinctual behavior may be important to the long-term relationship between mother and baby. Other studies show that mothers who undergo early separations from their infants are more likely to abuse them later on. Some breast-feeding experts believe that the skin-to-skin contact of breast-feeding creates a long-term bond that may help prevent parents from battering their children.

In many societies, mother-infant bonding stretches out into a lengthy interlude that anthropologists call "the transitional." The newborn is understood and treated as what has been called an "exterogestate fetus," a fetus gestating outside the womb, still tied to the mother by the umbilicus of her breast. This idea is so deep that it is woven into the language. In the central African country of Rwanda, the word *ingobyi* can mean either the human placenta or the sheepskin used to carry the infant on the mother's back.[12] During the transitional, a gradual physical separation from the mother plays itself out until the child emerges as an individual, still cared for and supported but no longer dependent on the mother's body. In different cultures, the transitional takes radically different forms. It is basically nonexistent in a Western hospital where the mother and the child are separated at birth and the baby is bottle-fed. At the other extreme, women of the Chenchu tribe of India do not wean their children from the breast until they are five or six years old.

Many traditional cultures (those that are preindustrial, rural, and tribal) have lengthy and intimate transitionals. Mother and baby sleep together. The baby suckles frequently during the night, often dozing with the nipple in its lips. The mother carries the child everywhere, usually in a sling, and nurses it on demand.

This constant suckling is a matter of survival. It ensures a nonstop milk supply. Such children usually thrive for the first year, then face a danger period during the second year, as they gradually begin to eat solid foods and to encounter their first dose of food-borne bacteria and parasites.

In addition to basic survival, the transitional has other important functions. The building blocks of the child's psychosexual nature are cemented at this time. And in many traditional cultures, the transitional is a time when the community mothers the mother, allowing her special privileges, rest, and recuperation from the pregnancy.

In Crocodile Village, that small rice-growing community in Thailand where Chat breast-fed eleven children to increase her merit store for a good rebirth, women were by custom entitled to a postpartum holiday known as "lying by the fire."[13] Villagers believed that since childbirth left a woman cold and wet, she must lie by the fire to warm her body and dry out her insides. Free from all household chores, she lay by a low fire for from five to eleven days, bonding with her baby and establishing breast-feeding. "Lying by the fire" was seen as an act of virtue.

In the tropical rain forest of Zaire, new mothers are rubbed all over with a red dye prepared from the bark of a tree. Having sex with their husband is taboo. Instead, they are sent away to live with their own clan and relieved of heavy work for eighteen months. Baby and mother spend that time constantly together. At the end of eighteen months, the mother weans the baby, holds a big party, and returns to her husband.

The taboo on intercourse during breast-feeding, while by no means universal, can be found in cultures worldwide. Many cultures believe that sperm poisons the milk, or simply, that it is a bad idea to get pregnant again before the child is weaned. These taboos, however, are not necessary to ensure child spacing. Prolonged, frequent suckling is an effective, if not foolproof, method of birth control. Although women can become pregnant while breast-feeding, the pituitary hormone prolactin, produced by the infant's suckling, delays ovulation and menstruation. Possibly a less conscious reason for the taboo is to ensure good bonding with the child and to leave the mother free to enjoy a sensuous, intimate relationship with her baby during those important early years.

Traditional cultures had all kinds of rituals and galactogogues, which are potions for ensuring good breast milk. Written in 1550 B.C., the *Papyrus Eber*, one of the earliest medical encyclopedias, gave these instructions: "To get a supply of milk in a woman's breasts for suckling the child, warm the bones of a swordfish in oil and rub her back with it. Or, let the woman sit cross legged and eat fragrant bread of soured durra. While rubbing her parts with the poppy plant."[14]

It is hard to know whether or why these rituals worked. The warmed fish-bone massage may have been quite relaxing. The poppy plant sounds scratchy, but maybe it had an opiate effect. Some traditional galactogogues, the rooster soup in North China, the fried ginger, jaggery, and black pepper in India, the herbal teas and infusions in various parts of the world, may have contained vital nutrients that improved breast milk. But some of the rituals were clearly based on sympathetic magic. In ancient Hawaii, women hung freshly picked vines dripping with white sap over their breasts while they prayed to the gods Ku and Hina for a good milk supply. Given the psychological nature of oxytocin release, it is likely that any kind of magic a woman believed in would probably help.

Although these practices harmonized with successful breast-feeding, many traditional cultures were surprisingly ill-informed about colostrum, that yellowish liquid which is produced before the milk. Today's scientists are convinced of its many health benefits, but the majority of traditional cultures viewed it as a kind of poisonous pus.

The colostrum was drained, either manually expressed or sucked and spat out by a community member assigned to the task.

In many ways, the history of breast- and bottle-feeding reflects the history of Western civilization. In the beginning, breast-feeding was universally practiced. That it was worshipped as one aspect of the life-giving Great Goddess, one face of the power of the feminine, seems likely from the statuettes and images of milk-giving goddesses found around the world. For millennia, divine mothers—Ishtar, Isis, the Virgin Mary, and many whose names we have forgotten—were portrayed suckling young gods. For millennia, virtually all mothers nursed their young.

It is hard to put a finger on the moment when breast-feeding began to lose universal acceptance. A good guess would be the advent of organized cities. But nearly as far back as written history goes, we have examples of aristocratic women who did not nurse their own children. Sharing of breast milk must have gone on for as long as people lived in groups. In tribal cultures, if a mother died in childbirth or could not nurse her young, another lactating woman fed the baby. But when a wet nurse worked for a noble mother, the relationship lay along the axis of power, not mutual support.

The first reference to wet nurses dates from the third millennium B.C.[15] The flowering of Babylonian culture included legal contracts between wet nurses and their employers. The Code of Hammurabi stated that a wet nurse who substitutes another infant for a dead suckling without the parent's knowledge shall have her breast cut off in retribution. At the time of the pharaohs, royal women coveted the prestige of being wet nurse to the young kings. Pharaohs had several wet nurses, some of whom merely put the infant to the breast for a brief, ceremonial display. Wet nurses served aristocratic women in ancient China, Greece, and Rome, and the custom fanned out through Western Europe with the Roman occupation. Wet nurses were particularly in demand in cultures that exposed or abandoned babies. In Greece and Rome, unwanted infants were left on rubbish heaps, and it was the custom for people in search of slaves to go there and choose a healthy-looking baby to raise. Lower class or slave women were hired to nurse babies picked off rubbish heaps. In England, between 1500 and 1800, the use of wet nurses spread among the gentry and wealthy merchants and finally, by the nineteenth century, to women of relatively modest means. There were, however, always exceptions; a few highborn women insisted on nursing their own children. Indeed, near the end of the eighteenth century, under the influence of Rousseau, it briefly became fashionable for upper-class women once again to breast-feed their babies.

Sermons and tracts, written from the time of the Greeks and throughout the Middle Ages and Renaissance, ranted against the practice of employing wet nurses. The science of lactation, which changed little from the Greek era to the Renaissance, held that breast milk was white blood. The infant, already accustomed to its mother's blood, should not be shifted to another woman. It was commonly believed that the wet nurse's physical attributes and character traits could be assimilated through her milk. There were also warnings that children would come to love the wet nurse more than their natural mother, and indeed, sometimes that happened.

Why did highborn women, in spite of these beliefs and warnings, refuse to nurse their children? Aristocratic women, particularly in the Middle Ages and Renaissance, were virtual baby factories. Their primary purpose was to furnish abundant heirs for the bloodline. Without the contraceptive effects of lactation, which had been well-known since prehistoric times, they could produce up to sixteen or eighteen children in a lifetime instead of the four or six birthed by women in sustenance cultures who nurse for three or four years. There were also social considerations. With busy social schedules and household duties, nursing a child was not always practical. As time went on, employing a wet nurse became a status symbol, a sign of refinement and breeding, and a means by which a merchant or shopkeeper's wife could identify herself with a higher social circle. (It would be a mistake, however, to portray the growing use of wet nurses as woman's vanity. Up until the nineteenth century, husbands decided the matter of how the baby would be fed.)

During the nineteenth century, wet-nursing took on nightmarish qualities. With the flourishing of factories, the old systems of village life and cottage industry had broken down and many women needed to work away from their infants. The call for wet nurses rose dramatically. Aristocratic families insisted that the wet nurse live in their home and leave her own child behind, since it was believed she would nurse her own to the detriment of the family's baby. It was "fallen" or desperate women who would take these jobs. Those in need of wet nurses prowled the "lying in" hospitals to find such women. Although employment as a wet nurse paid well, it often meant the death of the nurse's own child. The wet nurse had to send her child out to a cheaper wet nurse or to the notorious "baby farms," where children, hand-fed or insufficiently nursed, died like flies. Sometimes the arrangement was little more than a contract to "dispose" of the child for a fee.

Outside of England the situation was even worse. In Russia, huge foundling homes farmed orphans out to wet nurses. The infant mortality rates in such placements averaged 45 percent. Wet-nursing became a vehicle for the spread of syphilis, which had menaced Europe since the fifteenth century. In France as well, large foundling hospitals were established with special infant drop-off doors. People could anonymously place an infant in the cradle, then push the revolving door to swing the infant indoors where the nuns would find it. Wet nurses were always scarce, and some of these institutions found direct suckling from goats or asses preserved more infants than hand-feeding. Goats entered the feeding room bleating, searching for their assigned infants, whom they could recognize. Pushing back the covers with its horns, the story goes, a goat would straddle the crib and give suck to the infant. As these animals were not susceptible to syphilis, they were frequently used to feed syphilitic babies. Because of the belief that character traits were absorbed through the milk, many physicians abhorred this practice. It was said to make infants "fierce and not like men," or "very swift and nimble."[16]

In the American colonies, infant abandonment was rare, and foundling homes were never established. Women in the southern colonies tended to use African slaves as wet nurses, even though visitors were shocked by the practice. In fact, there was some anxiety that children suckled by their mammies would grow up with slave accents and "pick-a-ninny" ways. Wealthy women in the northern colonies employed poor, white wet nurses, while Puritan women breast-fed their own as an act of piety.

Hand-feeding or "dry-nursing" has existed since the Stone Age, although to a much lesser degree than maternal breast-feeding and wet-nursing. People probably hand-fed only as a last resort, when the mother died or did not have enough milk or when the infant had mouth deformities, such as cleft palate, which prevented it from suckling. Nursing artifacts have been found, especially in infant graves: Neolithic feeding horns from the Sudan, a terra-cotta spouted vessel from ancient Egypt, watering can and boat-shaped feeders from the eighteenth century, sucking bottles and drinking tubes. Usually, some combination of unpasteurized cow's milk, bread crumbs or flour, and sugar was poured into the infant's lips.

Throughout most of history, hand-feeding was an act of desperation, one which often led to the death of the child. Curiously, in scattered communities, primarily in northern countries, mothers used hand-feeding as a matter of course. A few communities in Germany, Scandinavia, and northern Italy hand-fed almost exclusively, starting in the fifteenth century, and considered breast-feeding swinish and repulsive. It is not known how this custom began or what the infant mortality rates were. Possibly, people with long traditions of hand-feeding developed methods that worked better than in the rest of Europe. Colder northern climates may have kept milk from going bad as quickly.

During the course of the nineteenth century, the practice of baby farming fell under increasing criticism, and wealthy families slowly became aware of the social repercussions. By the mid-nineteenth century, most of Europe and parts of America were struggling with the disastrous wet-nursing situation, and the scientific community had become intensely interested in the subject of infant nutrition. The discovery of the germ theory and pasteurization promised to make safe infant formula possible for the first time in history. Chemists learned about crucial differences between human milk and cow's milk. Infant formula companies applied the new knowledge and started mining a new market, using physicians as their gateway into women's pocketbooks. During the first few decades of this century, the era of "scientific mothering," bottle-feeding made enormous gains in popularity. Woman stopped going for advice to other women and stopped learning the old ways from female relatives and neighbors. Instead, they learned new ways to care for their babies from experts, their doctors. Women wanted to do it the modern way. By mid-century, breast-feeding had become the exception and bottle-feeding, the rule.

In a sense, breast-feeding has been a casualty of the industrial revolution and our changing way of life. In tribal or sustenance or cottage-industry communities, people's lives were less segmented. People lived and worked among the birthing, growing, and dying of humans, animals, the crops, and forests or grasslands around them. Wealth came from nature, just as milk came from a woman's breasts. Holding, touching, and nursing the infant was an integral part of the pattern of life. But with the change to a cash and consumption economy, breast-feeding no longer fit. Women began to work outside the home, and their role as nurturers devalued. Breast milk does not mesh with the industrial ideology, the model of wealth in which things of value are manufactured, packaged, and exchanged for cash. The cash value of breast milk could not compare to a day's wages; the value of "lying by the fire" or mothering the mother had been forgotten long ago.

Today, virtually all physicians and public health agencies recommend breast-feeding, yet few babies get a full year of it. The Western world is still primarily a bottle-feeding society. Habits have improved since the nadir of breast-feeding in 1959, when only about 20 percent of women breast-fed one week after parturition;[17] almost no one breast-fed beyond a couple of months. In 1995, about 60 percent of American women started out breast-feeding; only about 22 percent were still doing it at six months of age[18] and an estimated 6 percent at the end of one year.[19] More than half of American women begin breast-feeding, but few follow through for a year or more. Part of the reason for low rates of extended breast-feeding is the difficulty of balancing full-time work and breast-feeding. But the mixed messages we are sending young mothers make breast-feeding even more difficult. In many hospitals, even mothers who say they want to breast-feed are given bottles of milk or glucose water, just in case. When they leave the hospital, they go away with a free gift of commercial products, including a bottle and a couple of cans of infant formula. These gifts and provisions have a silent way of undermining a woman's confidence that breast-feeding will work. To put it in perspective, imagine this scenario:[20] A young man is about to have his first experience of sexual intercourse. To ensure the utmost hygiene, the event will take place in a hospital room. A nurse enters to explain the procedure. "A lot of young men have difficulties with sexual intercourse," says the nurse. "Sometimes they don't have enough energy or their penis gets sore and chapped. Sometimes their partner is not receptive and won't cooperate. Sometimes they just can't rise to the occasion. It's best to do it the way nature intended, but in case you have any problems, you can always use this."

The nurse points to an artificial penis lying on a tray at the young man's bedside table.

"Don't feel embarrassed or guilty if it doesn't work out as you hoped," says the nurse. "Most men end up using the artificial penis sooner or later. At eight o'clock I'll bring your partner for an intercourse session. If she doesn't get enough, you should probably follow up with the artificial penis."

This kind of advice is what women too often receive in the hospital. The medical profession may mean well, but hospital procedures, the insistence on standardized routine, on treating mothers and babies as sick people, on weighing and measuring—all this can be antagonistic to breast-feeding. I still remember the routine in the hospital where I spent the first two days of my daughter's life. I was given two bottles. One contained a brown-colored, strong-smelling antiseptic, which I was to paint on my nipples before I nursed. The other was a bottle of glucose water which I was instructed to offer my daughter after she finished nursing. I had always been a good patient, and I wanted to do what was best for my baby, so I followed orders. She eagerly latched on, then winced and drew back, obviously repelled by the taste of the antiseptic. Luckily, I had already had the experience of nursing my first baby. I never questioned that my daughter would want to nurse, and I was sensible enough to wash the noxious liquid off. If I had been more naive and continued to follow orders, my daughter would have started her life on glucose rather than colostrum, and who knows if I could have ever established breast-feeding. The areolas of lactating breasts secrete a substance that keeps the nipples clean. I think it is a sad commentary on our culture's attitudes toward the female body that this hospital's staff thought a woman's nipples would not be clean enough to put in her baby's mouth. A common complaint among women who stop breast-feeding is that the baby refused the breast. I wonder how often that terrible-tasting antiseptic made the baby turn away.

Though some of their procedures may be antithetical to breast-feeding, hospitals cannot take the blame for our rather puny rates of breast-feeding. Some hospitals have made real commitments to encouraging breast-feeding by making available "rooming in" with the baby sleeping in the mother's room, by sponsoring nursing support groups, and even, occasionally, by refusing the almost ubiquitous free aid of formula companies.

Still, breast-feeding goes counter to many of our ways of thinking—to the hidden paradigms of our culture. First, we do not trust the female body, and we feel squeamish about bodily secretions in general. Then, we value breasts for their erotic appeal. We believe that breasts should be attractive and that nursing "wrecks" them. Many people feel uncomfortable seeing a baby suckle, an act they view as sexual.

In addition, our culture embraces an industrial or scientific mode of thinking. Many people feel more secure feeding an infant milk that can be sterilized and measured, rather then something unseen that comes out of a breast. And most people, accustomed to running their lives by the clock, find it inconvenient and perhaps unreasonable to meet the erratic demands of an exterogestate fetus.

During the last decade, reams of research have been published about why women do and do not breast-feed. Poorer, less educated, younger women in less stable circumstances tend not to breast-feed. Teenage mothers, preoccupied with breast sexuality, frantic about losing their freedom, and insecure about what other people think, almost never breast-feed. Well-educated, financially secure women with a network of supportive friends are more likely to breast-feed then less advantaged women. Clearly, the social milieu is a major influence in women's decisions about infant feeding. And a firm commitment to it seems to be the determining factor in breast-feeding success. Women who really want to nurse and whose husband, mother, and friends think it is a great idea, find the will, the belief, and the way to make it work.

When a woman puts a child to her breast, she is giving of herself in a way that is ancient and instinctual. She is also bound, on some level, to scrape against her sense of her own personal rights, her duties, and her identity as a woman. "I loved breast-feeding," one woman told me. "But I didn't like feeling so tied down." My own experience with breast-feeding was mostly a happy one; it made me feel good about myself, and it bound me to my children. But I still remember one especially unromantic moment in my breast-feeding career. I was tired, and the baby I held in my lap had been tugging insistently at one nearly empty breast for quite a while. I looked down, and the breast appeared long and skinny, similar to an animal teat. Suddenly, I had a vision of my baby as a largish parasite, a soft, white larva, sucking out my vital juices. Luckily, it struck me as mostly humorous and only a little bit horrible.

People in Western cultures do not like parasites; we place a high value on freedom and autonomy. A woman's desire to bond with the infant, to submerge herself in its needs, to be everything for another human being, and to be loved as never before—all that does battle with her desires for independence, for separation, her own space, her own time, her own achievements. This is not a new dilemma. Helene Deutsch wrote about this in 1945: ". . . the longing for reunion is from the beginning in conflict with the urge for liberation."[21] The pull-and-tug between self and children has no easy resolution; it is something parents always need to balance and weigh.

Then there is the forbidden thing that makes breast-feeding even more difficult. In our culture, women are allowed to give when they breast-feed but not to get back. If a woman were permitted, even encouraged, to feel sensual pleasure in nursing, as has been true in many non-Western cultures, her needs and the infant's needs, her satisfaction and the infant's satisfaction, could find a better balance. Breast-feeding is a deep human connection. It is about people with needs holding each other and finding relief and satisfaction. It involves two people blending together, egos dissolving. The problem is that we are accustomed to limiting such intimacy to the realm of adult sexuality. A woman's sensuality is reserved for her husband or lover and, according to our paradigms, has no place in the crisp, clean realm of motherhood. As it is, such pleasure is so taboo that some women experience it as discomfort or disgust. And women who nurse too long or too publicly are thought to be "doing it for themselves" or to be "forming unnatural dependencies."

It is clear that confusion between the sexual and nurturing functions of women's breasts is a key issue in breast-feeding in our culture. I think it is probable that, were we not so taken with the breast as a sexual object, breast-feeding could go on unhindered by the aura of being gross or embarrassing. Unfortunately, the breast complex has a way of replicating itself. I suspect that our culture's bottle-feeding habits actually help create our obsession with breasts. Ironically, the more we crave breasts, the less we are willing to give them to the infants who will make up our future world.

PART THREE: SEX

Chapter 7

Circles of Desire

As long as I have had a sex life, I have always enjoyed the breast caress. I cannot imagine making love without it. When my breasts are touched, I feel as though all the gates to all the streams have been opened, and the water is flowing homeward. I imagine a benevolent substance has been released in my body, infusing me with bliss. It feels like crying without the sadness.

So it surprised me to learn that many women do not share this pleasure. "It drives me crazy," one woman told me. "Every time we make love he grabs my breasts. Why can't he leave them alone just once?" I have heard enough of these comments to set me to wondering why my breasts are so responsive. Is it genetic predisposition? Do I descend from a long line of women with extra libido stored in their breasts? Or are there other factors? Maybe the inadequacy and the rejection I felt as an adolescent and projected onto my small breasts has eroticized them. Maybe having my breasts kissed by my lover heals that feeling of isolation. My breasts are accepted; my adolescent pain is answered with passion.

Currently, I believe the reason may go back to the earliest months of my life. My mother gave birth to me in the spring of 1944. A caring, well-educated woman who studied books on child rearing, she wanted to do her absolute best for me. So she did something quite unusual for the era; she nursed me for the first four months of my life. It is all recorded in my faded pink baby book. I suckled well after the first three days. She kept me on a four-hour schedule with a 2 a.m. feeding. I was introduced to Pablum at six weeks and the bottle at sixteen weeks. By the age of five months, I was weaned from both breast and bottle and was eating Pablum, cream of wheat, and various baby foods spooned out of little jars. Five months of suckling may have seemed a fair indulgence in the United States of 1944, but on a worldwide basis, it is extremely short.

Under likes and dislikes, the baby book notes that at the age of two I refused to eat hot cereal, custard, or anything of a similar texture. At three, I would gag when Pablum-like substances found their way into my mouth. The baby book does not say, but I imagine that in my unconscious, the link between losing the breast and eating Pablum gave that most innocent of cereals a bad rap.

I do not know when I started sucking my thumb, but I remember that I did not stop until it was time to enter first grade. Despite the noxious substances my parents painted on my water-logged thumb, I would not give up the vice until I knew I absolutely had to. My parents did their best for me according to the beliefs of the time, but it seems clear to me that I did not get enough suckling.

My baby book records that I was a stubborn little girl. I suspect that my psyche made up its mind that breasts were home and heaven and never quite gave up that conviction. When I grew up and began to have a sex life, my psyche remembered that breasts are where pleasure and satisfaction live. I identify myself as heterosexual, but sometimes when I see another woman who has handsome breasts, I feel a little thrill of attraction. I have really only noticed this in the last three or four years, but maybe all along I was unconsciously longing for the missing breast and fulfilling that yearning through the erotic feelings in my own breasts. This explanation feels right to me. It draws my whole life together from infancy to the present. It seems to have psychological truth, but it does not necessarily have "scientific" truth.

Sexology is a young science, an odd mixture of medicine, psychology, and sociology. Research in sexuality often goes begging for funding. Because of this lack of funds, basic studies that should have been done, have not. "Indeed, the fact that no large-scale study on American sexual habits has been conducted since the Kinsey volumes now stands as a major embarrassment, resulting in our inability to answer even the most basic questions," wrote Carole S. Vance,[1] editor of *Pleasure and Danger: Exploring Female Sexuality* (Thompson, 1984). Since Vance wrote those words in 1991, another large study, *The Social Organization of Sexuality* (Laumann et al., 1994), has come out, but it tells us almost nothing about breasts.

We do know what happens to our bodies, the physiological responses that take place when people have sex. Drs. William Masters, Virginia Johnson, and staff observed couples making love in the laboratory, measured the bodily changes, the secretions, the colors, and the temperatures and presented the results in their book *Human Sexual Response* (1966).

Masters and Johnson reported that as a woman becomes aroused, her breasts may take on a mottled, pinkish appearance, known as the sexual flush. Her nipples become erect, hardened by involuntary contractions of muscle fibers. Nipples may elongate as much as a centimeter and swell by one-half centimeter in diameter at the base. As her excitement increases, her breasts swell as much as 25 percent in size, and the bluish venous patterns become more marked. Blood rushing to the breasts causes the swelling. The areolas also become engorged, so much that sometimes the nipples appear to lose erection. Breasts that have nursed infants appear to swell less, probably because the veins that drain them become so efficient during lactation.

After orgasm, the areolas immediately deflate, constricting so that they look grooved or ridged while the nipples remain erect. In fact, the areolas' quick shrink act can be used as a marker of orgasm. Without orgasm, they diminish much more slowly and do not appear corrugated. Women over fifty show little or no swelling of their breasts and areolas during sex. Their nipples, however, seem to stay erect longer than those of younger women.

These dramatic physiological changes show that breasts participate fully in a vibrant sexual experience, but that is not necessarily what women report. Alfred Kinsey and the staff of the Institute for Sex Research at Indiana University found that only about half the women they questioned said they enjoyed having their breasts stimulated. Only about 11 percent touched their own breasts during masturbation.[2] If what women do when they masturbate represents their true desires unadorned and unsocialized, Kinsey's findings suggest that breasts are not that important to most women's sex lives.

While only one-half of American women enjoy having their breasts touched when they make love, most men like to touch them. And apparently, women let them do so. Kinsey reported that 98 percent of couples born after 1910 who had much sexual experience engaged in breast petting; 87 percent also had oral contact with the breasts.[3]

We cannot be sure these statistics and preferences reflect contemporary experience. There has been a sexual revolution since Kinsey did his work in the 1940s and 1950s; people today may feel more free to experience sexual pleasure or at least to talk about it. Yet my unscientific interviews with women seemed to corroborate Kinsey's findings. About half of the women I talked to said they enjoyed erotic breast play, and about half of them said they did not. Half the women are, at best, enjoying it because it pleases their lovers; at worst, they are only putting up with it. Women vary enormously, from those who attain orgasm simply from having their breasts stimulated, to those who cannot bear to have them touched.

Why these differences? We know nipples are rich with nerve endings and that stimulating them releases oxytocin, a hormone associated with sexual arousal. We know breasts become engorged and swell, and nipples become erect. So why do a large percentage of women feel no sexual pleasure in their breasts? Why are women's subjective experiences so varied?

Part of the explanation may be physiological. People have different thresholds of pleasure and pain. Some women's breasts become extremely sensitive just before or during their menstruation, and they find their lovers' touch painful at that time. At the other end of the spectrum, a woman wrote to *Playboy*'s advice column that she likes to roughen her nipples with an emery board to keep them sensitive enough to enjoy erotic touch.

In some cases, a woman's lack of response to the breast caress must surely result from a mismatch between her sensitivity and her lover's technique. Monica, a woman in her early forties who has had many lovers and regularly experiences multiple orgasms, told me that breast stimulation leaves her cold. She only feels pleasure in her breasts when she flirts with men. "When I am attracted to someone, it feels like electricity shooting out of my breasts," she said. "But having them stroked or sucked doesn't do a thing. It hurts during my period."

In her long career of lovemaking there was one exception. "Once I had a one-night stand with a Greek professor. He pushed my breasts together so the nipples were very close and flicked his tongue back and forth between them. It was wonderful. It brought that electricity. It was subtle and light, very nice." Maybe most of Monica's lovers simply do not know the right technique. Probably, poor technique explains why some women do not respond sexually to the breast caress. Sex therapists tell me that women often complain that men touch their breasts too roughly. Unfortunately, North Americans are notoriously poor at communicating what they specifically do and do not like. Bernard Apfelbaum, director of the Berkeley Sex Therapy Group, summed it up this way:

> Masters and Johnson observed that men tended to be clumsy and insensitive in touching women's breasts. They even found women wincing in pain, especially when they're menstruating. Women weren't complaining. Obviously the women were enduring it because they thought the men were enjoying it, although probably the men were doing it because they thought the women were enjoying it. That's typical, you know; nobody knows for sure. . . People just aren't talking that much in sex.[4]

No doubt many of us have much to learn about being more sensitive lovers, but I do not believe what arouses people can be summed up in techniques. People can be so different from one another. What they like to do in bed and who they like to do it with can be quite specialized, even fanciful. Dr. William Masters (1997) told me that one woman in the Masters and Johnson's lab could reach orgasm by having the small of her back rubbed. "Most people wouldn't call that erotic, but it was to her," he said. "It depends on how we individually orient ourselves."

The annals of fetishism are replete with case histories of people who are aroused by sights, sounds, smells, and behaviors that on the surface would not seem sexual at all. For instance, kleptomaniacs have been known to experience orgasm when they touch fabric that they intend to steal. Such cases are extremes; most of us have less startling preferences. Among my acquaintances, one woman loves to have her toes sucked; one man really prefers to masturbate while his lover snuggles up next to him (although he knows this is self-centered and only occasionally gives in to the urge). One woman must have men of a different race for her lovers; one man has only loved short, heavy-set women. From all the possible methods of arousal, individuals narrow down their preferences to some quite specific patterns. Whether or not a woman responds to the breast caress depends on what Dr. Ethel Spector Person, a professor of clinical psychiatry at Columbia University School of Medicine, has called the "sex print." "The sex print is an individual's erotic signature," Dr. Person wrote. "It signifies that the individual's sexual potentiality is progressively narrowed between infancy and adulthood."[5] Although people can learn and incorporate new pleasures into their repertoire, the cluster of acts, fantasies, and situations one person finds arousing, once discovered, remain pretty consistent. That does not mean an individual cannot function with a different type of partner or in a different style of lovemaking, but deeply personal arousal, the feeling of full erotic abandon, may be missing.

Why and how we acquire our individual sex print remains something of a mystery. As with all great mysteries, thinkers disagree about where to look for the answers. But any exploration of the sex print must begin with the theories of Sigmund Freud. It is currently fashionable to debunk the father of psychoanalysis: his morals, his method, and his thought. Nonetheless, his writings on infant sexuality and the unconscious have saturated twentieth-century thought, and they remain an essential starting place for understanding sex.

Freud believed that an unstoppable well of sexual energy, what he called drive, springs from the body and that it takes different forms as human beings mature. Libido first lives in the infant's mouth. In the oral stage, the drive finds release when the infant sucks on the breast or bottle. In *Three Essays on Sexuality* (1975), Freud wrote, "No one who has seen a baby sinking back satiated from the breast and falling asleep with flushed cheeks and a blissful smile can escape the reflection that this picture persists as a prototype of the expression of sexual satisfaction in later life."[6] The mouth latches on with rhythmic suckling, but the infant is dependent and not in control. The mouth receives or loses the breast or bottle at the will of the mother.

In the second stage, the sexual energy moves to a new zone. The anus stands in for the erotic mouth and the feces for the breast. The infant gains the same sensual pleasure of surrounding an object and the satisfaction of release. But now the small self can control the

[margin note: Sex print]

holding in or letting go of the erotic object, sometimes much to the frustration and annoyance of the parent.

Later, the energy moves to the phallic zone, the penis or the clitoris, which replaces breast and feces as the erotic object. The young child delights in the autonomy of playing with his or her magic organ.

Once the libido has settled in the penis, it has arrived at its final destination. The phallus becomes the reigning object of desire. The keystone of Freudian theory is the Oedipal stage, during which a boy, in his fear of castration, rebuffs his father and clings to his mother. A girl, on the other hand, becomes jealous of the penis, and her longing for the magical organ turns into an incestuous desire for her father.

Freudians often view breasts as a poor substitute for the penis. The original erotic act is an infant's mouth suckling a breast, and in mature sexuality, the vagina is supposed to stand in for the mouth and the penis for the breast. Some Freudians even go so far as to suggest that, through its orgasmic contractions, the vagina sucks the penis the way a baby's mouth suckles a breast. Needless to say, many Freudian psychoanalysts believe women associate their own breasts with their fathers' penises.

Here is an example from the psychoanalytic literature of how the breast/penis association could simmer in the unconscious of a woman and how it could affect her arousal patterns, her sex print.[7] Joan is a twenty-seven-year-old married woman who complains of anxiety attacks and pain in her nipples. She tells her analyst that she hates her breasts. She wears a bra when she sleeps. The bra stays on when she takes a shower because she cannot bear water running over her nipples. The thought of nursing a baby brings her to the point of nausea. She and her husband, Charles, have a reasonably good sex life, but her unwillingness to let him play with her breasts during lovemaking has become a point of resentment. She tells the analyst she feels that if Charles were to press her breasts, her nipples would fly off like the cork of a bottle.

In the course of the analysis, a complex history emerges involving an overbearing mother and a sweet but ineffectual father. During one session, Joan talks about wanting to squeeze her husband's penis so hard the glans would pop off like a cork out of a bottle. The similarity to the image of her nipples as corks alerts the analyst to a breast/penis association. A few weeks later, while she is looking at her husband's penis, Joan suddenly remembers that between the ages of three and five she used to take showers with her father. Subsequently, she dreams that her father walks by while she lies in bed holding a man's penis.

The analyst speculates that, as a small child standing in the shower with her father's penis at eye level, Joan experienced a desire to touch it with her hands and her mouth. How natural for a child to want to touch and taste, but this desire was so forbidden, she could never acknowledge it. In the unconscious, her father's penis became equated with her own nipples. The frightening penis taboo was displaced onto the less frightening breasts, where the psychological dramas could be acted out. When the repressed childish urge to touch her father's penis came close to the surface, she responded with queasy feelings about her own nipples.

As Joan dredges up memories and starts to understand these connections, she gradually becomes able to take showers without wearing her bra and to begin feeling pride in, rather than distaste for, her breasts. At the same time, her understanding of her parents becomes less stereotyped, and she lets go of some of the old resentments. Unfortunately, the analysis was not finished at the time the analyst wrote up the case history, so we do not know whether her breast sexuality changed. Presumably, showering braless may have been the first step toward allowing her husband some gentle touching of her breasts. We do not know whether her breasts could ever become erotically sensitive.

I am willing to believe that, for Joan, her breasts symbolized her father's penis. But I do not believe that equation works for most women. Some women love the penis. I do; I think it is a truly wonderful organ. It possesses a splendid combination of toughness and tenderness and the ability (and courage) to penetrate another human being. But the penis really belongs to male sexuality. I do not think it makes sense to define my sexuality in terms of not having one, and in this belief, I follow in the footsteps of many female thinkers. Defining women's sexuality around the penis seems too much like another patriarchal con job.

I think penis envy is a beautiful metaphor for women's social situation. Making lower wages, getting smaller portions at dinner, talking less in meetings, being taken less seriously, waiting for that phone call, changing the baby's diapers, taking care of the aging parent, and wiping up the dog's vomit—women have lots of reasons to be envious and wish they were wearing the pants. I wish I had man's power and a man's wage scale, but I get along quite nicely without the penis. If I want to understand my own breasts, I must look elsewhere.

Freud pictured a natural drive that could be repressed, damaged, and/or perverted by culture. Another major school of thought takes entirely the opposite point of view. It claims that sex actually requires culture to give it form and meaning. The cultural constructionists (many of them from the fields of sociology and anthropology) believe that sex, like speech, is founded on biological potential but that its patterns are learned and conditioned. All cultures must include reproduction in their sexuality. But apart from that, the customs, the behaviors, and their meanings change from culture to culture. Anthropologists say that even identical acts have different meanings in different societies.

When it comes to breasts, anthropologists have discovered startling variations in different societies' sexual practices. In many societies, people do not think of breasts as erotic, nor do they touch or stimulate them before or during coitus. In others, however, breasts are essential. Among the Lepcha, a population of farmers and hunters living in the southeastern Himalayas, fondling the breast is the only form of foreplay. An anthropologist reports that breast stimulation is so essential among the Indonesian Alorese that "to pull a girl's breast" stands as a euphemism for intercourse. Young men try to lay hands on a woman's breast because they believe that she cannot resist such a caress. At dances, one young man said, "our hands move about at random and touch a girl's breast. That makes her spirit fly away and she has to sleep with a man."[8]

In most cultures, men stroke their lovers' breasts with their hands, but in some cultures, sucking is the norm. The fishermen of Truk, an island in the central Carolines, say sucking helps a woman reach orgasm.[9] Their neighbors living in the east central Carolines rub their noses against the woman's breasts while making love.

Interestingly, there seems to be no correlation between the breast's erotic appeal and whether or not women habitually hide or bare them. We Americans find the hidden and forbidden to be particularly exciting, but that mindset may not be cross-cultural. "The habit of concealing the breasts during everyday life bears no direct relation to the importance assigned to breast stimulation as a form of erotic play," wrote Clellan Ford and Frank Beach, authors of *Patterns of Sexual Behavior* (1951). "The Apache, Trukese, and Dunsun cover the female breast and this area is stimulated during sexual activities. With these few exceptions, however, in all the societies which use this form of caress the upper part of the woman's body is usually bare."[10]

Even within America, different subcultures have somewhat different sexual practices. According to Kinsey (1953), well-educated people are more likely to kiss, lick, or suck the breast than those with little education. People born before 1900 were less likely to have oral contact with the breast than people born after 1900.[11]

According to the cultural constructionists, when lovers take each other in their arms, they are performing a series of learned motions or scripted behavior. A script is usually something for actors in a play, and that exactly describes the act of making love. Foreplay is a ritual drama. Kisses and caresses have erotic meaning for us; they are symbolically imbued behavior that releases erotic feelings and physiological reactions such as blood rushing to the sex organs. If not, why would we become aroused watching other people making love on the screen or reading about it in a book? The meaning of the acts, not the actual touch of skin on skin, excites us.

As proof, the cultural constructionists point out that a physical act can be erotic in one situation but not in another. When a man touches a woman's breast in a romantic situation, they may both become aroused. But in the doctor's office, a woman's breast is palpated, and usually neither doctor nor patient find the act erotic in the least. The doctor's eyes drift to the ceiling and his face takes on an impersonal look. The patient feels awkward and uncomfortable.

What do the cultural constructionists make of infant sexuality, which was so important to Freud? They dismiss it. They say infant and childhood sexuality really does not exist as such. We may see children doing something we define as masturbation or as sex play, but they are not having a sexual experience as we know it. Sexuality really begins at adolescence when society recognizes young men and women as having sexual natures.

According to the cultural constructionists, cultural influences and individual experience form our individual sex print. Some of the women I interviewed showed definite signs of having had their sexuality shaped in this way. When women had suffered a good deal of teasing or other negative attention about their breasts in late childhood and early adolescence, they tended not to enjoy breast stimulation. A good example is Julie, a twenty-year-old woman in her junior year of college. She has very large breasts, which she suddenly developed in the fifth grade before any of her schoolmates showed signs of maturing. One week, she and her friend were making fun of the flat-chested little girls wearing training bras, and the next week her mother and grandmother were taking her to JC Penney's to get a real bra. "I was pretty traumatized," Julie said. "I don't remember my personal feelings about my body, but socially, it was hard. I felt really weird about the whole thing."

Ever since fifth grade, Julie has worn baggy clothes to camouflage her large breasts. Nevertheless, boys and men of all ages have pursued her; she has never lacked boyfriends. She often draws attention when she walks down the street; a kind of attention she does not appreciate. "If you have big breasts you're a slut," she said. "Right now tight shirts are in style. I'd love to wear them but I can't. It would be all cleavage and all tits. Guys would just drool. I don't want to be part of that. I don't want to be looked at like that. People think of me as a person with nice boobs. It's so shallow."

On an emotional level, Julie's breasts have been coopted. When I asked her whether she feels pleasure in them when she makes love, she seemed uncertain. "It's weird because it feels like it's not really me," she said. "They're not really part of me. They've never been neglected, but men touch my breasts for their pleasure, not for mine."

Then she told me about something upsetting that had happened to her recently. "It was with this disgusting guy I had instant relations with," she said. "He was just totally into my boobs. He sits on my chest and puts his penis between my breasts and, like, masturbates. I think it's just repulsive. I've done it with two different people. Once my boyfriend kind of got into it. It was kind of degrading, kind of gross. But I thought, OK that's cool. The other guy was really disgusting. You're just lying there. If they're considerate they won't do it in your face. I wouldn't feel comfortable using somebody else's body like that. That experience pushed me over the edge. I'll never do it again."

Julie's aversion to breast eroticism has been formed by learning and experience, starting at puberty. Although the larger culture says breasts are sexy, her own experience has alienated her from them to such an extent that it feels distant and impersonal when a lover touches them. All those men grabbing at her have created in her a barrier to breast sexuality.

A woman's experiences as a mother can also alter her sex print. A friend told me her breasts lost some of their erotic quality when she began nursing babies. She still enjoys having her breasts stroked but can no longer abide oral contact. "I don't like it when a man sucks on my breasts," she said. "I feel like, why do you want to do that? That's for babies." Perhaps the same kind of sexual uneasiness that keeps many women from nursing has made it impossible for her to enjoy a man's mouth on her breasts. My friend comes from a long line of women who prided themselves on propping the bottle rather than wasting their time holding the baby. To say her family was not supportive when she nursed her babies would be an understatement. Her father once harshly muttered, "This is disgusting," and stomped out of the room so he would not have to watch. Under this pressure, she may have compartmentalized her feelings, so effectively cutting off sexuality from suckling, that she never got the sexuality back again.

Both the Freudian and the cultural constructionist explanations of the sex print have some serious shortcomings. Psychologists say changing people's sexual preferences and obsessions is extremely difficult, if not impossible. But if sexuality is socially taught, as the constructionists say, why can't it be retaught and relearned?

The Freudian theory, as mentioned, has a masculine bias that no longer seems acceptable or true. In addition, the notion that sexuality is a drive that seeks discharge seems to be a narrow way of understanding sexual experience. Orgasm is not everything. People fulfill other goals in sex: sensuality, ecstasy, spirituality, comfort, and oblivion.

There is a third way of understanding sexual arousal—a paradigm suggested by Ethel Spector Person.[12] This approach forms somewhat of a synthesis between Freud and the cultural constructionists and makes liberal use of object relations theory. I have saved this interpretation of sexuality for last because it seems to me most inclusive and because it depends on the other two. The key element is sensual pleasure, the delight in skin-to-skin contact, of being held and soothed, caressed, warmed, rocked, the feeling of fullness, and the feeling of release. Sensual pleasure provides the basis for sexuality's continuum from cradle to grave.

In our mothers' arms, we learn whether the world is a kind or a cruel place and whether this all-powerful parent finds us lovable or annoying. This experience takes place in an ocean of touch, taste, and smell. In this sensual soup, the infant's mind develops and consciousness begins to take shape. Dr. Carol Rinkleib Ellison (1993), clinical psychologist and author of sexuality textbooks and a book on women's sexuality, told me that parental warmth is crucial to developing a sexual nature. "Through her breasts," she said, "a mother passes on an appreciation of sensuality and skin contact to the next generation."

The early pleasures and frustrations may not be sexual as we know sexuality, but they become etched in memory as a sensual experience. When we mature and begin to have sexual fantasies and adventures, these early unconscious memories come into play. Our bodies remember the feeling of being merged with another human being and seek to repeat it. Our mouths retain the desire to open and touch our beloved.

The culture speaks to us through our mothers' skins. Society teaches mothers how much holding and nursing is appropriate and desirable. Infants assimilate culture through physical contact, the milk from the mother's breast and the relaxation or tension in her body.

When we grow up, the motive behind sexual behavior is not really that of drive seeking release, as the Freudians would have it. The motives can vary, but many of the most compelling ones are reworkings of that first relationship. In sex, women and men try to fulfill desires for dominance and submission, for dependency and independence, and for acceptance and merging with another.

An acquaintance named Susan told me about poignant desires left over from a difficult infancy that for years played havoc with her sex life. She did not begin to understand her desperate cravings for love until she attended a Zen Buddhist retreat. After four hours of meditation trance, she began reexperiencing her first weeks of life, with memories that swept over her in waves of nausea and anguish. She saw herself as a baby who had been nursed for one week, then put away emotionally for the rest of her infancy. "I was a neglected child ever after," Susan said. "I screamed for six months, but my mother only picked me up every four hours." Susan's mother subsequently confirmed that this had been the case.

Susan played out this early abandonment over and over again with her lovers. She desired them desperately, and if they tried to pull back, she would scream at them until she was out of breath. They usually responded, not surprisingly, by abruptly leaving her. At thirty-eight she became pregnant, and the baby's father disappeared when she was four months along. "The last thing I heard from him was a postcard saying 'See you next week,'" Susan recalled. "I'd never been so thoroughly dumped in my life." When Joshua was born, she was still grieving over her latest abandonment. Her labor was difficult and ended in a caesarian. Her breasts were swollen, but the milk would not flow. Susan wanted very much to nurse and tried everything she could think of. Unfortunately, she did not have knowledgeable counseling or understand that a woman must relax before her milk can let down. She was still so distraught about being rejected that she could never release more than a few drops.

Joshua is as tall as his mother now. She could not nurse him, but Susan has loved him thoroughly, and he has helped to heal her feelings of isolation and abandonment. She finally has a lover who shows no signs of wanting to leave her. Their sex life, she says, is very good. She loves having her breasts caressed. She finds it exciting to have her lover ejaculate between her breasts—the very act that Julie found so demeaning. "I like the semen in my face or on my chest," she said. "I have a primitive, earthy nature. I get really excited at the man's excitement."

Susan has large breasts and is able to suck them herself, an act of self-stimulation she finds extremely erotic. She has also slowly introduced her present lover to the enjoyment of having his breasts sucked. "He was too repressed to tell me, but after he relaxed with me, I discovered it. I enjoy it," she said. "I get oral pleasure."

Susan's experiences with breast-feeding (her own and her son's) have been full of sadness and disappointment. But in her sex life, she can give and receive the oral pleasure that did not work out for her or her baby. She told me that when she makes love, she feels an awakening of innocence, a sense of childhood regained.

Whether the sex print is instinctual, culturally constructed, or a little bit of both, a woman's breast sexuality tells a story about who she is and how the world has treated her. Lee is a fifty-five-year-old professional woman who drives a little red sports car. She has had a hard life, and it became difficult early. As a baby, Lee was so tiny she would fit in a shoe box. "I didn't want to eat," she said. "My mother had to slap me to keep me awake." By the time she was seven, she knew she was somehow different. "I didn't know I was a lesbian," she said. "I just thought I wanted to be a boy." Lee grew up in Los Angeles during World War II. Her family lived in a poor neighborhood among "Okies and Arkies," hill people who had migrated west. She found great comfort in the big-bosomed country women so different from her thin mother. "Very heavy-set women," she said, "who wore no shoes and no underwear. They just threw a dress on. Big-breasted women. They would just grab hold of you and smother you in their softness."

In the sixth grade, Lee became enchanted with a schoolmate who wore angora sweaters over her large breasts. "The boys would tease her, probably because they were attracted to her. I would defend her against the boys, probably because I was attracted to her too."

When her own breasts began to develop, she hated them and hid the bras her mother bought her. Her brothers teased her about having small breasts. Secretly she was glad, but on a social level, she felt humiliated about having "no chest." Going to high school in the Marilyn Monroe era, she wore padded bras. In the 1970s, she threw them away and has not worn one since.

For years, Lee tried to ignore her sexuality, but it was difficult. Her dreams and sexual fantasies about breasts mingled with dislike of her own breasts. She could not love her breasts until she finally allowed herself to love another woman. "It was exciting to my breasts to stimulate her breasts," Lee said. "To imagine touching breasts can make my nipples get hard."

"Sometimes we liked to smear our breasts and our private parts with honey, then lick the honey off. The creams. The strawberries. We were using the body as a sort of a table."

Lee's long distaste for her breasts paralleled her uneasiness about being a woman. When she finally understood that she was not a misbegotten man, but a woman who loves women, she could begin to appreciate her breasts. Those early memories of the big, comforting women and her first burning attraction to her sweater-wearing schoolmate provided the groundwork for enjoying erotic pleasure in breasts—her own and her lover's. For her, the profound drama of her life has been the long self-denial, followed by the relief and celebration of accepting who she is. Her relationship with breasts has been the subplot, knit tightly to her life's central theme. Over the years Lee's breasts have become larger, and she has developed a touch of vanity about them. "Sometimes I like to dress manly and dapper and feel my masculinity," she said. "Sometimes I like to wear women's clothes. Women—and men too if they want—can enjoy looking at my breasts. Now I can be big-breasted," she said. "I can even enjoy wearing a little cleavage."

The sex print is as unique as the fingerprint. Each person is a little (sometimes more than a little) different from every other person. In my interviews with women, I did, however, find one consistent pattern: a link between teasing about breasts in childhood and a lack of receptivity to erotic feelings in the breasts. As discussed in Chapter 2, adolescent girls are astonishingly vulnerable; many of them feel horribly unsure of who they are and what they are becoming. I was never teased or tormented about my breasts, but I recall one incident in sixth grade when a boy very gently let me know he noticed that I was starting to develop. My breasts were no bigger than bee stings at the time, and I felt like the rug had been pulled out from under me. I was shocked and mortified that he had noticed, and I am grateful that no one mentioned my breasts again for many years. I feel sad that so many girls are subjected to comments, and I fear that the attention and taunting narrows their sexual potential. It seems a sorry price to pay for our cultural obsession.

It is strange living in a body with a sex organ that is also a public institution. For breasts are institutions, with vaunted attributes and a dogma of myths and beliefs. Living with genitals is comparatively simple and unproblematic. As long as they function, it does not really matter what they look like, and people rarely judge and comment on them in public.

Breasts, however, carry so much cultural weight that they often do not function as well as they might. Our sex lives are sensitive and telling parts of us, a little like our dream lives. In our dreams, wonderful and horrible things happen. It is the time when the monsters come out, or we can suddenly fly. For some women, breasts carry unconscious memories that stretch back to birth and span the breadth of adulthood, with a history that seems to enrich their erotic lives. But for too many, the monsters are grumbling in the background, and when a lover touches their breasts, the women wince in pain.

Chapter 8

Breast Men

What is a breast man? Who is he? What makes him so crazy about breasts? These questions seemed important to me because, I reasoned, breast men ought to embody a concentrated form of society's breast fetish. If I could understand the breast man, I might grasp the key to the cultural obsession. I started with the cliches I had heard: that breast men are rough, tough cream puffs, that they are primitives, and that they are insensitive clods. The stereotypes, of course, proved to be untrue. The search for the elusive breast man took me down some fascinating and surprising paths.

I began looking for answers by asking people who called themselves breast men to tell me all about their feelings about breasts. The first person I interviewed was Henry, a sixty-two-year-old retired educator who has been married to the same woman for forty years. Henry's thing about breasts goes back to the fifth grade when he first noticed the older girls on the school bus. His fascination grew during his teenage years. "I had a lusty, busty cousin," he said. "Boys were at a premium in the 1940s, and girls were all over the place. All my cousin's friends came over. They had these fancy bathing suits. I was a country bumpkin so they felt safe with me. I always associated with older girls; they had bigger boobs. I was so interested in girls I'd do anything." The big girls would pet and tease him and brush their breasts against him. "The feeling was electric," he said. "The fine hairs would stand up on the back of my neck, and then la la land. I'd get real shaky: tingles, then fantasies."

Henry described himself as a hunter who is drawn by a certain kind of game, a specific kind of visual presentation. As hunter, he becomes aware of breasts, excited by breasts packaged with enchanting semi-exposure. "I like them big. I don't like them saggy," said Henry. "I like cleavage but not flaunting it. A well-wrapped package is more interesting. I like the hint. I like to be teased." He must be the aggressor; he does not like forward women. He is offended by pornographic films or brazen display. He remembers during his army days, being taken to a restaurant where the waitresses, dressed like Daisy Mae, would flip up their tops and flash their breasts at customers. That turned Henry off. He wants the erotic display subtle enough that he has to discover it himself. If all this comes together—the right breasts with the right presentation in the right situation, then the magic happens. "Something in the mind unlocks," Henry said, "and it gets me."

Is the something that unlocks in Henry's mind a breast fetish? The answer hinges on how we define fetish, a word that has been loosely used and has accumulated a number of different meanings. In urban youth culture, it is, at the time of this writing, hip to play at fetishism, with games and costumes of rubber and leather.

The word fetish, however, dates back to the fifteenth century Portuguese word "feitiço," meaning charm or power object. Portuguese sailors exploring West Africa used it to describe native religious practices. If African villagers believed a material object, such as an amulet or a charm, contained divine power, the Europeans called the object a fetish. Never mind that medieval Europeans believed fragments of the holy cross and vials of the Virgin's milk could perform miracles; that was not a fetish. From the beginning, the word developed as a way to distance the racial other from the good Christian. The fetishist was someone alien who worshipped the bizarre. The concept of fetishism was picked up by nineteenth- and early twentieth-century anthropologists, who were particularly fascinated by fetish objects of human form. As the meaning of the word began to change, two parts of the concept stayed with it. First, a fetish always involves the transfer of power from an original source onto a substitute. Second, a fetishist is someone who operates outside the circle of what is conventionally considered "normal and good. "

In the nineteenth century, the newborn science of sexology adopted the word fetish to describe sexual obsessions that deviate from the only good, right, and normal behavior, namely heterosexual intercourse. The new science made lists and categories of "perversions," which included fetishism along with homosexuality, transvestism, and other exotic behaviors. Like the religious fetish, a sexual fetish displaces power from the source to a substitute object—be it a shoe, a rubber raincoat, or a breast. Today the word perversion has fallen into disrepute, but the less loaded term paraphilia (meaning pleasure in things beside or beyond) serves a similar purpose. Paraphilias include practices such as fetishism, transvestism, bestiality (sex with animals), and sadomasochism.

The explanation for how a person develops a fetish has evolved since Freud wrote that fetishism operates as a screen for castration fears and a substitute for the mother's missing penis.[1] At the moment of denial and repression, according to Freud, the boy fixes upon some object near at hand—a shoe, an undergarment, or maybe his rubber pants, and invests it with erotic energy. Psychologist Robert Stoller (1985) argued that men do not fear loss of their penis so much as loss of their masculinity. The idea of merging with a woman frightens them so they "partialize" the woman, focusing on just the breasts to avoid the full impact of the woman. In other words, the real love object ought to be a woman, not a body part. Because of fear, the man turns his erotic energy away from the woman and invests it in a part of her. He can get excited about her breasts without worrying about all the complexities of who she really is, complications that might quell his ardor.

A prime example of a man partializing a woman appeared in a 1971 article in the *Journal of Sex Research*.[2] This case history told of a twenty-year-old white man, R. B., who broke into an apartment, tied up a housewife who was alone in the premises, gagged her, and stared at her naked breasts. Then he left, went home, and masturbated. When the man was apprehended, he said he usually achieved orgasm by looking at pictures of nude women; he had no intention of raping or harming the woman; he just wanted to look at her breasts.

The actual diagnosis of this man's behavior was scopophilia. Scopophilia is the psychological term for sexual pleasure derived from looking. This technical word has some overlap with voyeurism, though voyeurism implies extra pleasure in lurking secretly and feeding off other people's lives. Scopophilia simply means visual erotic pleasure. Freud maintained that scopophilia is an instinctual element of all sexuality.[3] It became a dysfunction only when looking took over as the central act, rather than a precursor to more intimate, mutual activities. R. B.'s little escapade of breaking into an apartment and tying up a stranger surely involved more than simply looking. If he had stuck to his girlie magazines, however, R. B. might have remained just one of millions enjoying a little private scopophilia, satisfying himself by looking at pictures of breasts.

R. B. clearly had a fetish; but what about Jason, a man I interviewed who also likes to look at pictures? A thirty-five-year-old mechanical engineer who owns a large collection of pornography, Jason first became interested in pornography reading his father's *Playboy* magazines at about age five. "At the time it was just interesting seeing people with their clothes off," he said. When he was twelve his parents divorced, and within a year or two he got his own subscription. For several months he managed, by arriving first at the mailbox, to keep this secret from his mother. Ultimately, she caught on and canceled the subscription. Despite his mother's best attempts, however, Jason's fervent curiosity persisted; by the time he was fourteen or fifteen, he had read Masters and Johnson, and Kinsey, and owned his own copy of *The Joy of Sex*. Somewhere in his mid-teens, he said, the magazine pictures became arousing. Since then he has continued to buy and collect all kinds of pornography, from the mainstream to the hardcore and the bizarre. He likes amateur pornography best because sometimes it is fresh and original. Jason is not interested in peep shows with live models or in strip joints or even in videos; he is specifically attracted to print material. "I think the paper product is just something that can be readily available," he said. "You can pick up a magazine or something when you're in the mood. You don't have to go out and interact with clerks and all that. It's just right there. It's more controllable."

Apparently pornography appeals because it brings satisfaction without complications. Even though Jason sometimes uses pornographic pictures rather than turning to real women, he does not see it as a problem. He has maintained a number of serious, long-term relationships. "Other than having a pretty avid interest in sexuality in general, I haven't found my interest in pornography comes out in my sexual activities with partners," he said. "My ex-wife used to complain a lot that I was always trying to put her in the poses from magazines, but I don't remember actually trying to say, 'You have to be like this,' and contorting her into a position. So I don't know whether she had a valid complaint." Jason is an enthusiastic breast man, and he likes all kinds of breasts. "Everybody's just a little bit different and that's always interesting," he said. "But I don't think I have any specific preferences of colors or sizes." The only breasts he does not like are the balloon-like silicone implants that he sees more and more in mainstream pornography. He does not like "to see somebody with just these humongous breasts and the skin all stretched tight." That kind of fantasy does not work for him. He would rather look at amateur pornography with more realistic, imperfect bodies.

It does not seem useful to call what Jason does a fetish. Using pornography does fall outside the circle of what is usually thought of as good and proper, but judging by the strength of the thriving pornography industry, many people do use it. Moreover, pornography refuses to stay in the margins; it has seeped into mainstream media. "A fair amount of advertising that I see nowadays for women's products," Jason said, "are photographs that would almost be equivalent to *Playboy* magazine in the 1960s." Jason claims that pornography is purer and more honest than advertising that exploits women's breasts.

The standard definition calls pornography depictions of erotic behavior that are intended to cause sexual excitement. They may be more subtle and tasteful than skin magazines, but we see such depictions daily. With its sophisticated film, television, and print images of the female body, Western society is shot through with scopophilia. Jason's personal habit grew out of early childhood experience, and it was probably perpetuated by his desire for a quick, easy, controllable outlet. Similarly, media imagery trains most people in Western societies to enjoy a scopophilic buzz. Often the virtual images, outshining the real, elicit the erotic response. If Jason is a fetishist, then so are many of us.

Just as some women's magazines are now showing images that used to be reserved for *Playboy*, Western society as a whole has become much more sexually liberal. Some behaviors that used to be called paraphilias have entered the mainstream and been dropped from the list. When perversions were first described in the late nineteenth century, focus on breasts counted as a fetish. Now it is so widespread, it is no longer considered a paraphilia. But according to Stephen Levine, a psychiatrist who treats patients at the Center for

Human Sexuality at University Hospitals of Cleveland and Case Western Reserve, focus on breasts could be classified as a paraphilia if it overshadows or dominates the relationship with the woman.[4] "Unlike other paraphilias," Levine said, "this one passes as normal." But it is difficult to tell what is normal from what is passing as normal. To make the distinction between a fetish and normal sexuality even fuzzier, different levels of fetishism have been categorized. They range from (1) a slight preference for a specific kind of partner or object, to (2) a strong preference, to (3) a condition where a certain kind of partner or stimulus must be present in order for sex to take place.[5]

Of all the breast men I talked to, Jeff was the most open and enthusiastic about his craving for breasts. A well-educated, independent producer, Jeff grew up in a theatrical family in the Los Angeles area. Now fifty, he has had a series of passionate relationships during his adult life—all of them with large-breasted women. "Breasts are synonymous with female affection," he told me. "I was always attracted to well-developed women." In his fantasies, breasts are abundant and nurturing. In one of his favorite fantasies, he lies passively while five women run their breasts over his body. In another, he is an arbiter of breasts. "I would get off on twenty women walking and I had to judge which had the best breasts," he said. "The fantasy is that by judging, I get to look at them all. It's like chocolate. You might like one kind best, but you still love them all. Oh, and I like chocolate syrup on breasts, and whip cream. That's a lot of fun: putting it on and licking it off."

For Jeff, breasts are soft, delicious, and fulfilling. "I like touching them and the smoothness of it all and the silkiness of it all," he said. "If I'm in the submissive position with them in my mouth, I feel nurtured, warmed, comforted. Fondling them from the top is a different feeling. It's all coupled with fantasy. It's a part of the dream feeling."

The crucial nature of the fetishized object to sexual performance is one measure of a well-developed fetish. Jeff admits, with some remorse, that it would be a real problem for him to make love with a woman who had had a mastectomy. Small breasts, on the other hand, would be possible but far from ideal. He does not care what the shape and texture are as long as breasts are large.

Hearing Jeff articulate his absolute adoration for breasts made me wonder about the idea I had often heard that breast men are people who did not get enough suckling and mother love when they were babies. Because most people in the Western world do not benefit from frequent or lengthy breast-feeding, it is tempting to think our inordinate interest in breasts may result from frustrated oral needs. Object relations literature in the 1950s and 1960s promoted this notion, presenting many case studies of dependent people who, as infants, had been starved for the breast. These visceral memories continued to haunt them, sometimes coming out in a strong attraction to breasts. I asked all the breast men I interviewed whether they had been breast-fed. Some said no; some were not sure; only one man was certain he had been. To prove anything, a comparative study of breast men and men who do not identify as breast men would have to be done. When I asked if Jeff had been breast-fed, he said he was not sure. "My parents said that the milk was not good," he said, "I spit it out." Jeff's mother is dead, and the truth about what happened at his mother's breast cannot be known. Possibly baby Jeff spit up, and his mother mistakenly assumed her milk was no good. It is intriguing that he believes that he had bad milk as a baby and today loves to indulge in whipped cream, licked from his lover's breasts.

If lack of oral satisfaction during infancy really explains the existence of breast men, then we would have to account for why women are not sexually turned on by breasts. It may be that growing one's own breasts satisfies that ancient need. Since women have their own breasts, they do not need to look outside themselves. I would argue, however, that many women are attracted to breasts, though they do not always experience the attraction in a sexual way. Perhaps few women would say they are turned on by breasts, but how many millions of girls play with Barbie dolls and get crushes on busty movie stars? How many women buy cleavage-enhancing bras or have breast-enhancing surgery? Heterosexual women may not be caressing other women's breasts, but one way or the other, many of them crave breasts.

Karen is a married, heterosexual woman who says she is fascinated with breasts. She was breast-fed and has many fond childhood memories of breasts. Her family had a roly-poly cook on whose lap she loved to sit and gaze at the swell of the woman's breasts. And she can remember the ecstatic comfort of snuggling between the large breasts of her maternal grandmother. But the memories are not all warm and romantic. Her grandmother grew sick with breast cancer, and Karen had the shock of visiting her sickbed, seeing a large, raised growth on her grandmother's breast and thinking, "So that's what cancer looks like." Later, when she developed breasts, her sisters taunted her, saying, "You are going to be enormous, just like Grandma." Still, at fifty-five, Karen finds the sight of breasts both beautiful and erotic. She swims two or three times a week and likes looking at other women's bodies in the locker room. However, she maintains that her attraction to breasts is sensual, not sexual. "It doesn't make me horny," she told me.

It is interesting that many of the breast men described breasts as sensual, comforting, and relaxing and spoke of their experience as a continuum that included both the sensual and the sexual. Jeff said, "For me, comfort blends into sexual feelings." Jason described breasts as, "like a smile, relaxing, soft, round, changing form and textures." Apparently the soft sensuality of breasts can be sexual in one context but not in another. Karen is a psychotherapist who has a good deal of education in human sexuality and human nature. That education and experience allows her to accept her fascination with breasts for what it is and not hide it from herself. Many women may be just as fascinated with breasts, but they translate that impulse into an array of culturally approved feelings such as concern about displaying their own breasts or idealizing the breasts of a model or movie star.

Thinking about models and movie stars brings me to a third and final definition of fetishism. Beyond its meaning as a religious artifact and as a sexual fixation, the word fetish also has a political meaning. Karl Marx wrote about commodity fetishism in capitalist societies.[6] Marx thought that worth is inherent in the laborer, not the product. He deplored the way the factory system and marketing separated the product from the laborer, so that people valued the product while the laborer was diminished and demeaned. Marx was borrowing the same fundamental idea that proved so useful to anthropologists and sexologists: the notion that power has been displaced from its origins onto an object. The object obscures and replaces social relations. I believe the concept of sexual fetishism helps explain the widespread fascination with breasts but add to it the concept of commodity fetishism, and you get a much fuller picture of what is actually going on.

In our contemporary society, commercial products are packaged as objects of desire. In advertising and the imagination, the sleek, new automobile is completely removed from dingy factory line scenes of the workers with their tools and their aching legs. Advertising pitches the sensuous experience of zooming ecstatically down highways. The product is supposed to provide not only transportation but other intangibles such as freedom, prestige, sexuality, and a fuller sense of self. It is not news that sex sells and that breasts have been used to sell every commercial product imaginable. In the process, breasts also become commodities; it is increasingly difficult to disentangle products from sex and sex from products. We are constantly presented with a dizzying display of beautiful things to have. Beautiful human body parts, particularly breasts, are so much a part of that display, it is difficult to distinguish them from all the other goods. Breast fetishism, Stephen Levine told me, "is more a political diagnosis than a psychiatric one. . . . Understanding it as a cultural fascination sheds more light than looking for individual pathology."

Levine added that because of the way breasts are used in the culture, it is common for adolescent boys to focus their sexual energy on them. Approaching women's breasts can become a rite of passage, at least according to one of the breast men I interviewed. "Growing up as a guy," he said, "feeling someone's breast was definitely a goal, like driving a four-speed. I used to dream about that—driving a stick shift, though I never dreamed about feeling a girl's breast." His first attempt at making it to "second base" came at a summer cottage. He and his best friend were sitting on a bed, each making out with a girl. He reached around his girl's shoulder and scored, only to realize shortly after that the protuberance he caressed was his friend's elbow. "A large number of boys are preoccupied with breasts," Levine said. "We expect mature people to move on in sexual development."

Sometimes that maturity is hard won, and the story Malcolm told me reminded me of how men have to struggle with the cultural breast fetish and learn to live with their own personal version of it. Malcolm is a forty-eight-year-old musician, successful on the West

Coast folk circuit. He grew up in a chaotic atmosphere. His mother had been a dime-a-dance girl in a saloon, an Alaska bush pilot, and a single mother with a series of husbands and lovers. She suffered several schizophrenic episodes and had lost all the family money. Malcolm loved and admired her deeply, but that did not keep him from going a bit wild. In the seventh grade, he and a group of four or five friends began methodically copping feels from ninth grade girls. They would spot a likely candidate in the school hallway's oncoming traffic, reach out at the last minute, feel her breast, then disappear in the crowd. It was an exhilarating, rebellious thing to do. Inevitably, they got caught and kicked out of school.

Malcolm has a clear memory of being smitten at age fourteen by a view of his cousin's wife's ample cleavage. "She was on one side of the bed with the baby, changing the diapers and leaning over with a square top that showed a very conspicuous optical view of her breasts. I was basically gawking, I suppose. And my cousin made some comment about that . . . He looked and me and she looked at me, and I was really embarrassed. But I couldn't stop."

Like many American boys, he grew up lusting for large, firm breasts. But as he matured, things changed. He has traveled widely and has had many lovers—about eighty by his estimate. Over the years, he learned to see women and breasts in less stereotypical ways. "I've been to Bali and I've seen the old grannies (with wrinkled breasts): beautiful, beautiful, beautiful women. I've been lovers with women who were flat as could be. I had a lover with unusual breasts; they were small and shriveled, and there wasn't any uniformity at all. A certain type of breast might be true to my fantasies, but not true to my realities."

His reality is that ten years ago he saw something on television that clicked in his brain, and he realized that although he liked breasts, he did not really like women. Since then he has worked at trying to mend that conflict and to build loving relationships with women. He is still a breast man, but he also calls himself a feminist. When he talked about what breasts mean to him today, he said, "My bottom line is the nurturing aspect of femininity. When I think of caressing and sexual intimacy, when I'm actively engaged with my lover's breasts, I feel gratitude."

I am moved, as I listen to Malcolm talk, by the sense of his struggling with his past. Thinking about his own formation, he described the images he saw in girlie magazines. "It breeds such illusions," he said. "Racially, politically, class-wise. Each photo shoot costs thousands and thousands of dollars, but people don't compute that. Big breasts, flat tummies, a lot of muscle. There's a lot of misinformation there. But you don't have a forty-eight-year-old man telling you this stuff as a twelve-year-old boy." We all live in both the past and the present; we walk around wrapped in memories from the past like layers of tissue paper. It was fascinating to think about the superimposed images of the young teen who copped feels from ninth-grade girls and the man who struggles to be a feminist, to take responsibility for the truth about himself, and to love women as fellow human beings.

Together, the concepts of commodity and sexual fetishism help explain why people in Western societies are so taken with breasts. What happens to us as babies combined with the commercial use of breasts creates a desire that expresses itself in many different ways. As I interviewed self-professed breast men and found out how varied they are, I kept asking myself why so many men are willing to use the term breast man to describe themselves. My search for breast women helped to clarify what the term means. I wanted to find lesbian or bisexual women who were fascinated with breasts and include their experiences in my research. Finding breast women turned out to be more difficult than I had imagined. Although I contacted lesbian therapists, lesbian community leaders, a lesbian sex-shop owner, and most of my lesbian friends, no one owned up to being or knowing a breast woman. When I tried to contact breast women through the Society for Human Sexuality list service, the only response I received was from a heterosexual woman who was "into my boyfriend's nipples."

Although I could not locate a breast woman, the lesbians who talked to me recounted a variety of erotic interests and behaviors. Mary, a woman in her forties who owned a successful business, said she was attracted to healthy, athletic, androgynous-looking women and could not imagine how anyone could consider breasts erotic. Her partner had recently given birth and was breast-feeding the baby. Mary loved watching her partner nurse. That made her feel tender, she said, but not sexual.

Kate, a twenty-seven-year-old sociologist, told me she remembered as a child being "hot" for Wonder Woman and other well-endowed cartoon characters. She is attracted to curves and enjoys the way breasts are soft and how they change and the nipples contract. She likes medium-sized breasts best; she finds big ones a little bit scary. But, she said, "I could be having this conversation about a lot of body parts." Her attractions were keyed more to a woman's personal style—her haircut, dress, and mannerisms—than to a specific part of the body.

The closest I came to a real breast woman was a tale one woman told me about a heavy-set, six-foot bartender in a gay bar in Madison, Wisconsin. The bartender received a phone call from an unknown woman who asked, "Hey, mama, you got big titties?"

"Why, yes I do," the bartender replied.

"If I ask you to dance, will you shake them for me?" asked the voice on the phone.

"Why, yes I will," the bartender said.

This was thrilling for the bartender. She was extremely flattered at this interest in her large breasts and talked about it all the time. It was a well-known story in the bar, fueled by repeated phone calls. My informant was present during one of the calls. Occasionally, the mysterious woman showed up for an ecstatic dance and those famous, shaking titties. But this gay bar story seems more public performance than private fetish. These phone calls were not harbored in the secret recesses of the erotic imagination; they took place in a noisy center of the lesbian community. A good deal of the bartender's joy came in the telling and retelling of the story. The phone calls and dances served as a communal celebration of lesbian sexuality.

According to Masters and Johnson (1988), lesbians caress each other's breasts with great sensitivity, which produces an intense erotic response in both the caresser and the caressed.[7] Unlike heterosexual men, they proceed slowly, building erotic feeling; they spend more time on each breast; they are solicitous about each other's sensitivity and pain level during menstruation. But lesbians are as varied and unique as heterosexuals; their behavior cannot be limited or contained by Masters and Johnson's description.

When it comes right down to acts of physical love, lesbians may lavish as much, more, or less attention on women's breasts than do people who call themselves breast men. Although the men I interviewed identified themselves as breast men, many of them just barely qualified for the level one breast fetish described earlier. In their minds, the term "breast man" stood for carnal man, a man who is sexual with women. Calling oneself a breast man is an acknowledgment that one is frankly attracted by the female body, and it signals an approach to women that focuses on the body. The lesbians I spoke with find open objectification of a body part much less acceptable. "I think there is really a taboo," Kate told me. "I think a lot of women associate this with pumped-up bikini models. If you say that you are into breasts, if you were to say you were a breast woman, then that would make you no better than those guys."

From this point of view, what is wrong with "those guys" is not what they do in bed but that they are ready and willing to talk about their sexuality in terms which objectify one body part—terms that allow one part of a woman, breasts, to stand for the whole woman. There are people with genuine breast fetishes that come from deep places in their psyches, but most breast men reflect and parallel the culture-wide fetish. It is a shared fetish—one that depends not only on a person's infantile relationship with his or her breast-feeding mother, but on his or her relationships with the entire culture.

Combine a scopophilic society with an active advertising industry and the technology to disseminate images, and you get a process that objectifies, judges, and makes commodities of women's bodies, particularly their breasts. There is a gender symmetry to this. While men ogle and judge breasts, women criticize and agonize over their own breasts. While men are hunters of breasts, women consciously work to display their breasts.

According to the theories, at the heart of a sexual fetish is a fear and avoidance of something, and there is an accompanying displacement of energy from its source to a symbolic object. I do not buy Freud's theory that castration fear underlies all fetishes. According to Stephen Levine, fetishes and other paraphilias can serve as a defense against a number of life traumas.[8] An all-consuming fetish helps people forget about the trauma of childhood abuse, an unstable sexual identity, or intolerable feelings such as guilt, anxiety, and anger. Compulsive sexual behavior can be a way of retreating from the responsibilities and difficulties of life.

By all the images of breasts, and all the breast implants and uplift bras, by all the slang words for breasts, and all the people who call themselves breast men, we know that a good deal of energy goes into breasts in our culture. Amid the complexity in which we live, it is difficult to find out why energy is being displaced onto breasts, to understand what we are turning away from, or to name the fear. Perhaps it has to do with the trauma of loneliness and the fear of intimacy. Perhaps it is a horror of the feminine and a fear of women's growing power. Perhaps it is a cringing away from the earthly cycle of reproduction, decay, and death, a reality we try to replace with beautiful commodities and permanently youthful breasts.

PART FOUR:
THINKING ABOUT BREASTS

Chapter 9

How the Woman Got Her Breasts

Between 1967 and 1997, an interesting dialogue about breasts took place among a group of scholars of evolution. They asked the question: "Why do women have permanently enlarged breasts?" The breasts of all other mammals swell only during lactation then shrink away when the milk dries up. Only women go about with full, rounded breasts even when they are not making milk. The theory of natural selection holds that evolution has favored the best adaptations. Therefore, permanently enlarged breasts must have evolved for a reason. What could that reason be?

Since we cannot go back to the past to find out what actually happened, we must infer from clues available today. Evolutionary theories are based on three sources of information: archeological finds, our knowledge of modern-era, "stone age" peoples, and the study of primates, particularly the chimpanzee, with which we share 99 percent of our DNA.

As a source of information, million-year-old bones do not tell us much about what is happening at the level of organs, flesh, and skin. When it comes to the shape of a skull or the size of the teeth, evidence has been found and can be dated. We have, however, evolved important nonskeletal traits that set us apart from the other primates. The bones do not tell us when or how we lost hair or developed our characteristic breasts. Even though scholars can make educated guesses based on available data, there is no way to test and verify them. Theories about the evolution of breasts are all speculation.

In 1967, Desmond Morris opened the breast evolution debate in his bestselling book *The Naked Ape*. *The Naked Ape* was fresh and titillating at that time. It found a receptive readership in an era that took great pleasure in smashing stodgy conventions. The book offered to strip our species of its civilized pretensions and show man for the animal he really is. Morris, a British zoologist, claimed breasts evolved as sexual signals.

Morris found the underpinnings for this claim in Darwin's theory of sexual selection.[1] Darwin developed this theory to explain traits that seem to exist solely to help attract a mate. The theory states that individuals with features that entice the opposite sex have a better chance of reproducing, even if these features have no other survival value. If peahens, for instance, prefer to mate with males who have fancy tail feathers, evolution will select for this trait, propagate it, and even exaggerate it. Although we still have no other theory to explain some of the extravagances of nature, sexual selection is still controversial and open to question.

Morris wrote that breasts evolved as sexual ornaments developed specifically to promote pair bonding. He based this idea on a life-style Morris and other scholars in the 1960s believed early hominids lived. The scenario was known as "Man the Hunter," because it hypothesized that hunting drove evolutionary development. When our early ancestors emerged from their fruit- and leaf-eating jungle life to the sun-scorched savannas of Africa, goes the theory, they began to hunt big game. To cooperate in the hunt and develop better tools, early hominids needed bigger brains and bigger heads. Because women's pelvises could not accommodate those expanding crania, hominids evolved giving birth at an earlier point in fetal development, began delivering semi-fetuses who required complete care for years. Women, taken up in this task, became dependent upon men for the meat they hunted. They had to have some way to be sure that their mates would come home with the food. That way was sex. Women stopped going into periodic estrus and instead became permanently receptive. The woman's willingness to mate at any time drew the man to her and pair bonds were formed. The man got exclusive sexual rights over the woman and the assurance that her children would carry his genes. The woman got food to help her survive while she cared for her child.

Within this scenario, Morris theorized that breasts developed to encourage face-to-face intercourse. Breasts, he wrote, mimic buttocks. Most primates, Morris claimed, practice quick, impersonal, rear-entry intercourse. Early hominids, normally attracted to rounded buttocks, would transfer this erotic interest to the two round swellings in the front. With face-to-face intercourse, mating partners could enjoy the nuances of emotional expression. These intimacies strengthened the pair bond. Moreover, once proto-humans stood upright and walked around on two legs, a frontal sexual signal would have become more important. Chimpanzees move on all fours, with prominent rump and hidden chest. The chests of bipedal humans are much more conspicuous than their bottoms.

Could one body part develop to mimic another? Morris found a precedent for rump-chest echoing in the gelada monkey, popularly called the bleeding heart baboon. The female's pink estrus swellings are outlined by a line of white swollen bumps along the margin of her colored rump. On her chest she has a hairless pigmented area surrounded by a necklace of pearly nodules, a replica of what is on her behind. Her pink chest color changes hue and intensity in the same cyclic rhythms as her bottom. Geladas live in polygynous groups so the pair bonding argument could not explain this rump-chest echoing. They do, however, have prominent chests, more visible than their rumps. Although quadrupedal, they go about on their haunches foraging for seeds and plants on the grassy plains of Ethiopia, keeping their trunks erect.

Morris did not say specifically when breasts were supposed to have evolved. New findings are always emerging, but at this writing, the earliest hominid skeletons appear to date from over four million years ago. (If it proves to be a true hominid, the recently discovered *Ardipithecus ramidus* may push back our origins even earlier.) The first hominids, the Australopithecines, were probably ape-like beings who walked upright. Although popular illustrations sometimes show hairy Australopithecine females with human-like breasts, that probably does not reflect a reasonable estimate of when breasts evolved. Instead, these anachronistic breasts most likely reveal the illustrator's desire to humanize early hominids and to add a little sex appeal. Humans may, in fact, have descended from a separate and distinct line than Australopithecines. The earliest generally accepted human ancestor is Homo erectus, who existed between 200,000 and 1.6 million years ago. Anthropologists believe these hominids lived together in small bands, cooperatively hunted meat, and shared food. They made tools and had the use of fire. If

Morris' theory is true, permanently enlarged breasts would have evolved during this period.

After Morris, nobody said much in print about the evolution of breasts until the 1980s, when suddenly, scholars took up the question and published a flurry of articles, refining and debating Morris' assertions. Much of the work continued to assume that female hominids were beholden to males for food and protection, but now scholars began bolstering their theories with the principles of sociobiology. Sociobiology, a controversial form of classic Darwinism, was brought to public attention in 1975. Sociobiology is the study of the relationship between behavior and natural selection. It examines the genetic origins of behavior and, conversely, the behavioral origins of morphology. The successful individual, it argues, is the one who reproduces viable offspring. Therefore, evolution favors traits that lead to reproductive success. A central concept is parental investment, which measures the amount of energy it takes for each parent to ensure his or her offspring will thrive. The way the arguments run, parental investment often seems a battle between the sexes. Each parent's goal is to get as much as he or she can while investing as little as possible. The ideal solution for either mate would be to breed, leave the partner with the job of rearing the baby, then go on to engender more babies. When sociobiologists considered the evolution of permanently enlarged breasts, they asked the question: "How do enlarged breasts increase a woman's ability to carry on and bequeath her genes to the next generation?"

In 1981, John Cant (Department of Anthropology, University of Colorado) published an article hypothesizing that both enlarged breasts and fatty buttocks evolved to show that females had enough fat to bear and nurse infants. His argument says that when male primates do not have to invest much in their infants, they will copulate with any female who permits. But in humans, male investment is high. Human hunter-gatherers had to provide for their infants for an extended period. Therefore, it was in the male's best interest to find a healthy female capable of having and nursing babies. Males would not actually size up females and calculate whether they had enough fat to make it through the dry periods. It would not work on a conscious level. The male would mate with the female because she was sexy; she gave him that certain feeling. But unconsciously, he would be attracted to the body signals that showed she could reproduce.

Cant argued that fat on breasts and buttocks would be the only unmistakable sign of extra fat. Fat on the belly could be mistaken as a sign of malnutrition. Fat on the wrists or ankles would be an unmistakable sign but not a good idea because it would impede mobility. Since hominids assumed an upright stance, it would make sense for fat signals to develop on both the front and the back.

To buttress his argument, Cant pointed to the San bushmen of the Kalahari, one of the last stone-age-type, hunter-gatherer groups. Before being exposed to modern culture, the San underwent periods when little food was available and people lost weight. During seasons of plenty, people gained weight and women became pregnant. The group experienced an annual baby boom nine months after times of abundance. They must have understood that fat on the body meant women were fertile.

There are problems with Cant's theory, however. His claim that fat is necessary for reproduction and that a good deal of the bulge in breasts and buttocks is made up of fat holds true for many women. But fat on the breasts could be confused with lactation. If mother nature were looking for a reliable sign of fat content, why not pick upper-arm fat. A nice, plump layer of fat would not impede mobility and could not be confused with anything else.

Shortly after this article came out, another by G. G. Gallup (1982) (Department of Psychology, State University of New York at Albany) appeared. Gallup agreed that breasts were sexual signals, but that what they showed was not fat content but ovulatory potential. Plump breasts served as a signal that a woman could reproduce. Such a signal is not necessary among primates because their bottoms swell and turn pink during their periodic estrus. After our hominid ancestors lost estrus, males could not tell whether females were capable of reproducing. The presence of enlarged breasts would give this information. Gallup wrote that prepubertal girls have flat chests and postmenopausal women have fallen breasts. Only women in their reproductive years have puffed up breasts. Of course, lactating women have swollen breasts, and they are not good candidates for insemination. To explain this anomaly, Gallup argued that the swelling of lactating breasts served to secure the pair bond and hold the man to the woman during a period of high need.

Although this argument seems reasonable, it also has some problems. The pink swelling of primate estrus tells the male when the female is ovulating; breasts do not. Although, in general, the budding of breasts comes as a sign of maturation, the size and shape of breasts are not reliable indicators of ovulation. Some women's breasts fall before they give birth; others have rounded breasts well into old age. Lactating women have the fullest breasts of all, but they do not usually ovulate.

Perhaps the most complicated and speculative theories are those that claim breasts evolved as deceptive sexual signals. Anthropologist Robert L. Smith (1984) argued that female hominids developed "subtle stratagems" that would secure maximum support from reluctant males. Their unconscious evolutionary strategy was to confuse males about what was actually going on inside their bodies. To accomplish this goal, evolution produced concealed estrus and permanently enlarged breasts. Hominid females needed to get the best possible genes for their children and the most security for themselves. They entered pair-bond relationships, in which they exchanged sexual favors for help from their mates. But it was not to their advantage to be continually under their mates' watchful eye. If they could have intercourse on the side, they could possibly get better genes and even some extra goods. According to this theory, hominid females developed permanently swollen breasts to confuse their mates and to make them think they were lactating and, thus, temporarily infertile. A lactating woman did not have to be kept away from other men. Breasts mollified the female's mate and reassured him so that he loosened his hold on her and let her wander off by herself. As the millennia wore on, hominids got used to permanently swollen breasts and started experiencing them as attractive in and of themselves.

In 1987, Bobbi Low and colleagues (School of Natural Resources, University of Michigan) developed another theory that claimed breasts evolved as deceptive signals. Low claimed that enlarged breasts evolved to make the male believe the female could make lots of high quality milk. In a parallel development, hips developed fat pads to appear wider, so the male would think the female could easily bear children. But fatty breasts are a deceptive signal because fat is not milk-producing tissue. Women evolved deceptive signals because they were less "expensive" than the real thing. Growing and maintaining real mammary tissue might take more energy. Real wide hips might impede movement.

This argument was soundly attacked in the literature, though, through it all, Bobbi Low continued to respond with more articles defending her position. Critics argued that breast size has nothing to do with a woman's ability to nurse. Nor does external hip size affect successful birthing. Twentieth-century Americans who seldom view birthing and nursing may believe in these relationships, but early hominids, presumably less buffered from bodily processes, would not be fooled. Moreover, males who are attracted to deceptive signals would be put at a reproductive disadvantage and, thus, would not prevail.

Taken as a group, all these theories claiming that breasts evolved as sexual signals are steeped in ethnocentric assumptions. They assume that men are attracted to breasts. That may be true for most men in America today, but it is certainly not true in many other cultures. Many cultures view breasts solely as udders that provide milk for babies. Men in these cultures take no sexual interest in them at all. The unquestioning assumption that breasts are sexy tells us that many scholars in the mid- to late- twentieth century had no idea how culturally conditioned their breast fetish was. The fact is, nobody has any way of knowing how Homo erectus felt about breasts.

In addition, the "Man the Hunter" scenario that provided the backdrop for these theories has been discredited today. "Man the Hunter" held that bipedalism, tool making, sexuality, and social organization all evolved in response to men hunting meat while women squatted passively by the fire. A surge of feminist scholarship in the 1970s and 1980s produced and reviewed studies of modern hunter-gatherers. Their work showed that women in some societies hunt. In others, women provide significant quantities of food through gathering.[2] Among chimpanzees, females, not males, do most of the toolmaking.[3] And in most primate societies, female choice has a strong influence on mate selection.[4]

Moreover, all the theories assume that monogamous pairing is the universal human mating pattern. In reality, humans are among the few species that practice what is known as "facultative monogamy"; they are monogamous under some circumstances and poly-gynous under others. Almost 90 percent of human societies have practiced polygyny.[5] If we look at our primate relatives, only 37 or 18 percent are monogamous.[6] The rest are polygynous. There is no way of knowing what mating system prevailed during the evolution of permanently enlarged breasts and little if any support for assuming our proto-human ancestors enjoyed monogamous love.

The theories assume that early hominids traded food for sex. We have some evidence that leads us to believe Homo erectus shared food and that archaic Homo sapiens cared for weaker members of the group. However, we do not know that breeding pairs shared or protected each other.

Do we see females trading sex for meat in chimpanzee society? Yes and no. In her field research, Jane Goodall observed male chimpanzees hunting the infants of red colobus monkeys or baboons that they snatched from their mothers and killed instantly by biting through the skull. As the shell-shocked colobus mother scurried away, a great squabbling would begin, with troop members snatching at the carcass and begging for scraps. Some chimpanzees shared and some did not, but the most privileged recipients of meat were females with the swollen pink bottoms of estrus. So there is evidence that a sexually attractive female is more likely to be given meat. However, among Tai chimps in Guinea, males hunt cooperatively. In order to get the meat, they must organize to cut off their victim's escape routes. After the hunt, the males share with one another.

Apparently both food sharing and hunting techniques have a lot to do with the particular environment and social group. Early hominids scavenged or hunted in groups. Individual males may have shared with their mates, but it is just as likely that the entire group shared the meat. Maybe food and other goods were distributed with the best portions going to high-status individuals. On the other hand, maybe bands of early hominids gave according to group members' needs. We just do not know.

Reading the theories for what they tell us about cultural assumptions held between 1967 and 1997, we learn that many well-educated theorists understood sexual bonding as an exchange of sexual favors for material goods. They apparently believed men desire sex more than women do and men, more than women, control resources. They seem to have imagined some kind of prehistoric battle of the sexes where calculating, bosomy bimbos latched on to ugly but powerful cavemen. These scenarios bring to mind Mafia movies in which the standard couple is a curvy, blond floozy wearing glittery jewels strutting along on the arms of a short, dog-faced Mafia don. Because most of the theories were written during the Reagan era, they may reveal a cynical side of the family values equation. They assume that relationship is based on a calculated exchange of goods. Beneath the sacred family unit, they discover the primitive marketplace.

Not all the discussion, however, took place on one side. In response to the breasts-as-sexual-signals theories, other scholars spoke out during the same period, arguing that breasts evolved to further the survival of women and to improve the breast-feeding relationship. In 1986, Frances Mascia-Lees (Social Science Division, Simons Rock of Bard College) and colleagues argued that permanently enlarged breasts evolved as part of natural selection for greater fat. This theory sees breasts as part of a whole system, rather than organs that evolved separately. Hominid body fat probably increased while hominids lived in the semi-arid African savannas. Females had to nurse for several years while still spending their energy gathering food. Individuals who accumulated fat would have a buffer against hard times. In addition, fat tends to produce estrogen, and the presence of this estrogen may have been a crucial factor in the loss of estrus and permanent sexual receptivity. Unlike the claim that enlarged breasts evolved as *signals* of nutritional fitness, this theory says they evolved as *by-products* of greater fat. This is an important distinction. The theory sees breasts not as sex objects but as part of a unified system of body fat and hormones.

A year later, an article by Judith Anderson (Department of Psychology, Simon Fraser University) argued along the same lines. Anderson focused most of her energies on defeating the idea of breasts as deceptive signals. In the process, she proposed other possible explanations. Fat in breasts could serve as insulation, she argued, keeping milk at a temperature that is good for babies. Or human breast enlargement may function to make breasts long enough to hang conveniently down to the mouth of a baby held in the crook of the arm. Primate infants can cling to chest hair, but human babies, lacking this opportunity, need access to larger, more pendulous breasts.

Other scholars postulated swollen breasts evolved to benefit babies instead of their fathers. In 1972, Elaine Morgan in *Descent of Women* built on Sir Alister Hardy's hypothesis that humans went through an aquatic stage which accounts for our hairlessness and our layer of subcutaneous fat. She wrote that enlarged breasts provided something for infants to hang onto, small floating buoys in the water. It would have to be in the water. Anyone who has ever had a breast knows that, under our normal terrestrial circumstances, having a child swinging from a breast would be unthinkably painful. If the aquatic theory could be substantiated, then floating breasts would deserve a closer look. Unfortunately, there is absolutely no physical evidence to back up the theory.

Noel Smith (Department of Psychology, State University of New York at Plattsburgh) postulated that enlarged breasts developed as soft, pillow-like appendages to comfort infants. To back up this idea, he pointed to well-known experiments examining the relationship between infant monkeys and wire mesh surrogate mothers. Infant monkeys deprived of their mothers will, when alarmed, cling to a soft, surrogate mother instead of seeking comfort in a hard, wire mesh, milk-giving surrogate. The infants preferred something soft to comfort them over something to eat. Human infants, Smith argued, have a profound psychological need for comfort. Soft human breasts fulfill that need.

A final theory, developed by Cambridge University Royal Society Research Fellow Gillian Bentley, argued that enlarged breasts co-evolved with changing facial structures. The earliest hominids had muzzles that jutted out as monkeys' do. Slowly, as brains enlarged, jaws and teeth grew smaller. As the hominid infants' faces became flatter, the flat, primate-style chests would pose a threat to their breathing. A jutting face suckles well at a flat chest, but rounded breasts work better for flat-faced infants.

Many of these ideas could work well together. A million years or more ago, Homo erectus females dug and foraged on the dry savannas of Africa, carrying their nursing infants on their hip or in a sling. Because their energy needs were high, evolution selected for greater body fat. As their faces grew flatter, their breasts grew rounder to accommodate the nursing infant. Their breasts became pendulous and hung down to reach the infant's mouth. And breast softness comforted their infants, giving them the security they needed to grow up, survive, and reproduce. After women evolved permanently enlarged breasts, men in some, but not all, cultures, began to find breasts sexually attractive. Some men were so attracted to breasts, they could not believe this desire was anything less than fundamental to human nature.

This second set of theories shows that some scholars objected to the "primal prostitute" scenario of the sexual-signal theories. They wanted to develop theories that would present women as independent from such relationships. In gender politics, this point is extremely important to make. If breasts evolved as sex objects, that establishes sexism as natural and pulls the rug out from under women's attempts to own their bodies.

Except for Bentley's theory, which is under development as I write, all the anti-sex object theories came out in the 1980s. That was supposed to be the backlash decade, a time when some claimed feminism had been stamped out. Theories that early hominid females' bodies developed as a whole unto themselves, not in response to the sexual tastes of their mates, show that feminism was still stirring. Theories about breasts evolving in response to infants' needs show that the primary function of breasts was not entirely forgotten.

We will never be certain why our foremothers evolved away from estrus and toward permanently enlarged breasts. Many of the theories seem convincing. They all give us something to think about. Evolutionary theories are journeys in search of the truth, but they also serve as metaphors and justifications for our present-day culture as myths of origins we spin in response to the questions that trouble us. Women and men are going through an ongoing struggle to understand what it means to be a certain gender and how it is possible to find balance, mutuality, and ways to love. As we work through this puzzle, we are torn among theories that say, in effect, that breasts are for men or for babies or for deceiving women's mates but never just for women. It would be nice to have a clean and simple theory, one that somehow rises above women's history of surviving for millennia by pleasing, by manipulating, by influencing, and by nurturing.

The evolution of permanently enlarged breasts is an important development whose meanings exceed what any one theory can contain. Women's bodies are mysterious and multipurpose. We are living in a great web of life along with men, children, and other women. We cannot separate ourselves from all the others, any more than we can separate our breasts from the rest of our being. Our bodies, minds, and psyches interact with an ingenuity and elegance that seems bigger than any one element. Maybe this very complexity is one of the reasons breasts are so compelling. They have become symbols, signifiers, stimulants, comforts, providers, and givers of pleasure. Today, breasts grow on women's bodies in a great variety of shapes and sizes. Who knows—maybe they are still evolving. Certainly, their meaning and significance continue to evolve.

Chapter 10

The Great and Terrible Breast

People are storytelling animals. They love stories for the pure pleasure of telling and hearing them told, and they need them for emotional reasons. Stories help us work through anxieties or explain mysteries or justify our feelings and actions. We are constantly running stories through our minds and repeating them to ourselves and other people. Into those stories people weave their assumptions, prejudices, hopes, and fears. You can tell a good deal about people from the stories they tell.

In the late-twentieth-century Western world, people tell a rich variety of stories about breasts. The Internet is full of breast implant horror stories that portray breasts as sites of mutilation and gateways for disease. Women in La Leche League meetings tell stories about breasts that nurture and comfort babies. Woody Allen, in his movie *Everything You Always Wanted to Know About Sex but Were Afraid to Ask* (1972) portrayed cultural breast obsession as a giant breast (cup size 1000 triple-X) that has broken loose and is rampaging through the countryside, threatening civilization as we know it. Together, all these stories about breasts portray a cultural icon filled with complex, ambiguous meanings.

When we look at myths from the distant past, much of this complexity recedes, and a starker picture emerges. The details are lost, but it is easier to see the broad outlines of belief. There are many legitimate ways of understanding myths and fairy tales. Some mythographers look for historical clues; others see myths as explanations of natural events. The politically minded use them to elucidate the power structure of a culture. Jungians see myths as images of archetypal psychological patterns, the dreams of the collective psyche. Most myths have many variants, and interpreters tend to pick the version that suits them best.

The oldest images and tales about breasts tell us that they were once worshipped, probably as symbols of the life stream that nurtures human existence. Peche-Merle, a cave in south-central France contains a hidden breast sanctuary.[1] Twenty thousand years ago, Stone Age people worshipped in the tiny cavern where a wreath of breast-like formation hangs from the low ceiling. The slow drip of dissolved minerals formed stalactites the size and shape of human breasts, even down to nipples made of lime. The lower parts of several of the stalactites have been painted black, the color of fertility and of mother earth. Maybe the people sensed a divine presence as they entered the cave and felt their way deep into its core. They had to bend a little in the corridor just before the entrance, where they encountered first a row of red disks then a single stalactite breast circled in red. Maybe as they sat in the sanctuary, they heard the rhythmic bonging of the shaman's club against a stalagmite in an adjacent chamber and then the sound of bird-bone whistles as the ecstasy swept over them and the ritual began.

Although the sanctuary at Peche-Merle is one of a kind, its stalactite breasts number among hundreds of Stone Age breast artifacts that must have had religious purpose and meaning. In addition to the often faceless, armless, and legless Venus statuettes with their enormous breasts, Stone Age people sculpted breast-shaped pendants and beads. Breast pendants have been found in more than fifty Paleolithic sites, ranging from Palestine to France. The breast was probably an enduring symbol, like the cross of the Christian era. And like the cross, the breast may have been a visual reference to a story that everybody knew.

Many people told stories about a mother breast that existed at the foundation of the world or, at least, at the start of human life. In the beginning, there were enormous breasts that let down milk, and we were fed by them and they gave us life. So true to the human experience is this basic concept that traces of it have been found nearly everywhere in the world.

The pre-Christian Siberians, for example, worshipped a goddess called "Milk Lake Mother" or "Lake of the Milk."[2] They imagined her in different forms, sometimes simply as a great white lake in the sky. Sometimes they described Lake Milk Mother as a woman with "breasts as large as leather sacks," who lets down life, as a mother lets down her milk.

Creation myths attempt to get at the mystery of how matter organizes itself into life forms. If the creator begins by dividing the light from the dark, then we are witnessing the power of discipline, of mind over matter. When the Creator lets down life the way a mother lets down milk from her breasts, she is transforming through her body; she is divine matter. A good example of this principle is Adumla, the Norse cow mother who stood in a world of ice and let down four rivers of milk that sustained the rest of creation.

The concept of giving life through the breasts did not stop with a simple outpouring of food. It provided the foundation for stories with much more complex and sophisticated meanings, such as the stories told about the Egyptian goddess, Isis. The breast milk of Isis played a crucial role in the investment and transfer of power and also provided for the afterlife of human souls. Beloved by the Egyptians for 4,000 years, later adopted by the Greeks and Romans, Isis was worshipped well into the sixth century after Christ. Isis was a mainstay, a trustworthy center, and by the way, a single mother.

Isis seems distinct and different from other Egyptian breast goddesses. Nut, for instance, was a sky mother sometimes pictured as a beautiful, naked woman whose star-spattered body stretches across the sky above her lover, Geb, the earth. Once they were one creature, but after they split into two, her breasts hung down, watering the earth with life-giving rain. She is so huge and distant, Nut resembles a force of nature.

Stories about Isis, by contrast, depict her with the passions of a woman and the powers of a god. After her husband Osiris was murdered and his corpse dismembered, the grieving Isis took action. She found and reassembled his remains, hovered above them, and managed thus to become pregnant. By his birth, her son Horus offered the promise of reincarnation, a concept that became a major tenet of Egyptian religion.

Isis possessed a ruthless intelligence and gifts of magic and healing. Once, when she hid Horus in the papyrus while she went out to find food, a scorpion bit her son. She found him dead, and she lamented, "My breasts are full, but my bosom is empty."[3] Isis swiftly brought the child back to life, and under her protection,

Horus ascended to the throne and became the first pharaoh. Every subsequent pharaoh would be the reincarnation of Horus, so each pharaoh was Isis' son and received his power from her. Pharaohs were born weak, it was believed, and Isis' milk made them strong. Egyptian artists made images of the various pharaohs enthroned on her lap and nursing from her breasts. Her milk was a transforming substance, a conduit that carried divine power to the pharaohs. The hieroglyph for Isis was a throne because nobody could posses the throne except through her, by imbibing her breast milk. When the pharaohs died, Isis nursed the infant souls of the dead. By this act, she also promised resurrection for all humanity.

Isis was not the only powerful breast goddess. The many-breasted Artemis held sway over Ephesis. She was different from the Greek Artemis, and we do not have a rich source of stories about her. We know about her primarily from three statues, one dating from the fifth century B.C.E. and the other two from the first Century B.C.E. She is a puzzling figure who stands rigid and upright like a column. The Bible says her statue was a holy object that fell from the sky. Above her treelike lower half, she has a naturalistic face and hands, but on her chest, hang rows and rows of breasts. Scholars disagree about those breasts; some think they aren't really breasts at all but some other kind of decoration. They may represent the testicles of bulls sacrificed in her honor. It is said that to honor her during spring rites, celebrants sang or danced themselves into states of ecstasy and had wild and indiscriminate sex. In the frenzy, young men ran amok through the streets, took up knives, and castrated themselves. Some scholars believe the objects hanging on the goddess' chest represent the shorn testicles of her worshippers.[4] But early Greek writings called them breasts. The meaning of Artemis' breasts remains a mystery. Are they the answer to all our infantile needs, the assurance that we will be fed, that there will be comfort and nourishment enough to go around? Or are they badges of her fearsome might, the wild ecstasies of her worship, and the sacrifices she demanded?

Although quite different from each other, Artemis and Isis were both powerful breast goddesses in ancient times. They were beings of self-contained might. The milk from their breasts represented a stream of power. Some time after their stories were told, a great shift took place in the human understanding of breasts. Breasts had been venerated, but after the shift, they became objects to be dominated. Sometimes they were feared; sometimes they were desired, but one way or the other, they had to be possessed. This change coincided with enthusiasm for aggressive warrior heroes, the worship of dynamic, masculine gods, and the growth of city states. This cultural shift did not happen all at once; it came in phases, appeared at different times in different places, and was never entirely complete. Shadows and shreds of the old intermingled with the dominant new. Moreover, myths and tales overlapped the boundaries, dragging mixed meanings along with them.

The Greek myths talk about breasts in a new and different way. The new ethos bloomed in the Greek city state of Athens, which produced so much of the art and literature that would form the basis of Western thinking. By the fourth century B.C.E., Greek women were confined to home and hearth as breeders and housekeepers, while aristocratic men reserved their highest love and admiration for other men. Although the cult of Isis and her divine milk still comforted many, especially women and the poor, male gods dominated the Greek pantheon. These gods killed monsters, hurled lightening bolts, and seduced or raped multitudes of mortal women.

Athenians told stories about goddesses, but their immortal breasts were no longer all-powerful and benevolent. Now they served as foils for the hero's guile or might. Hera, the queen of the gods, provides a good example of the new attitude toward breasts. Her power was interpreted as shrewishness. Greek myths tell about her vanity, her jealousies, and the punishments she wreaked on the innocent victims of her philandering husband's lusts. At the same time, her breasts attracted Zeus' divine cupidity. In the early years before Zeus married Hera, he lusted for her, but she resisted his advances. One day she found a stiff, cold cuckoo, just barely alive. Filled with pity, she picked up the creature and warmed it between her breasts. To her great surprise, the bird was actually Zeus in disguise, and he quickly transformed himself and took advantage of his intimate position. This myth portrays Hera's breasts in a more modern way than do the old tales of the mother goddesses, Isis and Artemis. Hera's breasts are both compassionate and erotically vulnerable. Perhaps her act of bringing an ailing bird to her breasts echoes the old idea of mother goddess as sustainer of nature. But now she has become an object of desire, one who can be tricked and dominated by a god.

In another story, Zeus had a liaison with the mortal woman Alkemene, who consequently gave birth to a son, Heracles. Fearing Hera's jealousy, the woman exposed the infant boy in a field. But soon afterward the goddess Athena led Hera to the field, where she discovered the child. Athena pitied Heracles and persuaded Hera to nurse him. Hera put Heracles to her breast, but the child latched so violently that Hera screamed in pain and angrily flung Heracles from her. At that, milk spurted out from her breasts, filled the skies, and formed the Milky Way. Heracles got only a few drops, but they sufficed to build his great strength. Later, when Hera tried to kill him by putting two serpents into his cradle while he slept, he crushed them with his hands.

Many cultures have believed our galaxy, the Milky Way, represented the scattered drops of milk from the mother goddess' breasts. In this story, Hera's breast milk has the power to create the galaxy and endow a hero with strength. Unlike Isis, she does not let down her milk with love and compassion. The milk has to be coaxed out of her, and she feels pain in giving it. The story puts the hero and the mother in opposition; he attacks her breasts and escapes with the precious drops of milk.

It's interesting that such breast-biting stories exist in other cultures, including one in East Indian mythology and another in Native American stories of the Pacific Northwest. The stories are always about the infant years of future heroes and community leaders, men who show their ferocity early, at the breast. Symbolically, biting the breast is a form of attacking the mother goddess. The great mother breast that held sway for so many thousands of years eventually took on a negative aspect, as a new kind of feeling swept over certain parts of the world. The time had come for initiative, for conquering nation-states, and for individual glory. Little patience remained for a great mother who gave birth, nourished the world, and then reclaimed life, taking it back into her dark womb. The mother breast must have seemed static, overwhelming, and dangerous.

As male-centered religions pushed the old, mother goddess religion deeper and deeper into the shadows, The idea of wild and dangerous breasts haunted folk tales. South German and Polish legends told of wild, disheveled women who ran through the forest flinging their long, pendulous breasts over their shoulders as they ran. These pagan, forest demons were probably remnants of the old religion given a negative interpretation in later years. Their frightening breasts were wild and erotic, uncontrollable, and sometimes uncanny.

One disturbing story about frightening breasts comes from Turkey. In this fairy tale, a young hero set out on a quest. A holy man warned him about huge, female demons called devs. "If you should meet a dev," said the holy man, "throw chewing resin into her mouth and embrace her right nipple. If you do this, she will tell you the way; if not, she will kill you."

Sure enough, the young man encountered a dev, threw resin into her mouth, grabbed her right nipple and sucked. She said, "Oh you human, if you did not grasp my right nipple I would crunch you between my teeth and mix you with my chewing resin. Where are you going?"[5] She sent him on to her two sisters, and he managed to appease each by sucking her nipple before proceeding on to the next adventure. These demons are similar to negative mother goddesses. The hero gains what he wants by suckling their breasts, but there is no indication that they let down holy milk. Instead, his sucking does something to or for the devs. Maybe it appeases their lust or raises their maternal instincts or makes some other connection that stimulates them to unlock their secrets and give the information. The negative goddesses are a threat; they are to be overcome, to be used, manipulated, and tricked by the hero.

While tales of wild women haunted the Christian era, Christianity offered the succor of a pure and sanctified breast. Christians of the Medieval and early Renaissance cherished the Virgin Mary as a divine presence, overflowing with both purity and mother love. Like Isis before her, Mary was frequently represented as a mother nursing the Christ Child, but Mary's milk existed not just for Christ, but for all Christians.

During the Medieval period, people sought the Virgin's milk as a cure to physical and spiritual ills. One legend tells how Saint Bernard's mouth was covered with sores and blisters. He was so far gone with torment and fever that his brother monks gave him up for dead. The Virgin came to him in a vision, put her breast to his oozing lips, and granted him three drops of her milk. Her holy moisture immediately effected a cure, not only of his body but also of his soul.

During this period, many holy shrines had vials of the Virgin Mary's milk, mysteriously preserved, living proof of divinity. Calvin made the dry remark that "There is no town so small, nor convent . . . so mean that it does not display some of the Virgin's milk. . . . There is so much that if the holy Virgin had been a cow, or a wet nurse all her life she would have been hard put to it to yield such a great quantity."[6]

Though she was never officially a goddess, people prayed to the Virgin, and their passion for her grew at times to levels of great intensity. Based on her study of fourteenth century Tuscan paintings, Margaret Miles (1986) argued that people cleaved to the breast-feeding Virgin Mary during the years of crop failure, of starvation, and the black plague, when the masses of people were anxious about whether there would be enough food. They lived with a deep sense of vulnerability and of the closeness to death. The Virgin offered her breast to these hungry people. Paintings show her with milk spurting from her breasts or holding out one breast, almost as though the viewer were invited to suckle. Perhaps the appeal of Mary's breasts went right to the unconscious, but often the association between the Mother of God and food was quite explicit. She is frequently surrounded with grape leaves, bread, or other images of food.

If the Virgin's bare breast offered nourishment to the people, it had another message for the Aristocracy, according to Miles. Noble women were constantly admonished to breast-feed their babies but rarely did so. The tension in the culture about breast-feeding gave the sight of Mary's breast a powerful edge. Here was the perfect mother. She offered her breast as noblewomen should but so seldom did. In doing so, she gave proof of her humility.

Mary's appeal, however, was not limited to her ability to nurture. Mary's breast-feeding was understood as a loving sacrifice made not just for her baby but for all Christians. One classic theme painted during this period is the intercession of Christ and the Virgin. In a fresco by an unknown Florentine of the early fifteenth century, Christ kneels on the left of God, pointing to the wound in his side and gesturing toward the Virgin's breast. The Virgin kneels to the right, embracing a group of penitent sinners with one hand while with the other she holds out her breast. Just as Christ points to his death wound in asking for God's mercy on the sinners, so Mary points to her breast. The wound and the breast are the salvation of humankind. The blood and the milk nourish and purify the sinners.[7]

This idea that holy breast milk acts as a conduit for salvation bears a strong resemblance to the ideology surrounding Isis and her divine breasts. In fact, some scholars believe the Cult of the Virgin descended from the Cult of Isis, but there are some real differences. The pharaohs received their power from Isis. Christ, on the other hand, did not owe his holiness to Mary. On the contrary, her deification came through him. Still, the Virgin Mary could be understood as a Christian incarnation of the old nurturing goddesses—a feminine deity whose breasts gave comfort, healing, and mercy. She has existed as such, an enclave of feminine power within a masculine structure, her popularity waxing and waning for over a thousand years.

Stories about and pictures of breasts from the Stone Age through the Christian era tell about breasts that were sacred, powerful, desirable, and dangerous. Though narratives about the Virgin Mary are an important exception, on the whole, stories show a shift away from worship of breasts to domination of them. The power struggle around breasts is especially clear in stories about the loss or sacrifice of a breast. Tales of the Amazons probably took shape around 3,000 years ago, though the first literary rendition of the battle between the Amazons and the Greeks dates from 700 B.C.E. They were told and retold in many versions by the Greeks and Romans, and then by the Christians. The name Amazon comes from the Greek *amazos*, meaning without a breast. Amazons were fierce warriors who hurled axes as they thundered along on horseback. Capturing, raping, or killing them figured as great signs of masculine achievement for Greek mythical heroes, including that old breast-biter Heracles.

Amazons lived without men. Some said they crippled their own men children and used them for lovers. Others claimed they mated with neighboring cave-dwelling men, staying with them only long enough to get pregnant. They kept the daughters and gave their infant sons back to the fathers. The Amazons burned off their daughter's right breast so that it would not interfere with use of the bow. The strength that would have gone into that breast poured into the muscles of the shoulder; Amazons made excellent archers. Some stories said Amazons did not give their daughters breast milk, which would feminize them. Instead, they raised them tough and mean by feeding them mare's milk.

These stories can be interpreted as ways the masculinist cultures— Greek, Roman, and Christian—dealt with their fear of the old feminine powers. "Stories about Amazons," writes Bernice Schultz (1942), "filled many psychological needs of classical Greeks."[8] As with the wild women and the devs, the Amazon stories represented powerful women as brutal, mannish separatists. Legends about heroes such as Heracles and Theseus struggling with and dominating Amazons echoed the need at home to establish patriarchal order and the rights of fatherhood. Depicting Amazons as fierce and masculine counteracted any latent tendency to succumb to the seduction of the old mother cults or to throw oneself on the mercy of an Isis or an Artemis.

The removal of the breast symbolized ruthlessness and a lack of nurturing femininity in these warrior women. Contemporary women who lose a breast to cancer sometimes fear they will not be able to attract men. Desirability was not an issue in the legends, which include many stories about heroes engaging sexually with Amazon captives and queens. The sacrifice of the breast meant that the Amazons were giving up something important in exchange for their power; it was impossible for women to have such might and still retain the essential nurturing quality of femininity. The removal of the breast stands for a separation or fragmentation of feminine power and a loss of its sacred, life-giving element. Not all the stories mention the missing breast, and most Greek sculptures and friezes show Amazons as two-breasted. However, the images often depict a male warrior hero slashing or stabbing an Amazon in the breast. One way or the other, their breasts were not intact.

The legends of the Amazons have persisted and been used by different interest groups. They have had enduring value; even today people gain a certain effect by calling a woman an Amazon. Few people, however, know the story of Sheen Billy. This obscure Scottish tale brings up once again the struggle between feminine and masculine power in which breasts play a unique role. It never became widely known, probably because it is too strange and complicated to be politically or emotionally useful to very many people. It stands as evidence, however, that the old struggle still found its way into stories, at least through the mid-nineteenth century. This story appeared in a dusty collection titled *Popular Tales of the West Highlands* (Campbell, 1890-1893). A traveling tinker named Mac-Donald recounted it to the collector sometime before 1860.

Sheen Billy was the son of the King of Eirinn. Every day he and his twelve comrades played shinny (a game like hockey) with silver shinny sticks and a golden ball. Living such a delightful life, the handsome lad grew long-limbed and strong. Little did he suspect, as his silver shinny struck the gold ball, that hardship lay ahead. His wicked stepmother had procured an enchanted shirt, which she gave him and urged him to wear. Sheen Billy refused at first, but eventually he gave in. He pulled the garment over his head, buttoned it up, and then he was trapped. The shirt was really a beithir—a great, magical snake—and now Billy was enchanted and under its spell. He wandered away from the safe kingdom and his boyish games and happened upon many dangerous adventures.

After years of wandering, one day he came to the house of a wise woman and her beautiful daughter. The daughter at once fell in love with Billy and told her mother she must have him.

"It will cost thee much sorrow," said the mother.

"I care not," said the girl. "I must have him."

"It will cost thee thy right breast," said the mother.

"I care not if it costs me my life," said the daughter.

Seeing that her daughter was adamant, the wise woman prepared a huge caldron filled with wild plants and herbs. The two women stripped Billy down to his shirt, and he stepped into the cauldron. The beautiful girl stripped to her waist and joined the boy she desired in the enormous cast-iron vessel. The wise woman stood nearby and handed her daughter a large knife. As the wise woman's herbs started to work, the shirt began to quiver. It writhed and contorted until mother, daughter, and Billy could all see its true serpent form. Immediately the great snake sprang for the girl. It sank its teeth into her breast and held tight. The girl took her mother's knife and cut off her breast, freeing herself from the snake and Billy from the spell. The girl married Sheen Billy, and after the wedding, a golden breast was fashioned, and she wore it for the rest of her life.

In this story, the power of the goddess is divided among the three women—the stepmother, the wise woman, and the girl, all of whom have magical abilities. The stepmother represents everything hateful about the old feminine powers. The snake, a familiar of goddesses since Paleolithic times, is her weapon for binding up the young prince. The wise woman with her healing herbs represents the good face of feminine power. The daughter, by contrast, is a transitional figure, as she steps away from the wise woman ways to embrace the prince. She is allied with the old powers but attracted to Sheen Billy, the bright and shining beauty of the masculine.

The scene in the cauldron with the man, woman, and snake brings to mind another famous scene, where the serpent tempts Eve to eat of the fruit of the knowledge of good and evil. It is that snake, representing the temptation of feminine knowledge, which holds Sheen Billy in its grip. At that moment in the cauldron, the girl reverses the story of Eve. She offers her own rosy fruit for the snake to bite and, taking up a knife, disengages herself from the old ways of female power. She has sacrificed a breast, not as the Amazons in a quest for power but as symbol of power gladly given. In its place, she gets a man-made breast, golden and shiny as Sheen Billy, around whom she will revolve like the earth around the sun.

The wise woman's daughter may be forgotten, but people are still telling stories about breasts. A late-twentieth-century revival of stories about goddesses shows there is some life left in them yet. And twentieth-century women have added their voices to the story-telling chorus. Some of the stories they tell, such as the ones in the pages of this book, are terribly sad—stories of loss and disease or stories of embarrassment and exploitation. But they also tell stories of desire and fulfillment, stories of self-knowledge—uplifting and funny stories about breasts. These days breasts seem to be too wrapped in sexual meanings to be widely regarded as sacred symbols. Nonetheless, nearly every week some newspaper story is published that discusses the magical quality of breast milk, which prevents a host of diseases and promotes a growing number of good human traits. Women are telling breast feeding stories that show their wonder at discovering the transformative power of their breasts—a power that they believe nurtures and transforms not only the baby, but also the woman and the world.

Chapter 11

Breasts Unbound

Liz Baldwin did not expect her legal career to revolve around breast-feeding issues. Kathy Dettwyler did not set out to become an authority on cross-cultural breast-feeding practices. Kayla Sosnow certainly did not plan to get arrested for going top free in the national forest.

People just do not start out in life with ambitions to change the way the world thinks about and treats breasts. Breast activism is not a standard career option. When the repercussions of the great American breast fetish touched these three women's lives, however, they responded, bringing to bear their particular talents and skills. They are not the only women in the Western world who are working on issues about breasts. They are, however, all outstanding women who refused to accept the status quo. They are working to demystify breasts, to redefine them as healthy, functional body parts, and to create a world where women can have more comfortable relationships with their bodies. I do not agree with everything each of these women thinks and says about breasts, nor do they all agree with one another. But they all provide models for how women can fight back, insist upon what they know is important, and articulate their personal visions.

In 1982 Liz Baldwin and her husband-to-be set up a joint law practice in Miami Beach, Florida. When she became pregnant four years later, she expected to give birth and return to work. "I was running around telling everybody 'I'm no Susie Homemaker,'" she said. "'You're not going to find me sitting around all the time nursing.' I used to joke, 'Nobody gave me any instincts when they were passing them out.' But when my first baby was born, the world stopped."

Nothing seemed as important as this helpless infant. Her son was a needy baby who wanted to suckle every forty-five minutes, so Baldwin did sit around all the time nursing. She still tried to work, but the logistics became so difficult, she decided, with some regret, to stop practicing law. Instead, she became involved with La Leche League. La Leche League International is an American organization that exists solely to promote breast-feeding. It was founded by seven breast-feeding mothers in 1956, when breast-feeding was at an all-time low. Since then it has expanded enormously and now operates in sixty-six countries. Although it engages in many education and outreach projects, the essential part of its work goes on in small, local groups set up to give breast-feeding women encouragement and advice. Since North Miami Beach had no group, Baldwin signed up to be a La Leche League leader. Today, she is still a volunteer who holds meetings, answers breast-feeding questions, and provides information for women in her area.

In 1991, a controversial legal case hit the national media. A young mother lost custody of her child, apparently for extended breast-feeding. This posed a threat to everything La Leche League stood for, and across the country, women who were breast-feeding toddlers were frightened and confused. Was something wrong with breast-feeding a three-year-old? Could it really be illegal? At the request of La Leche League, Baldwin researched the case and found it to be much more complicated than the news stories told. The mother in question had said and done inappropriate things that made the authorities fear she would abuse her child. Baldwin began explaining the case, reassuring worried mothers and fielding reporters' questions. Soon she was appearing on television, saying to audiences, "You have a constitutional right to breast-feed. There is no law that tells mothers how long they can breast-feed."

Baldwin did not earn a cent from the case, but she received a flood of legal calls from all over the United States. After the initial flurry abated, calls kept coming and have continued at a rate of about sixty a month. The case brought her instant notoriety and threw her back into practicing law.

That does not mean Baldwin returned to her office. She had had a second child by then and was still a nursing mother, so she answered the calls at home. "Nobody knew whether I was sitting in a housecoat nursing my baby or I was sitting in a suit behind a fancy desk in an office," Baldwin said. "As long as I had a mute button on the telephone, I was ready and raring to go."

Today, Liz Baldwin is the foremost legal authority on breast-feeding issues in the United States. Her fingerprints are all over recently enacted laws that protect a woman's right to breast-feed in public. Although women have theoretically always had that right, indecency statutes have been invoked, and in some cases, local ordinances have been passed to keep them from doing so. Baldwin provided information to Florida State Representative Miguel de Grandy, who went on to craft legislation that not only assured the right to breast-feed in public but included language that said breast-feeding must be encouraged. After that, Baldwin provided free legal expertise and help in writing statues to many other states. Between 1995 and 1997, twelve states enacted breast-feeding legislation. "Many times I'll work with whoever is sponsoring the bill or their aide on how to handle problems or amendments to it," she said. "In whatever way they need, I'm there to help."

Although this is history-making work, it takes up only a small percentage of Baldwin's working time. What she does best and loves best is helping breast-feeding mothers settle divorce cases out of court. As a consultant and mediator, she negotiates parenting-time plans that preserve the breast-feeding relationship while also supporting the baby's bond with its father.

Settling is crucial, Baldwin says, because family law is not equipped to deal with breast-feeding. Judges routinely order long weekend or three-week summer visits for fathers of young children who may still be breast-feeding. Successful breast-feeding requires regular contact. A woman can pump out her milk for a while, but extended separations scuttle and ultimately sink the breast-feeding relationship. "Letting a judge decide your case, especially a custody case," said Baldwin, "is absolutely playing blind lotto with your child's life. Some people would like to see certain cases litigated to make law for other people. That's not fair. You've got to protect the individual mother and baby first."

Baldwin is opposed to rigid one-size-fits-all visitation formats, such as those that base visitation programs on the child's age. She believes strongly in parenting that responds to children's individual needs, and she feels each visitation plan must be negotiated on a case-by-case basis. This philosophy grew out of her own experience and what she learned from raising her two children. She started out trying to follow the baby book rules, but her fussy baby was not happy with standard treatment. "I had a choice of nursing him every forty-five minutes or letting him scream," said Baldwin. "All I knew was my heart told me not to let my baby cry. I couldn't stand it. And so I decided to be a bad mother and just let him nurse when he wanted to." She planned to nurse for six months but kept extending the date because her baby was not ready to wean. She nursed through her second pregnancy, then tandem nursed the two children. "I wasn't exactly sure what it was going to be like," Baldwin said, "but it turned out to be a very beautiful, wonderful experience that my baby and my toddler would sit there and play footsies with one another and hold hands while they nursed together."

As she continued nursing beyond the usual one or two years, friends and relatives pressured her to stop. She plunged into research on attachment-style parenting. What she read convinced her that children who are strongly bonded to their parents grow up to be happier and healthier. "Most babies don't nurse this long," she said. "I'm really way up on the scales. But both of them had food allergies. Both of them were high-needs kids, and they're happy, independent kids now." Each child stopped nursing on his own about the time he learned to read. "Eventually they weaned," she said. "Eventually the need goes away."

Baldwin does not think of herself as a radical person. She does not want to be called an activist, but she is working for a way of parenting that runs counter to the mainstream. She has a clear, specific idea of what breasts are all about. They are tools for nurturing babies, and she applies her considerable talents to protecting that function.

Baldwin's work has not made her rich. She does much of it pro bono. She has a big heart and will give almost anyone an hour or so of her time for free. Her kids object when she gets wound up in a case and spends hours on the phone. But she is doing the work she loves, both as a parent and as a lawyer. "I did not have a passion in terms of the law until it came to the breast-feeding cases," she said. "This is my passion."

*   *   *

When I e-mailed Kathy Dettwyler the question, "Do you like your own breasts?" she replied that was a "very ODD question that could only come from a perspective totally enculturated into the view that breasts MUST be viewed as sexual objects." She liked her breasts just fine, she explained, as well as she liked her toes or her ears. "My breasts have been very good to my children," she e-mailed back. "They worked just fine. . . But I'm done with my breasts. They are just there."

How could this woman have such neutral feelings about her breasts? That story begins in 1982 when a young anthropologist set off on an adventure that would decide the direction of her life. Excited and a little nervous, Katherine Dettwyler boarded the plane to Mali in West Africa. At her side sat her husband, Steven, also an anthropologist. On her lap she held fifteen-month-old Miranda, who snuggled and nursed at her breast. Dettwyler loved the bond with her first child. She had become pregnant in 1979, in the middle of the Nestlés' boycott. Many were protesting the milk company's campaign to sell infant formula in traditionally breast-feeding third world countries where people could not afford to buy wood to sterilize milk or bottles, so that bottle-feeding could mean the baby's death. Dettwyler planned to study the health effects of infant formula, but when the plane landed in Mali, she found herself in a new and different world. Everybody breast-fed; infant formula had made no inroads as yet. She restructured her project to study traditional beliefs and practices surrounding breast-feeding, weaning, and child-nutrition and found a whole universe of subtle meanings. Mothers in Mali, who go about unclothed above the waist in their compounds or rural villages, nurse their babies frequently in the fields, on public transportation, and even in the office. It was unthinkable not to breast-feed because breast-feeding formed the central bond of kinship and relationship in Mali. Malians use the same word *shin ji* for breast milk and for one's closest kin. As a kinship term, shin ji literally means "those who breast-fed from the same woman."

Dettwyler's thirty months of fieldwork in Mali led to another trip in 1989 and the book *Dancing Skeletons: Life and Death in West Africa* (1994). Dettwyler's writing is lively and accessible; *Dancing Skeletons* won the 1995 Margaret Mead Award from the American Anthropological Association and the Society for Applied Anthropology, and it became an academic bestseller.

Today, Katherine Dettwyler is an associate professor of anthropology and nutrition at Texas A&M. Her focus has not been limited to Mali. In her research, she tracks studies of breast-feeding in other cultures and trains the beam of her intelligence on issues surrounding breasts and breast-feeding worldwide. The meanings breasts carry for any particular culture directly influence the health and growth of children. Turning her anthropological analysis on the United States, she has criticized practices that undermine breast-feeding in this country.

At the root of our problem, Dettwyler says, lies our sexualization of breasts. Most cultures do not think of breasts as sex objects. When Dettwyler told women in Mali that Americans think breasts are sexually arousing, they were horrified. What a repulsive practice! But also what a hilarious one! "You mean men act like babies," they shrieked, collapsing in laughter. Sexual habits and mores, Dettwyler argues, are culturally constructed. Breasts do not naturally respond in sexual ways. And the sexualization of breasts is no laughing matter because it is so destructive. According to Dettwyler, sexualization of breasts harms babies because bottle-fed babies have on average more infant sickness and death, more life-long illnesses, and lower cognitive abilities than do breast-fed babies. It harms women because women who do not breast-feed have higher rates of breast and other cancers. It leads women to "participate in their own oppression by valuing their own worth on the basis of the size and shape of their breasts," causing them to "mutilate" their bodies with breast implant surgeries.

Physiological responses such as sexual arousal are conditioned by social assumptions, Dettwyler says. After spending twenty-four months of her young life in Mali, plus six more months as a nine-year-old, her daughter Miranda still thinks of termites as a delicious, crunchy snack. She salivates when an American might gag. By the same conditioning process, an American woman may feel sexually aroused when her breasts are caressed. There is nothing wrong with that per se, Dettwyler says. "I don't care a whit what people do in the privacy of their bedrooms. . . . There ARE cultures, such as many in India, where breasts are viewed as both sexy and maternal—where women are not classified as mothers or whores, but as sexy and maternal at the same time. It is clearly possible to view breasts as sex objects and still have a totally breast-feeding culture—India does it. But that is not how the United States has gone." Breast-feeding and sexualized breasts should not be mutually exclusive, she believes, but if a culture cannot live with both, then sexuality should give way to breast-feeding—a function that is infinitely more important.

In her writing, Dettwyler criticizes infant formula companies for distributing "public information" that reinforces this sexualization by presenting breast-feeding as something women do in private, wearing a negligee, and then only with very small infants.

Dettwyler is particularly alert to information that sexualizes breasts or prejudices people against breast-feeding. Although research and writing fit into her job description, she also carries on a letter-writing campaign on her own time, turning out hundreds of letters about breasts and breast-feeding issues. Once she wrote objecting to a *Time* magazine ad identifying the magazine's parenting Web page with a baby bottle. *Time* wrote back and said they would change it. One of her letters was partly responsible for a milk company's decision to kill an advertisement urging parents to feed babies its milk instead of formula. She often writes complaining about advertising that exploits women's breasts. "Anytime I see something I think is inappropriate, I write a letter," she said.

Dettwyler has produced groundbreaking research on extended breast-feeding. Her comparative primate research on breast-feeding takes into account factors such as life histories, length of gestation, age of eruption of teeth, and sexual maturity. Based on these variables, she argues that the natural weaning age for humans ranges between two and a half and seven years. She is conducting an on-going survey of long-term breast-feeding in the United States. Her results show that many mothers are not weaning their babies until age three or four, and that some have nursed even longer. Her record breakers are two women who nursed until their children were nine! One purpose of this work is to show that extended breast-feeding is not just done in remote and exotic cultures; it can work in our country too.

Because Dettwyler possesses a restless, rigorous intelligence and an ability to communicate with mass audiences, her voice has become a major influence in contemporary thought, in policymaking, and also in the lives of many individuals. Her second book, *Breast-Feeding: Bio-cultural Perspectives* (1995), co-edited with Patricia Stuart-Macadam, is selling well. She consults with lactation specialists, doctors, and nurses, using her influence and the weight of her research to promote breast-feeding. She gives popular lectures in the United States and abroad. Her work has been used in seven court cases involving mothers charged with sexual abuse for breast-feeding older children. And it has been used to set pediatric guidelines for breast-feeding and training third-world health workers.

Some people see the argument for breast-feeding as a conservative one—an attempt to shove women back into roles as mothers and housewives. Dettwyler strongly disagrees. "I'm the most feminist person I know," she told me. "I believe women should have all the same opportunities as men, get the same pay, and be judged on their accomplishments rather than how they look." She does not believe breast-feeding means women need to lower their horizons. She breast-fed all three of her children while building her career. She took them to work and breast-fed them during office hours and staff meetings. Dettwyler admits, however, that hers is a privileged career, and it would be much more difficult for a woman on a factory line to do the same. She argues that companies need to create baby-friendly workplaces, with innovations such as on-site day care, where women can come and nurse their babies periodically throughout the day. "If you look at other cultures around the world, there isn't this problem of the public-private split," she said. "Everybody's just working all the time, and their kids are with them all the time. I say you can have work and breast-feed your children."

Certainly Kathy Dettwyler has had both. Outspoken, energetic, and inquisitive, she seems to be one of those rare people whose abilities and temperament are a perfect match for his or her career. "Katherine is having a major influence on contemporary thinking where infant and child feeding and related maternal and child health issues are concerned," said James Akre, of the World Health Organization. It is thrilling, she says, to know that her work is making real changes in people's lives. "I love this stuff," she said. "My family is totally supportive. My colleagues at the university leave me alone. Because of this research, I've had enormous opportunities to travel and write and speak."

* * *

In February 1996, Kayla Sosnow went to jail for going bare-breasted in the Osceola National Forest. It happened like this: Sosnow was attending a gathering of the Rainbow Family in north-central Florida. The temperature had reached ninety degrees, and she and her friend Eric had taken off their shirts, borrowed a car, and gone to fetch water for the group. Since her college days, Sosnow had gone top free on certain occasions. "I just knew it was the right thing to do," she said. "I knew it was ridiculous that men had the right to go without a shirt and women didn't, so I was going to do something about it, which was just take my shirt off and be comfortable. I like to be free and natural."

When two forest rangers approached her and asked her to put on her shirt, she balked. They said, "We've got laws about nudity around here." Sosnow knew there were no such laws at the state level, so she asked, "Do you have a local ordinance?" At that point, the rangers radioed for backup.

While she was detained awaiting the arrival of reinforcements, Sosnow thought about what to do. "I wasn't there to stir up trouble or cause a scene, create a cause or make a statement," she said. "I was making my statement just by not wearing a shirt." She thought about what could happen and how she could make it all go away by just covering up. "I'm smart enough that the reality of the situation goes through my mind," she said. "But when it comes to a matter of justice, pragmatics go out the window."

The sheriff arrived with five more patrol cars. The officers approached her and asked her to put on her shirt. Sosnow replied, "What about all these shirtless males?" The officers gave her a choice—put on your shirt or go to jail. She refused to cover herself, so they grabbed her and arrested her. She spent four days behind bars before seeing the judge and being let out on bail.

In the Florida justice system, Sosnow continued to hold out for personal dignity and her own belief about what is right, and she found that strategy can get you into trouble. The charges against her kept changing—from obscenity to indecent exposure to disorderly conduct. The latter is the charge that has been used against top-free women in Florida since 1977. Despite that, if she pled guilty she would get off easy, Sosnow continued to plead innocent. Seven months after the arrest, she was finally found guilty of disorderly conduct and sentenced to thirty days in jail to be suspended after successfully serving five months probation, fifty hours of community service, payment of $600 in fines and fees, and a promise not to appear nude or partially nude in public for the next six months. Sosnow left the court feeling wretched. She asked herself, "What is wrong with me that my values are so foreign to the rest of society?"

At her first appointment, her probation officer asked Sosnow to sign a release requesting any organization that had information about her to give it to the probation department. Sosnow thought that was too broad and invasive and asked if it could be adjusted to reflect what was actually needed to verify that she was complying with conditions of probation. The probation officer flew into a rage and shouted, "There is no adjusting to be done! I call the shots around here!" By the time she finished shouting, Sosnow was in tears. When she left, she went across the street to the court library and filed an appeal. "I am not going to tolerate this treatment," she thought. "For what I did, I do not deserve to be treated like a criminal." Because she refused to sign the release, Sosnow was thrown back in jail on charges of violating probation and stayed there for sixteen days until the state attorney saw the form she had been asked to sign and dropped the charges against her. The probation department has since agreed to stop using that form.

Sosnow's stay in jail was not intolerable. "I mostly had good roommates," she said. "Most of the people didn't belong there. They were in there because they didn't know how to fight for their rights. The women in jail really dug me. They respected me because I was one person who was standing up and fighting for rights."

Even out of jail, the legal system was not through with Sosnow. As of this writing, she still has to go through her appeal—a process she thinks could take three to five years. She realized that her case was potentially precedent-setting and began organizing her defense. She found a good lawyer who was willing to take on her appeal for a flat fee of $1,000. The fee was quite modest for the work he would do, but for Sosnow it was a lot. At the time of the arrest, she was a graduate student and had very little money. She launched a fundraising campaign, asking for support from sympathetic organizations and individuals. "This campaign was organized very strategically," she said, "so I would have a high profile in all the right places and I wouldn't have to be subjected to having a high profile in the wrong places." With a good deal of time-consuming letter writing and speaking, she has raised the lawyer's fee and gained support from people across the country and from sympathetic organizations. The Naturist Society, the state and local branches of the American Civil Liberties Union, and the National Organization for Women are among her supporters.

With these efforts, Kayla Sosnow has become an organized top-free activist. She is one of at least sixteen known women who, in the last twenty years, have been arrested for going top free and have fought the charges. These women include Debbie Moore and Nina Shilling in Berkeley, Rosita Libre de Marulanda in New York City, and Gwen Jacob in Toronto. What they do is called "top free equality" or "top free liberation." It is not a coordinated movement but rather an effort that has sometimes been strategically organized, and sometimes the spontaneous act of women who doff their shirts on the spur of the moment, and after they are arrested, attract a group of supporters. Their court cases have made a difference. In 1996, the Ontario Court of Appeals overturned Gwen Jacob's conviction of indecent exposure. In 1992, the New York State Court of Appeals ruled that women have the right to go without their shirts wherever men can do so, as long as they do not behave in a lewd manner.

Kayla Sosnow plans to base her appeal on the Fourteenth Amendment's assurance of equal protection under the law. Although the top-free movement does not have a defined and delineated philosophy, one of its key ideas is equality with men. If men's chests are not obscene, why should women's be? If men can take off their shirts, why can't women? This prohibition, goes the argument, places a yoke on women. Men have the choice of going to strip joints and seeing breasts when they want, but women do not have the choice of uncovering their breasts. Men get to control the visibility of women's breasts.

Another important concept is that covering breasts lends them a sexual mystique. Writing about top-free equality, *Esquire* magazine complained that, ". . . in the end we are talking about a certain diminution of glamour. . . . Nothing is left to the imagination. . . . Bare breasts are a bit much, for instance, to contemplate by the copying machine." Voices on both sides of the issue acknowledge that keeping breasts covered keeps them sexy. This mystique is exploited by commercial interests who use images of breasts to sell products. "We're reclaiming our bodies," said Sosnow, "from the people who would use them to make money."

When I talked to Kayla Sosnow a year and a half after her arrest, she had a new job as an administrative assistant and was preparing for more graduate school and a career as a high school guidance counselor. She felt torn between her desire to build a career and her passions for top-free activism. If she wins her appeal, it could change Florida law. "The world," she said, "needs people to stand up against things that are wrong." At the same time, she worried about how the publicity would affect her career. Fighting this cause has given her a police record. How would that affect her future?

In some ways, Sosnow's battle for top freedom has given her less personal freedom. Because our culture associates breasts with sex, she feels she must be careful about her behavior. She's afraid to flirt or act overtly sexual. "I am so closely associated with this cause," she said, "that I don't want to be seen as an exhibitionist. I don't want to confuse the issue by giving people reason to suspect my motives."

On the other hand, becoming involved in top freedom has provided her an opportunity to use her knowledge and skills. She has strategically organized a campaign and spoken publicly on several occasins. It has made her think long and deeply about women's bodies and women's freedom, and she has learned about how the law and justice systems work.

Even though she has to worry about balancing her career and future security with her ideals, Sosnow said, "I feel best about my life when I have a cause. I feel best about my life when I'm doing something productive to change the world for the better."

"I'm not doing this for myself," she added. "If I were doing it just for myself, I would have quit a long time ago. I'm doing it for the women of Florida and for women in general."

When I asked Kayla Sosnow if she liked her breasts, she said, "Yes I do. I like them very much." She described them as smallish and slightly lopsided. They are round and perky, and they have a few hairs around the nipples. They are, she said, not perfect. Sosnow likes her breasts, but she recognizes that she judges them by society's standards. "Just because you're aware enough to understand society's pressures on you," she said, "does not make you immune to them."

She is right, of course. This is a time in history when people are thinking, writing, and talking about oppressive beauty standards that hold captive women's bodies and women's spirits. There have been major breakthroughs. Thirty years ago breast cancer was a secret shame; now, well-organized support and advocacy groups have taken the shame away and made it a public health issue. Fewer than 10 percent of women in the Western world breast-feed their babies for a year or more, but there are signs of improvement. Recently compiled statistics show a modest increase in breast-feeding in Americans, especially among lower economic groups. Women are going to court for the right to breast-feed in public and the right to take off their shirts at a picnic. These are real advances. Yet, during this same period, women have been eagerly snatching up the new cleavage-enhancing brassieres, and breast implant surgery remains a thriving business.

The great American breast fetish is alive and well, but more people are aware of it, and that means things are changing. I would like to see us face up to this obsession. By that I do not mean that breasts should be desexualized or that breast men should all go in for attitude adjustments. I would, however, like to see the majority of women feeling OK about their breasts. I would like to see breast-feeding become a natural and easy choice. I would like to stop seeing women judged by the size and shape of their breasts.

More and more women are, like Sosnow, living in a transitional world where they see through the cultural breast obsession but are still not immune to it. Cultural revolution does not happen in a day, or even, sometimes, in a generation. People have to live through it and carry it along. It is a burden, living with this ambivalence, this double-vision of our breasts. But somebody has to carry the load, and I believe the women at this time in history have the strength to do it.

Notes

Chapter 1

1. Rosen, Marjorie. *Popcorn Venus*. New York: Avon, 1973, p. 267.
2. Mead, Margaret. *Male and Female: A Study of the Sexes in a Changing World*. New York: Dell, 1971.
3. Mazur, Allan. "U.S. trends in feminine beauty and overadaptation." *The Journal of Sex Research,* 22 (1986): pp. 289-293.
4. Snyder, Mark, Elizabeth Decker Tanke, and Ellen Berscheid. "Social perceptions and interpersonal behavior. On the self-fulfilling nature of social stereotypes." *Journal of Personality and Social Psychology,* 9 (1977): pp. 656-666.
5. Franzoi, Stephen, L. and Mary E. Herzog. "Judging physical attractiveness. What body aspects do we use?" *Personality and Social Psychology Bulletin,* 13(1) (1987): pp. 19-33; Horvath, Theodore. "Correlates of physical beauty in men and women." *Social Behavior and Personality,* 7(2) (1979): pp. 145-151; Horvath, Theodore. "Physical attractiveness: The influence of selected torso parameters." *Archives of Sexual Behavior,* 10 (1981): pp. 21-24. Kleinke, Chris and Richard Staneski. "First impressions of female bust size." *The Journal of Social Psychology,* 110 (1980): pp. 123-134; Wiggens, Jerry S., Nancy Wiggens, and Judith Cohen Conger. "Correlates of heterosexual somatic preference." *Journal of Personality and Social Psychology,* 10(1) (1968): pp. 82-90; Wiggens, Jerry S. and Nancy Wiggens. "A typological analysis of male preferences for female body types." *Multivariate Behavioral Research,* 4(1) (1969): pp. 89-102.
6. Allende, Isabel. *The Infinite Plan.* Trans. Margaret Sayers Peden. New York: HarperCollins, 1991, p. 98
7. Schmitt, Raymond. "Embodied identities: Breasts as emotional reminders." *Studies in Symbolic Interaction,* 7(A) (1986): p. 242.
8. Coons, Philip, Haya Ascher-Svanum, and Kirk Bellis. "Self-amputation of the female breast." *Psychosomatics,* 27 (1986): pp. 667-668.
9. Schmitt, "Embodied identities," pp. 256, 261.

Chapter 2

1. Collins, John K. "Self-recognition of the body and its parts during late adolescence." *Journal of Youth and Adolescence,* 10(3) (1981): pp. 243-254.
2. See: Chodorow, Nancy. *The Mermaid and the Minotaur: Sexual Arrangements and Human Malaise.* New York: Harper and Row, 1976; and Rosenbaum,

Maj-Britt. "The changing body image of the adolescent girl." *Female Adolescent Development,* Ed. Max Sugar. New York: Brunner/Mazel, 1979, pp. 234-252.

3. Rheingold, Joseph C. *The Fear of Being a Woman: A Theory of Maternal Destructiveness.* New York: Grune and Stratton, 1964, p. 211.

4. Rierdan, Jill and Elissa Koff. "Representation of the female body by early and late adolescent girls." *Journal of Youth and Adolescence,* 9 (1980): pp. 339-346.

5. Rosenbaum, Maj-Britt. "The changing body image of the adolescent girl." *Female Adolescent Development,* Ed. Max Sugar. New York: Brunner/Mazel, 1979, p. 244.

6. Brooks-Gunn, Jeanne. "The psychological significance of different pubertal events to young girls." *Journal of Early Adolescence,* 4(4) (1984), p. 323.

7. Blos (1962), Deutsch (1944), and Kestenberg (1967), as cited in Rierdan, Jill and Elissa Koff. "Representations of the female body in early and late adolescent girls." *Journal of Youth and Adolescence,* 9 (1980): p. 340.

8. Meador, Betty DeShong. *Uncursing the Dark.* Wilmette, IL: Chiron, 1992, p. 55

9. Brooks-Gunn, Jeanne and Edward O. Reiter. "Role of the pubertal process." *At the Threshold: The Developing Adolescent,* Eds. S. S. Feldman and G. R. Elliott. Cambridge, MA: Harvard University Press, 1990, p. 20.

10. Brooks-Gunn, Jeanne, Denis Newman, and Michelle Warren. "The experience of breast development and girls' stories about the purchase of a bra." *Journal of Youth and Adolescence,* 23(5) (1994), pp. 551-552.

11. Ephron, Nora. "A few words about breasts: Shaping up absurd." *Scenes From Life,* Ed. Judy Blankenship. Boston: Little Brown and Company, 1976, p. 365.

12. Brooks-Gunn and Reiter, "Role of the pubertal process," Peterson, Anne C., Maryse Tobin-Richards, and Andrew Boxer. "Puberty: Its measurement and its meaning." *Journal of Early Adolescence,* 3(1-2) (1983): pp. 47-62.

Chapter 3

1. Quoted in Batterberry, Michael and Ariane. *Fashion: The Mirror of History.* New York: Greenwich House, 1977, p. 30

2. This amount of the Minoan civilization is based on the following sources: Cotterell, Arthur. *The Minoan World.* New York: Scribner, 1980; Hawkes, Jacquetta. *Dawn of the Gods.* London: Chatto and Windus, 1968; Payne, Blanche, Geitel Winakor, and Jane Farrell-Beck. *The History of Costume: From Ancient Mesopotamia Through the Twentieth-Century.* New York: HarperCollins, 1992; Russell, Douglas. *Costume History and Style.* Englewood Cliffs. NJ: Prentice-Hall, 1983; Trump, D.H., *The Prehistory of the Mediterranean.* New Haven: Yale University Press, 1980.

3. Neumann, Erich. *The Great Mother: An Analysis of the Archetype.* Trans. Ralph Manheim. Princeton, NJ: Princeton University Press, 1972, p. 128.

4. Cotterell, *The Minoan World,* p. 96.

5. For differing theories see: Blumer, Herbert. "Fashion: From Class differentiation to Collective Selection." *The Sociological Quarterly,* 10 (Summer 1969):

pp. 275-291; Cordwell, Justine and Schwartz, Eds. *The Fabrics of Culture: The Anthropology of Clothing and Adornment.* New York: Mouton, 1979; Flugel, John C. *The Psychology of Clothes.* London: Hogarth Press, 1950; Hollander, Susan. *Seeing Through Clothes.* New York: Penguin Books, 1978; Horn, Marilyn J. *The Second Skin: An Interdisciplinary Study of Clothing.* Boston: Houghton Mifflin Company, 1968; Laurie, Alison. *The Language of Clothes.* New York: Random House, 1981; Laver, James. *Taste and Fashion.* London: George G. Harrop, 1948; Roach, Mary Ellen and Joanne Babolz. *Dress, Adornment, and the Social Order.* New York: John Wiley and Sons, 1965; Russell, Douglas. *Costume History and Style.* Englewood Cliffs, NJ: Prentice-Hall, 1983.

6. See: Sproules, George B. "Behavioral science theories of fashion." *The Psychology of Fashion*, Ed. Michael R. Solomon. Lexington, MA: D.C. Heath, 1985, pp. 55-69.

7. For a good summary of theories of fashion see: Blumer, Herbert. "Fashion: From class differentiation to collective selection." *The Sociological Quarterly,* 10 (Summer 1969): pp. 275-291; and Sproules, "Behavioral science theories of fashion."

8. See: Batterberry and Batterberry. *Fashion*, pp. 23-29; and Russell, *Costume History,* pp. 14-27.

9. Hollander, *See Through Clothes*, pp. 3-4.

10. Keuls, Eva. *The Reign of the Phallus: Sexual Politics in Ancient Athens.* New York: Harper and Row, 1981.

11. Batterberry and Batterberry, *Fashion*, pp. 42-43.

12. Hollander, *Seeing Through Clothes,* p. 5.

13. Attributed by Kunzle, David. *Fashion and Fetishism: A Social History of the Corset, Tight-Lacing, and Other Forms of Body-Sculpture in the West.* Totowa, NJ: Rowman and Littlefield, 1982, pp. 65-66.

14. Laver, James. *The Concise History of Costume and Fashion.* New York: Charles Scribners Sons, 1979, p. 29

15. Kunzle, *Fashion and Fetishism*, p. 29.

16. See Kunzle, *Fashion and Fetishism*, p. 29.

17. Quoted in Kunzle, *Fashion and Fetishism*, p. 83.

18. Milford, Nancy, *The Sun King.* New York: Crescent Books, 1966, pp. 27, 45-47.

19. Laver, James, *Taste and Fashion,* p. 147.

20. Batterberry and Batterberry, *Fashion*, p. 197.

21. Kunzle, *Fashion and Fetishism*, p. 105.

22. Ewing, Elizabeth, *Dress and Undress.* New York: Drama Book Specialists, 1972, p. 79.

23. Ewing, *Dress and Undress*, p. 115.

24. Van Gelder, Lindsey. "The truth about bra-burning." *Ms.* (September/October 1992): pp. 80-81. See also: Kanin, Ruth. *The Manufacturer of Beauty.* Boston: Branden, 1990, pp. 110-111.

Chapter 4

1. Palfreman, Joe, Producer. "Breast implants on trial." PBS *Frontline, http://.pbs.org/wgbh/pages/frontline/implants/cron.html,* p. 6
2. The American Society of Plastic and Reconstructive Surgeons. Plastic Surgery Media Center. "1996 Breast Surgery Statistics," *http://plasticurgery.org/ mediactr/breast96.htm.,* p. 1.
3. U.S. Food and Drug Administration. *Breast Implants: An Information Update.* Washington, DC: Government Printing Office, 1996, p. 25.
4. Symmers, W. St. C. "Silicone mastitis in 'topless' waitresses and some other varieties of foreign-body mastitis." *British Medical Journal,* 6 (July 1968): p. 19.
5. Byrne, John A. *Informed Consent.* New York: McGraw-Hill, 1996.
6. "Escalation," *Newsweek* (October 25, 1966): p. 110.
7. "Bosom perfection—the new possibilities," *Vogue* (October 15, 1959): p. 127.
8. Biggs, Thomas, Jean Cukier, and Fabian Worthing. "Augmentation mammaplasty: A review of eighteen years." *Plastic and Reconstructive Surgery,* 69 (1982): p. 447.
9. USFDA, *Breast Implants,* p. 25.
10. Palfreman, "Breast implants on trial," p. 6.
11. USFDA, *Breast Implants,* p. 14.
12. Vasey, Frank V. and Josh Feldstein. *The Silicone Implant Controversy: What Women Need to Know.* Freedom, CA: The Crossing Press, 1993.
13. The "Mayo Clinic Study" (Gabriel, S.E., Kurland, W.M., Beard, L.T., Woods, J.E. and Melon III, L. J. "Risk of connective-tissue diseases and other disorders after breast implantation." *New England Journal of Medicine,* [June 16, 1994]: pp. 1607-1702) and the "Harvard Nurses Study" (Sanchez-Guererro, J., G.A. Colditz, K.W. Karlson, D.L. Hunter, F.E. Speizer, and M.H. Liang. "Silicone breast implants and the risk of connective tissue diseases and symptoms." *New England Journal of Medicine,* 332 [1995] pp. 1666-1670).
14. Wolf, Naomi. *The Beauty Myth: How Images of Beauty Are Used Against Women.* New York: W. Morrow, 1991.
15. Young, Tracy. "A few (more) words about breasts." *Esquire,* (September 1992): p. 146.
16. Longacre, J.J. "Surgical reconstruction of the flat discoid breast." *Plastic and Reconstructive Surgery,* 17(5) (1956): pp. 358-366.
17. For a fuller discussion, see: Latteier, Carolyn. *Cosmetic Breast Surgery: The Origins 1945-1968.* Thesis. Washington State University, 1997.

Chapter 5

1. Makin, Jennifer W. and Porter, Richard H. "Attractiveness of lactating females' breast odors to neonates." *Child Development,* 60(4) (1989): pp. 25-66.
2. The experiment is described in: Lichtenberg, Joseph. *Psychoanalysis and Infant Research.* Hillsdale, NJ: The Analytic Press, 1983, pp. 8-9.

3. Lichtenberg, *Psychoanalysis*, p. 8.

4. Klein, Melanie. *The Psychoanalysis of Children.* Trans. Alix Strachey. New York: Free Press, 1984, p. 55.

5. Segal, Hanna. *Introduction to the Works of Melanie Klein.* New York: Basic Books, 1964, p. 65.

6. See: Astor, James. "The breast as part of a whole." *Journal of Analytical Psychology,* 34 (1989): pp. 120-121.

7. Restak, Richard M. *The Infant Mind.* Garden City, NY: Doubleday, 1986, p. 8.

8. Maurer, Daphne and Charles. *The World of the Newborn.* New York: Basic Books, 1988, p. 61.

9. Otto Isakower presented a paper on trace memories of nursing at the breast at the Fourteenth International Psychoanalytical Congress in 1936. That paper appeared under the title of "A Contribution to the Pathopsychology of Phenomena Associated with Falling Asleep." *International Journal of Psychoanalysis,* 19 (1938): pp. 331-345. Subsequently, Geraldine Fink (1967) and William Easson (1973) reported identifying the phenomenon in their patients.

10. See: Mahler, Margaret, Fred Pine, and Ann Bergman. *The Psychological Birth of the Human Infant.* New York: Basic Books, 1975, p. 44; and Kohut, Heinz. *Self-Psychology and the Humanities.* New York: Norton, 1985, p. 119.

11. Eichenbaum, Luise and Susie Orbach. *Understanding Women: A Feminist Psychoanalytic Approach.* New York: Basic Books, 1983, p. 169.

12. Eichenbaum and Orbach, *Understanding Women,* pp. 169-174; Birksted-Breen, Dana. "Working with an anorexic patient" *International Journal of Psychoanalysis,* 70(29) (1989): pp. 29-38; Chernin, Kim. *The Obsession: Reflections on the Tyranny of Slenderness.* New York: Harper and Row, 1981; Sours, John A. *Starving to Death in a Sea of Objects: The Anorexia Nervosa Syndrome.* New York: J. Aronson, 1989.

13. Silverman, Lloyd, Frank Lachmann, and Robert Milich. *The Search for Oneness.* New York: International Universities Press, 1982.

14. Choderow, Nancy. *The Reproduction of Mothering.* Berkley: University of California Press, 1978, p. 57.

15. Berlin, Irving, "The Girl That I Marry." From *Annie Get Your Gun,* 1946.

Chapter 6

1. Case information from: Gaskin, Ina May. "Who is abusing whom?" *The Birth Gazette,* 8(2) (1992): pp. 11-12; and personal interview with Elizabeth Baldwin, J.D., April 18, 1997.

2. Baldwin, Elizabeth N., and Kenneth A. Friedman. "Breast-feeding legislation in the United States." *New Beginnings,* 11(6) (1994): p. 164.

3. Baldwin and Friedman, "Breast-feeding legislation" p. 164.

4. *Sun* news services and *Sun* staff. "Is breast-feeding in public places the last taboo?" *The Sun Daily Newspaper* (Bremerton, WA), (March 8, 1994): p. C5.

5. Van Esterik, Penny. "The cultural context of breast-feeding in rural Thailand." *Breast-feeding, Child Health, and Child Spacing: Cross-Cultural Per-*

spectives, Eds. Valerie Hull and Mayling Simpson. London: Croom Helm, 1985, p. 143.

6. Newton, Niles. "Breast feeding." *Psychology Today,* 2(1) (1968): p. 70.

7. Newton, Niles. "Interrelationships between sexual responsiveness, birth and breast-feeding." *Contemporary Sexual Behavior: Current Issues in the 1970s,* Eds. J. Zubin and J. Money. Baltimore: Johns Hopkins, 1973; Newton, Niles. "Trebly sensuous woman." *Psychology Today,* 5(2) (July 1971): pp. 68-71, 98-99.

8. Newton, "Interrelationships between sexual responsiveness," p. 81.

9. Debackere, M., Peeters, G., and Tuyttens, N. "Reflex release of an oxytocic hormone by stimulation of genital organs in male and female sheep studied by a cross-circulation technique." *Journal of Endocrinology,* 22 (1961): pp. 321-334.

10. Newton, "Interrelationships between sexual responsiveness," pp. 83-84, 91-94.

11. For pro-bonding arguments see: Kennell, John H. and Marshall H. Klaus. "Mother-infant bonding: Weighing the evidence." *Developmental Review,* 4 (1984): pp. 275-282; Klaus, Marshall, John Kennell, Nancy Plumb, and Steven Zuehlke. "Human maternal behavior at the first contact with her young." *Pediatrics,* 46(2) (1970): pp. 187-192; and Lynch, Margaret A. "Ill-health and child abuse." *The Lancet,* (August 16, 1975): pp. 317-319. For a summary of the literature with an anti-bonding bias, see: Meyers, Barbara J. "Mother-infant bonding: The status of the critical-period hypothesis." *Developmental Review,* 4 (1984): pp. 240-274.

12. Jelliffee, Derrick and Patrice. *Human Milk for the Modern World.* Oxford: Oxford University Press, 1978; p. 174.

13. Van Esterik, "The cultural context of breast-feeding."

14. Quoted in: Baumslag, Naomi. "Breast-feeding: Cultural practices and variations." *Human Lactation 2: Maternal and Environmental Factors,* Eds. Hamosh and Armand Goldman. New York: Plenum Press, 1986, p. 626.

15. The brief history of breast-feeding that follows is based on two excellent books by Valerie A. Fildes. *Breasts, Bottles, and Babies.* Edinburgh: Edinburgh University Press, 1986 and *Wet Nursing: A History from Antiquity to the Present.* New York: Basil Blackwell, 1988.

16. Fildes, *Breasts, Bottles, and Babies,* pp. 270-271.

17. La Leche League. "A brief history of La Leche League International." el. 1, *http://www.lalecheleague.org/LLLhistory.html.*

18. 1995 statistics for initiating breast-feeding through six months were produced by the Ross Laboratories Mothers' Survey and reported in: Ryan, Alan S. "The resurgence of breast-feeding in the United States," *Pediatrics,* 99(4) (1997): p. el 1; Ryan, A.S., W.F. Pratt, J.L. Wysong, G. Lewandowski, J.W. McNally, and F.W. Krieger. "A comparison of breast-feeding data from the National Survey of Family Growth and Ross Laboratories Mothers Survey." *American Journal of Public Health,* 81(8) (August, 1991): pp. 1049-1051.

19. No statistics for twelve months are available for 1995. Dettwyler reports that, in 1990, 6.2 percent of mothers in the United States were still breast-feeding when their babies were twelve months old. (Dettwyler, Katherine. "Beauty and the breast: The cultural context of breast-feeding in the United States." *Breast-*

feeding: Biocultural Perspectives, Eds. Katherine Dettwyler and Patricia Stuart-Mac-adam. Hawthorne, NY: Aldine de Gruyter, 1995.) Catherine Hoteri, a researcher for La Leche League International, confirmed that 6 percent "sounds reasonable" for 1995 (Personal communication, March 26, 1997).

20. Palmer, Gabrielle. *The Politics of Breastfeeding.* London: Pandora Press, 1988, pp. 29-31.

21. Deutsch, Helene. "The psychology of women" Volume 2. New York: Grune and Stratton, 1945, p. 279.

Chapter 7

1. Vance, Carole S. "Anthropology rediscovers sexuality: A theoretical comment." *Social Science and Medicine,* 33 (1991): p. 880.

2. Kinsey, Alfred C., Pomeroy Warden, Martin Clyde, and Paul Gebhard. *Sexual Behavior in the Human Female.* Philadelphia: W.B. Saunders, 1953, p. 161.

3. Kinsey, *Sexual Behavior in the Human Female,* pp. 253-257.

4. Apfelbaum, Bernard. Personal Interview, August 8, 1993.

5. Person, Ethel Spector. "Sexuality as the mainstay of identity: Psychoanalytic perspective." *Women: Sex and Sexuality,* Eds. C.R. Simpson and E.S. Person. Chicago: University of Chicago Press, 1980, p. 51.

6. Freud, Sigmund. *Three Essays on Sexuality.* Trans. James Strachey. New York: Basic Books, 1975, p. 48.

7. Woltmann, Adolf G. "The riddle of the Amazon." *Psychoanalytic Review,* 58(1) (1971): pp. 135-148.

8. Ford, Clellan S. and Frank A. Beach. *Patterns of Sexual Behavior.* New York: Harper and Row, 1951, p. 48

9. Ford and Beach, *Patterns of Sexual Behavior,* p. 47

10. Ford and Beach, *Patterns of Sexual Behavior,* p. 47.

11. Kinsey, *Sexual Behavior in the Human Female,* pp. 371, 399.

12. Person, "Sexuality as the mainstay of identity," pp. 44-47.

Chapter 8

1. For a summary of Freud's theory of fetishism, see: Moorjani, Angela. "Fetishism, gender masquerade, and the mother-father fantasy." *Psychoanalysis, Feminism, and the Future of Gender,* Eds. Joseph H. Smith and Afaf M. Mahfouz. Baltimore: Johns Hopkins University Press, 1994, pp. 22-25.

2. Berest, Jospeh J. "Fetishism—three case histories." *Journal of Sex Research,* 7(3) (August 1971): p. 238.

3. For a summary of Freud on scopophilia, see: Mulvey, Laura. "Visual pleasure and narrative cinema." *Feminisms: An Anthology of Literary Theory and Criticism,* Eds. Robyn Warhol and Diane Price Herndl. New Brunswick, NJ: Rutgers University Press, 1993, p. 434.

4. Levine, Stephen. Personal Interview, March 11, 1997.

5. North, Maurice. *The Outer Fringe of Sex: A Study in Fetishism.* London: The Odyssey Press, 1970, p. 27.

6. For a discussion of Marx's theory of commodity fetishism, see: Gamman, Lorraine and Merja Makinen. *Female Fetishism.* New York: New York University Press, 1994, pp. 28-37.

7. Masters, William, Virginia Johnson, and Robert C. Kolody. *Homosexuality in Perspective.* New York: HarperCollins, 1994, pp. 66-68; Masters, William and Virginia Johnson. *Masters and Johnson on Sex and Human Loving.* Boston: Little Brown, 1988, pp. 357-358.

8. Levine, Stephen B., Candace B. Risen, and Stanley E. Athof, "Essay on the diagnosis and nature of paraphilia." *Journal of Sex and Marital Therapy,* 16(2) (Summer 1990): p. 101.

Chapter 9

1. For an explanation of the theory of sexual selection and the debate surrounding it, see: Mayr, Ernest. "Sexual selection and natural selection." *Sexual Selection and the Descent of Man 1871-1971,* Ed. Barnard Campbell. Chicago: Aldine, 1972.

2. See: Ehrenberg, Margaret. *Women in Prehistory.* London: British Museum Publications, 1989; Fedigan, Linda Marie. *Primate Paradigms: Sex Roles and Social Bonds.* Montreal: Eden Press, 1982; Hamilton, M.E., "Revising evolutionary narratives: A consideration of alternative assumptions about sexual selection and competition for mates." *American Anthropologist,* 86 (1984): pp. 651-662.

3. Jurmain, Robert and Harry Nelson. *Introduction to Physical Anthropology.* New York: West, 1994, p. 387.

4. Hrdy, Sarah. *The Woman That Never Evolved.* Cambridge, MA: Harvard University Press, 1981, p. 24.

5. Relethford, John. *The Human Species.* Mountain View, CA: Mayfield, 1991, p. 257.

6. Hrdy, *The Woman That Never Evolved,* p. 36.

Chapter 10

1. Giedion, S. *The Eternal Present Volume I: The Beginnings of Art.* New York: Bollingen Foundation, 1962, p. 211.

2. Harva, Uno. *Finno-Ugric, Siberian Mythology.* New York: Cooper Square Publishers, 1964, pp. 413-416.

3. Budte, E.A. Wallis. *From Fetish to God in Ancient Egypt.* London: Oxford University Press, 1934, p. 498.

4. See: LiDonnici, Lynn. "The images of Artemis Ephesia and Greco-Roman worship: A reconsideration." *Harvard Theological Review,* 85(4) (1992): pp. 389-415.

5. Wickler, Wolfgang. *The Sexual Code.* Garden City, NY: Doubleday, 1972, p. 253.

6. Warner, Marina. *Alone of All Her Sex: The Myth and the Cult of the Virgin Mary.* Vintage Books, New York, 1983, p. 200.

7. See: Bynum, Caroline Walker. *Fragmentation and Redemption: Essays on Gender and the Human Body in Medieval Religion.* New York: Zone Books, 1991, pp. 102-107.

8. Schultz, Bernice Engle. "The Amazons in ancient Greece." *Psychoanalytic Quarterly,* 11 (1942): p. 544.

Bibliography

Chapter 1

Allende, Isabel. *The Infinite Plan.* Trans. Margaret Sayers Peden. New York: HarperCollins, 1991.

Ayalah, Daphne, and Isaac Weinstock. *Breasts.* New York: Summit Books, 1979.

Brownmiller, Susan. *Femininity.* New York: Simon & Schuster, 1984.

Butters, Jonathan, and Thomas Cash. "Cognitive-behavioral treatment of women's body-image dissatisfaction." *Journal of Consulting and Clinical Psychology,* 55 (1987): pp. 967-974.

Coons, Philip, Haya Ascher-Svanum, and Kirk Bellis. "Self-amputation of the female breast." *Psychosomatics,* 27 (1986): 667-668.

Dion, K. "Physical attractiveness, sex roles and heterosexual attraction." *The Bases of Human Sexual Attraction,* Ed. Mark Cook. New York: Academic Press, 1981, pp. 3-22.

Fisher, Seymour, and Sidney Cleveland. *Body Image and Personality.* New York: Dover, 1968.

Ford, Clelland S., and Frank A. Beach. *Patterns of Sexual Behavior.* New York: Harper and Row, 1951.

Foucault, Michel. *History of Sexuality Vol. I: An Introduction.* Trans. Robert Hurley. New York: Random House, 1978.

Franzoi, Stephen L. and Mary E. Herzog, "Judging physical attractiveness: What body aspects do we use?" *Personality and Social Psychology Bulletin,* 13(1) (1987): pp. 19-33.

Freeman, Rita. *Beauty Bound.* Lexington, MA: Lexington Books, 1986.

Horvath, Theodore. "Correlates of physical beauty in men and women." *Social Behavior and Personality,* 7(2) (1979): pp. 145-151.

Horvath, Theodore. "Physical attractiveness: The influence of selected torso parameters." *Archives of Sexual Behavior,* 10 (1981): pp. 21-24.

Kleinke, Chris, and Richard Staneski. "First impressions of female bust size." *The Journal of Social Psychology,* 110 (1980): pp. 123-134.

Mazur, Allan. "U.S. Trends in feminine beauty and overadaption." *The Journal of Sex Research,* 22 (1986): pp. 281-303.

Morrison, Denton, and Carlin Holden "The Burning Bra." *Sociology for Pleasure,* Ed. Marcello Tuzzi. Englewood Cliffs, NJ: Prentice-Hall, 1974, pp. 345-362.

Rosen, Marjorie. *Popcorn Venus.* New York: Avon, 1973.

Schmitt, Raymond. "Embodied identities: Breasts as emotional reminders." *Studies in Symbolic Interaction,* 7(A) (1986): pp. 229-289.

Snyder, Mark, Elizabeth Decker Tanke, and Ellen Berscheid. "Social perceptions and interpersonal behavior: On the self-fulfilling nature of social stereotypes." *Journal of Personality and Social Psychology,* 9 (1977): pp. 656-666.

Stern, Jane and Michael. *The Encyclopedia of Bad Taste.* New York: Harper-Collins, 1990.

Stone, Gregory P. "Appearance and the self." *Human Behavior and Social Progress: An Interactionist Perspective,* Ed. Arnold Rose. Boston: Houghton Mifflin, 1962.

Wiggens, Jerry S., and Nancy Wiggens. "A typological analysis of male preferences for female body types." *Multivarite Behavioral Research,* 4(1) (1969): pp. 89-102.

Wiggens, Jerry S., Nancy Wiggens, and Judith Cohen Conger. "Correlates of heterosexual somatic preference." *Journal of Personality and Social Psychology,* 10(1) (1968): pp. 82-90.

Wolf, Naomi. *The Beauty Myth.* New York: William Morrow and Company, 1991.

Chapter 2

Brooks-Gunn, Jeanne. "The psychological significance of different pubertal events to young girls." *Journal of Early Adolescence,* 4(4) (1984): pp. 315-327.

Brooks-Gunn, Jeanne, and Edward O. Reiter. "Role of the pubertal process." *At the Threshold: The Developing Adolescent,* Eds. Shirley Feldman and Glen Elliott. Cambridge: Harvard University Press, 1990.

Brooks-Gunn, Jeanne, Denis Newman, and Michelle Warren. "The experience of breast development and girls' stories about the purchase of a bra." *Journal of Youth and Adolescence,* 23(5) (1994): pp. 539-554.

Chodorow, Nancy. *The Reproduction of Mothering.* Berkeley: University of California Press, 1978.

Collins, John K. "Self-recognition of the body and its parts during late adolescence." *Journal of Youth and Adolescence,* 10(3) 1981: pp. 243-254.

Dinnerstein, Dorothy. *The Mermaid and the Minotaur: Sexual Arrangements and Human Malaise.* New York: Harper and Row, 1976.

Ephron, Nora. "A few words about breasts: Shaping up absurd." *Scenes from Life,* Ed. Judy Blankenship. Boston: Little Brown and Company, 1976, pp. 364-369.

Giovacchini, Peter. "The dilemma of becoming a woman." *Female Adolescent Development,* Ed. Max Sugar. New York: Brunner/Mazel, 1979.

Meador, Betty DeShong. *Uncursing the Dark.* Wilmette, IL: Chiron, 1992.

Peterson, Anne, Maryse Tobin-Richards, and Andrew Boxer. "Puberty: Its measurement and its meaning." *Journal of Early Adolescence,* 3(1-2) (1983): pp. 47-62.

Rheingold, Joseph C. *The Fear of Being a Woman: A Theory of Maternal Destructiveness.* New York: Grune and Stratton, 1964.

Rierdan, Jill and Elissa Koff. "Representation of the female body by early and late adolescent girls." *Journal of Youth and Adolescence,* 9 (1980): pp. 339-346.

Rosenbaum, Maj-Britt. "The changing body image of the adolescent girl." *Female Adolescent Development,* Ed. Max Sugar. New York: Brunner/Mazel, 1979, pp. 234-252.

Chapter 3

Banner, Lois W. *American Beauty.* New York: Alfred A. Knopf, 1983.

Batterberry, Michael and Ariane. *Fashion: The Mirror of History.* New York: Greenwich House, 1977.

Blumer, Herbert. "Fashion: From class differentiation to collective selection." *The Sociological Quarterly,* 10 (Summer, 1969): pp. 275-291.

Carter, Alison. *Underwear, The Fashion History.* London: B.T. Batsfield, 1992.

Cordwell, Justine and Schwarz, Eds. *The Fabrics of Culture: The Anthropology of Clothing and Adornment.* New York: Mouton, 1979.

Cotterell, Arthur. *The Minoan World.* New York: Scribner, 1980.

Cunnington, C. Willet and Phillis. *The History of Underclothes.* New York: Faber, and Faber, 1981.

Ewing, Elizabeth. *Dress and Undress.* New York: Drama Book Specialists, 1972.

Flugel, John. *The Psychology of Clothes.* London: Hogarth Press, 1950.

Gutwirth, Madelyn. *The Twilight of the Goddesses: Women and Representation in the French Revolutionary Era.* New Brunswick, NJ: Rutgers University Press, 1992.

Hawkes, Jacquetta. *Dawn of the Gods.* London: Chatto and Windus, 1968.

Hollander, Susan. *Seeing Through Clothes.* New York: Penguin Books, 1978.

Horn, Marilyn J. *The Second Skin: An Interdisciplinary Study of Clothing.* Boston: Houghton Mifflin Company, 1968.

Jacobus, Mary L. "Incorruptible milk: Breastfeeding and the French Revolution." *Rebel Daughters: Women and the French Revolution,* Ed. Sara E. Melzer and Leslie W. Rabins. New York: Oxford University Press, 1992.

Kanin, Ruth. *The Manufacture of Beauty.* Boston: Branden, 1990.

Kunzle, David. *Fashion and Fetishism: A Social History of the Corset, Tight-Lacing, and Other Forms of Body-Sculpture in the West.* Totowa, NJ: Rowman and Littlefield, 1982.

Laurie, Alison. *The Language of Clothes.* New York: Random House, 1981.

Laver, James. *Taste and Fashion.* London: George G. Harrop, 1948.

Laver, James. *The Concise History of Costume and Fashion.* New York: Charles Scribner's Sons, 1979.

Neumann, Erich. *The Great Mother: An Analysis of the Archetype.* Trans. Ralph Manheim. Princeton, NJ: Princeton University Press, 1972.

Payne, Blanche, Greitel Winakor, and Jane Farrell-Beck. *The History of Costume: From Ancient Mesopotamia through the Twentieth Century.* New York: HarperCollins, 1992.

Polhemus, Ted, and Lynn Procter. *Fashion and Anti-Fashion.* London: Cox and Wyman, 1978.

Roach, Mary Ellen, and Joanne Bubolz Eicher. *Dress, Adornment, and the Social Order.* New York: John Wiley and Sons, 1965.

Roach, Mary Ellen, and Joanne Bubolz Eicher. "The language of personal adornment." *The Fabrics of Culture: The Anthropology of Clothing and Adornment,* Eds. Justine and Schwarz Cordwell. New York: Moulton, 1979: pp. 7-21.

Rousseau, Jean-Jacques. *Emile.* Trans. Barbara Foxley. New York: Dutton, 1974.

Russell, Douglas. *Costume History and Style.* Englewood Cliffs, NJ: Prentice-Hall, 1983.

Sproules, George B. "Behavioral science theories of fashion." *The Psychology of Fashion,* Ed. Michael Solomon. Lexington, MA: D.C. Heath, 1985.

Squire, Geoffrey. *Dress, Art, and Society, 1560-1970.* London: Studio Vista, 1974.

Trump, D. H. *The Prehistory of the Mediterranean.* New Haven, CT: Yale University Press, 1980.

Van Gelder, Lindsey. "The truth about bra-burning." *Ms.* (September/October 1992): pp. 80-81.

Wolf, Naomi. *The Beauty Myth: How Images of Beauty Are Used Against Women.* New York: W. Morrow, 1991.

Chapter 4

American Society for Plastic and Reconstructive Surgeons. "Breast surgery statistics: Aesthetic and reconstructive surgery." *Plastic Surgery Information Service.* 5 pp. Online. Internet. (February 17, 1997).

Anderson, Lenore Wright. "Synthetic Beauty: American Women and Cosmetic Surgery." Doctoral Thesis. Houston, TX: Rich University, 1989.

Andreasen, Nancy, and Janusz Bardach. "Dysmorphobia: Symptom or disease?" *American Journal of Psychiatry* 134(6) (June, 1977).

Biggs, Thomas, Jean Cukier, and Fabian Worthing. "Augmentation mammaplasty: A review of eighteen years." *Plastic and Reconstructive Surgery,* 69 (1982): pp. 445-449.

Bordo, Susan. "'Material girl': The effecements of postmodern culture." *The Female Body: Figures, Styles, Speculations,* Ed. Laurence Goldstein. Ann Arbor: University of Michigan Press, 1991.

Bridges, Alan J., and Frank B. Vasey. "Silicone breast implants: History, safety, and potential complications." *Archives of Internal Medicine,* 153 (December 13, 1993): pp. 2638-2644.

Brunning, Nancy. *Breast Implants: Everything You Need to Know.* Alameda, CA: Hunter House, 1992.

Da Silva, G. "Accurate rules for preoperative marking in mammaplasty." *Transactions of the Third International Congress of Plastic Surgery.* Amsterdam: Excerpta Medical Foundation, 1964, pp. 50-59.

De Camara, Donna, James Sheridan, and Barbara Kammer. "Rupture and aging of silicone gel breast implants." *Plastic and Reconstructive Surgery,* 91(5) (1993): pp. 828-834.

Druss, Richard G., "Changes in body image following augmentation breast surgery." *International Journal of Psychoanalytic Psychotherapy,* 2(2) (1973): pp. 248-266.

Edelman, Helen S. "Why is Dolly crying? An analysis of silicone breast implants in america as an example of medicalization." *Journal of Popular Culture,* (Winter 1994): pp. 19-32.

Edgerton, M. T. and A. R. McClary. "Augmentation mamomalasty: Psychiatric implications and surgical indications." *Plastic and Reconstructive Surgery,* 21 (1958): pp. 279-305.

Edgerton, M. T. E. Meyer, and Jacobson "Augmentation mammoplasty II: Further surgical and psychiatric evaluation." *Plastic and Reconstructive Surgery* 27 (1961): pp. 279-302.

Faludi, Susan. *Backlash: The Undeclared War Against American Women.* New York: Anchor Books, 1991.

Hirschauer, Stefan. "The manufacture of bodies in surgery." *Social Studies of Science,* 21 (1991): pp. 279-319.

Kumagi, Yasuo, Abe Chiyuki, and Yuichi Shiokawa. "Scleroderma after cosmetic surgery: Four cases of human adjuvant disease." *Arthritis and Rheumatism,* 22(5) (May, 1979): pp. 532-537.

Kumagi, Yasuo, Yuichi Shiokawa, Thomas A. Medsger Jr, and Gerald P. Rodnan. "Clinical spectrum of connective tissue disease after cosmetic surgery: Observation on eighteen patients and a review of the Japanese literature." *Arthritis and Rheumatism,* 27(1) (January 1984): pp. 1-14.

Longacre, J. J. "Surgical reconstruction of the flat discoid breast" *Plastic and Reconstructive Surgery,* 17(5) (1956): pp. 358-366.

Malinac, J. W. "Breast deformities and their repair." New York: Grune and Stratton, 1950.

May, Elaine Tyler. *Homeward Bound: American Families in the Cold War Era.* New York: Basic Books, 1988.

Mellican, R. Eugene. "Breast implants, the cult of beauty, and a culturally constructed 'disease.' " *Journal of Popular Culture,* (Spring 1995): pp. 7-17.

Palfreman, Joe. Producer, "Breast implants on trial." PBS *Frontline, http://.pbs.org/wgbh/pages/frontline/implants/cron.html.*

Penn, Jack. "Breast reduction." *British Journal of Plastic Surgery,* 7 (1954-1955): pp. 356-371.

Roth, Linda. Director, Coalition of Silicone Survivors. Personal interview, February 3, 1997.

Spitzack, Carole. "The confession mirror: Plastic images for surgery." *Canadian Journal of Political and Social Theory,* XII (1988): pp. 29-50.

Stevens, Diane. Director, ImPart Inc. Personal interview, January 25, 1997.

Symmers, W. St. C. "Silicone mastitis in 'topless' waitresses and some other varieties of foreign-body mastitis." *British Medical Journal,* 3 (1968): pp. 19-22.

U.S. Food and Drug Administration. *Breast Implants: An Information Update.* Washington, DC: Government Printing Office, 1996.

Vasey, Frank V., and Josh Feldstein. *The Silicone Breast Implant Controversy: What Women Need to Know.* Freedom, CA: The Crossing Press, 1993.

Williams, Lena. "Woman's image in a mirror: Who defines what she sees." *The New York Times,* (February 6, 1992): A1.

Wolf, Naomi. *The Beauty Myth: How Images of Beauty Are Used Against Women.* New York: W. Morrow, 1991, p. 11.

Young, Irish Marion. *Throwing Like a Girl and Other Essays in Feminist Philosophy and Social Theory.* Bloomington: Indiana University Press, 1990.

Young, Tracy. "A few (more) words about breasts." *Esquire* (September 1992): pp. 141-146.

Chapter 5

Almansi, Renato J. "On the persistence of very early memory traces in psychoanalysis, myth, and religion." *Journal of the American Psychoanalytic Association,* 31(3) (1983): pp. 391-421.

Astor, James. "The breast as part of a whole." *Journal of Analytical Psychology,* 34 (1989): pp. 117-128.

Bermant, Gordon, and Julian Davidson. *Biological Bases of Sexual Behavior.* New York: Harper and Row, 1974.

Bettleheim, Bruno. *Symbolic Wounds: Puberty Rites and the Envious Male.* New York: Collier Books, 1962.

Birksted-Breen, Dana. "Working with an anorexic patient." *International Journal of Psychoanalysis,* 70(29) (1989): pp. 29-38.

Blum, Gerald. *Psychoanalytic Theories of Personality.* New York: McGraw Hill, 1953.

Chernin, Kim. *The Obsession: Reflections on the Tyranny of Slenderness.* New York: Harper and Row, 1981.

Chodorow, Nancy. *The Reproduction of Mothering.* Berkeley: University of California Press, 1978.

Dinnerstein, Dorothy. *The Mermaid and the Minotaur: Sexual Arrangements and Human Malaise.* New York: Harper and Row, 1976.

Easson, William. "The earliest ego development, primitive memory traces, and the Isakower phenomenon." *Psychoanalytic Quarterly,* 42(1) (1973): pp. 60-72.

Eichenbaum, Luise, and Susie Orbach. *Understanding Women: A Feminist Psychoanalytic Approach.* New York: Basic Books, 1983.

Elmhirst, Susanna Issacs. "The early stages of female psychosexual development: A Kleinian view." *Women's Sexual Development,* Ed. Martha Kirkpatrick. New York: Plenem, 1980, pp. 107-125.

Erickson, Eric. *Childhood and Society.* New York: W. W. Norton and Company, 1950.

Fairbairn, W. Ronald. *An Object-Relations Theory of Personality.* New York: Basic Books, 1982.

Fenichle, Otto. *The Psychoanalytic Theory of Neurosis.* New York: W. W. Norton and Company, 1945.

Fink, Geraldine. "Analysis of the Isakower phenomenon." *Journal of American Psychoanalytic Association,* 25 (1967): pp. 281-293.

Freud, Sigmund. *Three Essays on the Theory of Sexuality.* Trans. James Strachey. London: Imago Pub., 1949.

Fuerstein, Laura Arens. "Some hypotheses about gender differences in coping with oral dependency conflicts." *Psychoanalytic Review,* 76(2) (Summer, 1989): pp. 163-184.

Gooch, Shirley. "Infantile sexuality revisited: The agony and ecstasy of the mother-infant couple." *Journal of the American Academy of Psychoanalysis,* 19(2) (1991): pp. 254-270.

Isakower, Otto. "A contribution to the patho-psychology of phenomena associated with falling asleep." *International Journal of Psychoanalysis,* 19 (1938): pp. 331-345.

Klein, Melanie. *The Psychoanalysis of Children.* Trans. Alix Strachey. New York: Free Press, 1984.

Kohut, Heinz. *Self-Psychology and the Humanities.* New York: Norton, 1985.

Kramer, Selma, and Salman Akhtar. "The developmental context of internalized preoedipal object relations: Mahler's theory of symbiosis and separation-individuation." *Psychoanalytic Quarterly,* 57 (1988): pp. 547-576.

Lichtenberg, Joseph. *Psychoanalysis and Infant Research.* Hillsdale, NJ: The Analytic Press, 1983.

Liss-Levinson, Nechama. "Disorders of desire: Women, sex and food." Binghamton, NY: The Haworth Press, 1988.

Mahler, Margaret. *On Human Symbiosis and the Vicissitudes of Individuation.* New York: International Universities Press, 1968.

Mahler, Margaret, Fred Pine, and Ann Bergman. *The Psychological Birth of the Human Infant.* New York: Basic Books, 1975.

Makin, Jennifer W. and Richard H. Porter. "Attractiveness of lactating females' breast odors to neonates." *Child Development,* 60(4) (1989): pp. 25-66.

Maurer, Daphne and Charles. *The World of the Newborn.* New York: Basic Books, 1988.

Mendez, Anita, and Harold Fine. "A short history of the British school of object relations and ego psychology." *Bulletin of the Menninger Clinic,* 40(4) (1976): pp. 357-382.

Mitchell, Juliet. *The Selected Melanie Klein.* New York: Macmillan, 1987.

Moss, Donald. "On situating the object: Thoughts on the maternal function, modernism and post-modernism," *American Imago,* 46(4) (Winter 1989): pp. 353-369.

Padel, John." The psychoanalytic theories of Melanie Klein and Donald Winnicott and their interaction in the British society of psychoanalysis." *Psychoanalytic Review,* 7(3) (Fall, 1991): pp. 325-345.

Restak, Richard. *The Infant Mind.* Garden City, NY: Doubleday, 1986.

Ritvo, Samuel. "The Image and uses of the body in psychic conflict psychoanalysis." *Study of the Child,* 39 (1984): pp. 449-469.

Segal, Hanna. *Introduction to the Works of Melanie Klein.* New York: Basic Books, 1964.

Silverman, Lloyd, Frank Lachmann, and Robert Milich. *The Search for Oneness.* New York: International Universities Press, 1982.

Sours, John A. *Starving to Death in a Sea of Objects: The Anorexia Nervosa Syndrome.* New York: J. Aronson, 1989.

Spillus, Elizabeth Bott, Ed. *Melanie Klein Today: Developments in Theory and Practice.* New York: Routledge, 1990.

Stern, Daniel. *The Interpersonal World of the Infant.* New York: Basic Books, 1973.

Tamminen, T. M., and R. K. Salmelin. "Psychosomatic interaction between mother and infant during breast feeding." *Psychotherapy and Psychosomatics,* 57 (1991): pp. 78-84.

Chapter 6

Anderson, Peter. "The reproductive role of the human breast." *Current Anthropology,* 24(1) (February, 1983): pp. 25-38.

Apple, Rima. *Mothers and Medicine: A Social History of Infant Feeding, 1890-1950.* Madison: The University of Wisconsin Press, 1987.

Auerbach, Kathleen, and Jimmie Avery. *Nursing the Adopted Infant: Report from a Survey.* Resources in Human Nurturing, International, Monograph Number Five. Denver: Resources for Human Nurturing, International, 1979.

Baldwin, Elizabeth. Personal Interview. April 18, 1997.

Baldwin, Elizabeth, and Kenneth A. Friedman. "Breast-feeding legislation in the United States." *New Beginnings,* 11(6) (1994): pp. 164-167.

Baumslag, Naomi. "Breast-feeding: Cultural practices and variations." *Human Lactation 2: Maternal and Environmental Factors,* Eds. Hamosh and Armand Goldman. New York: Plenum Press, 1986.

Bloch, Ruth H. "American feminine ideal in transition: The rise of the moral mother, 1785-1815." *Feminists Studies,* 2 (June 1978): pp. 100-126.

Bloch, Ruth H. "Untangling the roots of modern sex roles: A survey of four centuries of change." *Sign: Journal of Women in Culture and Society,* 4(2) (1978): pp. 237-252.

Buxton, Karen, Andrea Carlson, and Ruth Faden. "Women intending to breastfeed: Predictors of early infant feeding experiences." *American Journal of Preventive Medicine,* 7(2) (1991): pp. 101-106.

Campbell, B., and W. E. Petersen. "Milk let-down and orgasm in human females." *Human Biology,* 25 (1953): pp. 165-168.

Cantratto, Susan Weisskopof. "Maternal sexuality and asexual motherhood." Women: *Sex and Sexuality,* Eds. Catherine R. Stimpson and Ethel Spector Person. Chicago: University of Chicago Press, 1980.

Carter, James P. "The ecology of the urban adaptation syndrome: The decline of breast-feeding." *Journal of Holistic Medicine,* 6(1) (1984): pp. 64-83.

Debackere, M., G. Peeters, and N. Tuyttens. "Reflex release of an oxytocic hormone by stimulation of genital organs in male and female sheep studied by a cross-circulation technique." *Journal of Endocrinology,* 22 (1961): pp. 321-334.

Dettwyler, Katherine. "Beauty and the breast: The cultural context of breast-feeding in the United States." *Breast-feeding: Biocultural Perspectives,* Eds. Katherine Dettwyler and Patricia Stuart-Macadam. Hawthoren, NY: Aldine de Gruyter, 1995.

Deutsch, Helene. *The Psychology of Women.* Volume 2. New York: Grune and Stratton, 1945.

Elia, Irene. *The Female Animal.* New York: Henry Holt, 1986.

Fildes, Valerie A. *Breasts, Bottles, and Babies.* Edinburgh, Scotland: Edinburgh University Press, 1986.

Fildes, Valerie A. *Wet Nursing: A History from Antiquity to the Present.* New York: Basil Blackwell, 1988.

Gaskin, Ina May. "Who is abusing whom?" *The Birth Gazette,* 8(2) (1992): pp. 11-12.

Hilts, Phillip. "Study find a decline in breast-feeding." *The New York Times,* (October, 3 1991).

Hoteri, Catherine. Researcher, La Leche League International. Personal Interview. March 26, 1997.

Jelliffe, Derrick, and E. F. Patrice. " 'Breast is best': Modern meanings." *New England Journal of Medicine,* 297(17) (October 27, 1977): pp. 912-915.

Jelliffe, Derrick B., and E. F. Patrice. *Human Milk for the Modern World.* Oxford: Oxford University Press, 1978.

Jelliffe, Derrick B., and E. F. Patrice. "The Preventive role of breast-feeding." *Prevention in Human Services,* 5(1) (1986): pp. 97-108.

Kaufman, Karyn J., and Lynne A. Hall. "Influences of the social network on Choice and duration of breast-feeding in mothers of preterm infants." *Research in Nursing and Health,* 12 (1989): pp. 149-159.

Kennell, John, and Marshall Klaus. "Mother-infant bonding: Weighing the evidence." *Developmental Review,* 4 (1984): pp. 275-282.

Kinkade, Sheila. "Fewer mothers now are breast-feeding their babies." *Washington Post,* (November 13, 1990): WH11.

Kitzinger, Sheila. *The Experience of Breastfeeding.* New York: Penguin Books, 1982.

Klaus, Marshall, John Kennell, Nancy Plumb, and Steven Zuehlke. "Human maternal behavior at the first contact with her young." *Pediatrics,* 46(2) (1970): pp. 187-192.

La Leche League. "A brief history of La Leche League International" el. 3, *http://wwww.lalecheleague.org/LLL history.html.*

Lynch, Margaret A. "Ill-health and child abuse." *The Lancet,* (August 16, 1975): pp. 317-319.

Makin, Jennifer W., and Richard Porter. "Attractiveness of lactating females' breast odors to neonates." *Child Development,* 60(4) (1989): pp. 25-66.

Mead, Margaret, and Niles Newton. "Cultural patterning of perinatal behavior." *Childbearing: Its Social and Psychological Aspects,* Eds. S. A. Richardson and A. F. Guttmacher. Baltimore: Williams and Wilkins, 1967.

Millard, Ann. "The place of the clock in pediatric advice: Rationales, cultural themes and impediments to breast-feeding." *Social Science and Medicine,* 31(2) (1990): pp. 211-221.

Miller, Lynda. "Idealization and contempt: Dual aspects of the process of devaluation of the breast in a feeding relationship." *Journal of Child Psychotherapy,* 13(1) (1987): pp. 41-54.

Myers, Barbara. "Mother-infant bonding: The status of this critical-period hypothesis." *Developmental Review,* 4 (1984): pp. 240-274.

Newton, Niles. *Maternal Emotions.* New York: Paul B. Hoeber, 1955.

Newton, Niles. "Psychologic aspects of lactation." *New England Journal of Medicine,* 277(22) (1967): pp. 1179-1186.

Newton, Niles. "Breast-feeding." *Psychology Today,* 2(1) (1968): pp. 68-70.

Newton, Niles. "Trebly sensuous woman." *Psychology Today,* 5(2) (July 1971): pp. 68-71, 98-99.

Newton, Niles. "Interrelationships between sexual responsiveness, birth and breast-feeding." *Contemporary Sexual Behavior: Current Issues in the 1970s,* Eds. J Zubin and J. Money. Baltimore: Johns Hopkins, 1973.

Palmer, Gabrielle. *The Politics of Breastfeeding.* London: Pandora Press, 1988.

Perry, Ruth. "Colonizing the breast." *Forbidden History: The State, Society and Regulation of Sexuality in Modern Europe,* Ed. John C. Fout. Chicago: University of Chicago Press, 1992.

Romito, Patricia. "Mother's experience of breast-feeding." *Journal of Reproductive and Infant Psychology,* 5(2) (1988): pp. 89-99.

Rossi, Alice. "Maternalism, sexuality and the new feminism." *Contemporary Sexual Behavior: Current Issues in the 1970s,* Eds. J Zubin and J. Money. Baltimore: Johns Hopkins, 1973.

Ryan, Alan S. "The resurgence of breast-feeding in the United States." *Pediatrics,* 99(4) (1997): p. el 12.

Sarlin, Charles. "The role of breast-feeding in psychosexual development and the achievement of the genital phase." *Journal of the American Psychoanalytic Association,* 29(3) (1981): pp. 631-641.

Stein, Alan, Peter J. Cooper, Ann Day, and Alison Bond. "Social and psychiatric factors associated with the intention to breast-feed." *Journal of Reproductive and Infant Psychology,* 5 (1987): pp. 165-171.

Van Esterik, Penny. "The cultural context of breast-feeding in rural Thailand." *Breast-Feeding, Child Health and Child Spacing: Cross Cultural Perspectives,* Eds. Valerie Hull and Mayling Simpson. London: Croom Helm, 1985.

Waletzy, Lucy R. "Husbands' problems with breast-feeding." *American Journal of Orthopsychiatry,* 49(2) (1979): pp. 349-352.

Woollett, Anne. "Who breast-feeds? The family and cultural context." *Journal of Reproductive and Infant Psychology,* 5 (1987): 127-131.

Chapter 7

Apfelbaum, Bernard. Director, Berkeley Sex Therapy Group. Personal Interview. August 8, 1993.

Bermant, Gordon, and Julian Davidson. *Biological Bases of Sexual Behavior.* New York: Harper and Row, 1974.

Chilman, Catherine S. "Some psychosocial aspects of female sexuality." *Family Coordinator,* 23(2) (1974): pp. 123-131.

Clifford, Ruth. "Subjective sexual experience in college women." *Archives of Sexual Behavior,* 7(3) (1978): pp. 183-197.

Cott, Nancy F. "Passionlessness: An interpretation of victorian sexual ideology, 1790-1850." *Signs: Journal of Women in Culture and Society,* 4(2) (Winter, 1978): pp. 219-236.

Davenport, William, H. "Sex in cross-cultural perspective." *Human Sexuality in Four Perspectives,* Ed. Frank Beach. Baltimore: Johns Hopkins University Press, 1976, pp. 113-163.

Ellison, Carol Rinkleib, PhD. Clinical Psychologist. Personal Interview. August 1993.

Fisher, Seymour. *Sexual Images of the Self: The Psychology of Erotic Sensations and Illusions.* Hillsdale, NJ: Lawrence Erlbaum, 1989.

Ford, Clellan S., and Frank A. Beach. *Patterns of Sexual Behavior.* New York: Harper and Row, 1951.

Freud, Sigmund. *Three Essays on Sexuality.* Trans. James Strachey. New York: Basic Books, 1975.

Fuerstein, Laura Arens, "Some hypotheses about gender differences in coping with oral dependency conflicts." *Psychoanalytic Review,* 76(2) (1989): pp. 163-184.

Gagnon, John, and William Simon. *Sexual Conduct: The Social Sources of Human Sexuality.* Chicago: Aldine Publishing Co., 1973.

Gagnon, John, and William Simon. *Human Sexualities.* Glenview, IL: Scott Foresman, 1977.

Gebhard, Paul H., Jan Raboch, and Jans Giese. *The Sexuality of Women,* Volume 1. London: Andre Deutsch Ltd., 1970.

Goleman, Daniel. "Sexual fantasies: What are their hidden meanings." *The New York Times,* February 28, 1984, C1.

Gray, J. Patrick. "Cross cultural factors associated with sexual foreplay." *Journal of Social Psychology,* 3 (1980): pp. 3-8.

Harrison, Richard J. *Man.* New York: Appleton-Century-Crofts, 1973.

Heiman, Marcel. "Sexual response in women: A correlation of physiological findings with psychoanalytic concepts." *Journal of the American Psychoanalytic Association,* 2 (1963): pp. 360-385.

Hite, Shere. *The Hite Report: A Nationwide Study of Female Sexuality.* New York: MacMillan, 1976.

Hoon, Emily Franck, and Peter W. Hoon, "Styles of sexual expression in women: clinical implications of multivariate analyses." *Archives of Sexual Behavior,* 7(2) (1978): pp. 195-116.

Hoon, Emily, John Wincze, and Peter Hoon. "An inventory for the measurement sexual arousability: The SAI." *Archives of Sexual Behavior,* 5 (1976): pp. 291-300.

Hyde, Janet. *Half the Human Experience.* Lexington, MA: D.C. Heath and Company, 1980.

Irigaray, Luce. *This Sex Which is Not One.* Ithaca, NY: Cornell University Press, 1989.

Janeway, Elizabeth. "Who is Sylvia? On the loss of sexual paradigms." *Women: Sex and Sexuality.* Ed. Catherine Stimpson and Ethel Spector Person. Chicago: University of Chicago Press, 1980.

Jesser, Clinton J. "Reflections on breast attention." *The Journal of Sex Research,* 7(1) (February, 1971): pp. 13-25.

Kaplan, E. Ann. "Sex, work and motherhood: The impossible triangle." *The Journal of Sex Research,* 27(3) (1990): pp. 409-425.

Kaplan, Helen Singer. "Breasts and your emotions." *Vogue,* V (July, 1979): pp. 169-177.

Kendrick, Douglas, and Sara Gutierres. "Influence of popular erotica on judgments of strangers and mates." *Journal of Experimental Social Psychology,* 25 (1989): pp. 159-167.

Kinsey, Alfred C., Pomeroy Warden, Martin Clyde, and Paul Gebhard. *Sexual Behavior in the Human Female.* Philadelphia: W. B. Saunders, 1953.

Kirkpatrick, Martha, Ed. *Women's Sexual Development: Explorations of Inner Space.* New York: Plenum Press, 1980.

Kitzinger, Sheila. *A Woman's Experience of Sex.* New York: Penguin Books, 1985.

Klein, George S. "Freud's two theories of sexuality." *Psychological Issues,* 9(4) (monograph 26, 1976): New York: International Universities Press, pp. 14-70.

Kremer, J. M. D., and H. P. den Dass. "Case report: A man with breast dysphoria." *Archives of Sexual Behavior,* 19(2) 1990: pp. 179-181.

Laumann, Edward O., John H. Gagnon, Robert T. Michael, and Stuart Michaels. *The Social Organization of Sexuality: Sexual Practices in the United States.* Chicago: University of Chicago Press, 1994.

Masters, William. Masters and Johnson Institute. Personal Interview. July 17, 1997.

Masters, William H., and Virginia E. Johnson. *Human Sexual Response.* Boston: Little, Brown and Company, 1966.

Mitchell, Juliet. *Psychoanalysis and Feminism.* New York: Vintage Books, 1974.

Mitchell, Juliet, and Jacqueline Rose, Eds. *Feminine Sexuality: Jacques Lacann and the Ecole Frudrenne.* New York: Pantheon, 1983.

Moulton, Ruth. "Multiple factors in frigidity." *Science and Psychoanalysis,* Ed. Jules Masserman. Volume 10, New York: Grune and Stratton, 1966, pp. 75-93.

Norris, Jeanette. "Normative influence effects on sexual arousal to nonviolent sexually explicit material." *Journal of Applied Social Psychology,* 19(4) (1989): pp. 341-352.

Ogden, Gina. "Women and sexual ecstasy: How can therapists help?" *Women and Therapy,* 7(2-3) (1988): pp. 43-55.

Person, Ethel Spector. "Sexuality as the mainstay of identity: Psychoanalytic perspective." *Women: Sex and Sexuality,* Eds. C. R. Stimpson and E. S. Person. Chicago: University of Chicago Press, 1980, pp. 36-61

Person, Ethel Spector, Nettie Terestman, Wayne A. Myers, Eugene L. Goldberg, and Carol Salvadori. "Gender differences in sexual behaviors and fantasies in a college population." *Journal of Sex & Marital Therapy*, 15(3) (Fall, 1989): pp. 187-197.

Simon, William, and John Gagnon. "Psychosexual development." *Trans-action* (March, 1969): pp. 9-17

Spellman, Elizabeth V., "Woman as body: Ancient and contemporary views." *Feminist Studies*, 8(1) (Spring, 1982): pp. 109-131.

Thompson, S. "Search for tomorrow: On feminism and reconstruction of teen romance." *Pleasure and Danger: Exploring Female Sexuality*, Ed. Carole Vance. Boston: Routeledge, Kegan Paul, 1984.

Tolman, Deborah. "Adolescent girls, women and sexuality: Discerning dilemmas of desire." *Women & Therapy*, 11(3-4) (1991): pp. 55-69.

Vance, Carole. "Anthropology rediscovers sexuality: A theoretical comment." *Social Science and Medicine*, 33 (1991): pp. 875-884.

Vincus, Martha, "Sexuality and power: A review of current work in the history of sexuality." *Feminist Studies*, 8(1) (Spring, 1982): pp. 133-156.

Wine, Jeri Dawn. "Women's sexuality." *International Journal of Women's Studies*, 8(1) (January-February, 1985): pp. 58-63.

Woltmann, Adolf G. "The riddle of the Amazon." *Psychoanalytic Review*, 58(1) (1971): pp. 135-148.

Chapter 8

Berest, Joseph J. "Fetishism—three case histories." *Journal of Sex Research*, 7(3) (August, 1971): pp. 237-239.

Blanchard, Ray. "The she-male phenomenon and the concept of partial autogynephilia." *Journal of Sex and Marital Therapy*, 19(1) (Spring, 1993): pp. 69-76.

Eve, Raymond, and Donald Renslow. "An exploratory analysis of private sexual behaviors among college students: Some implications for a theory of class differences in sexual behavior." *Social Behavior and Personality*, 9(1) (1980): pp. 97-105.

Ferriera, James M. "Fetishes and the fetishism in girlie magazines." *Objects of Special Devotion: Fetishism in Popular Culture*. Ed. Ray B. Browne. Bowling Green, OH: Bowling Green University Popular Press, pp. 33-44.

Forsythe, Craig. "Parade strippers: A note on being naked in public." *Deviant Behavior: An Interdisciplinary Journal*, 13 (1992): pp. 391-403.

Gagnon, John, and William Simon. *Human Sexualities*. Glenview, IL: Scott Foresman, 1977.

Gamman, Lorraine, and Merja Makinen. *Female Fetishism*. New York: New York University Press, 1994.

Levine, Stephen. Director, Center for Human Sexuality, Department of Psychiatry, hospitals of Cleveland University and Case Western Reserve University. Personal Interview. March 11, 1997.

Levine, Stephen B., Candace B. Risen, and Stanley E. Althof. "Essay on the diagnosis and nature of paraphilia." *Journal of Sex and Marital Therapy*, 16(2) (Summer, 1990): pp. 89-101.

Masters, William, and Virginia Johnson. *Masters and Johnson on Sex and Human Loving.* Boston: Little Brown and Company, 1988.

Masters, William, Virginia Johnson, and Robert C. Kolody. *Homosexuality.* New York: HarperCollins, 1994.

Moorjani, Angela. "Fetishism, gender masquerade, and the mother-father fantasy." *Psychoanalysis, Feminism, and the Future of Gender.* Eds. Joseph H. Smith and Afaf M. Mahfouz. Baltimore: Johns Hopkins University Press, 1994.

Mulvey, Laura. "Visual pleasure and narrative cinema." *Feminisms: An Anthology of Literary Theory and Criticism,* Eds. Robyn Warhol and Diane Price Herndl. New Brunswick, NJ: Rutgers University Press, 1993, pp. 432-442.

North, Maurice. *The Outer Fringe of Sex: A Study in Fetishism.* London: The Odyssey Press, 1970.

Schneller, Johanna. "Chest nuts." *Gentlemen's Quarterly,* (January, 1990): pp. 68-70.

Scodel, Alvin. "Heterosexual somatic preference and fantasy dependency." *Journal of Consulting Psychology,* 21(5) (1957): pp. 371-374.

Solomon, Rose. "Moon bosoms." *Ladies Home Erotica.* Ed. The Kensington Ladies' Erotica Society. Berkeley, CA: Ten Speed Press, 1984.

Stern, Jane and Michael. *The Encyclopedia of Bad Taste.* New York: HarperCollins, 1990.

Stoller, Robert. *Observing the Erotic Imagination.* New Haven: Yale University Press, 1985.

Stone, Leo. "On the principal obscene word of the english language." *International Journal of Psychoanalysis,* 35 (1954): pp. 30-56.

Wiggins, Jerry S., Nancy Wiggins, and Judith Cohen Conger. "Correlates of heterosexual somatic preference." *Journal of Personality and Social Psychology,* 10(1) (1968): pp. 82-90.

Wiggins, Nancy, and Jerry S. Wiggins. "A typological analysis of male preferences for female body types." *Multivariate Behavioral Research,* 4 (1969): pp. 89-102.

Chapter 9

Anderson, Judith L. "Breasts, hips, and buttocks revisited: Honest fatness for honest fitness." *Ethology and Sociobiology,* 9 (1988): pp. 319-324.

Bentley, Gillian, Cambridge University Royal Society Research Fellows. Personal communication. July 15, 1997.

Buss, D. "Sex differences in human mate selection criteria: An evolutionary perspective." *Sociobiology and Psychology: Issues, Ideas, and Findings,* Eds. C. Drawford., M. Smith and D. Krebs. Hillsdale, NJ: Erlbaum, 1987.

Cant, John. "Hypothesis for the evolution of human breasts and buttocks." *American Psychologist,* 117 (1981): pp. 199-204.

Caro, Tim M., and D. W. Sellen. "The reproductive advantages of fat in women." *Ethology and Sociobiology,* 11(1) (1990): pp. 51-66.

Ehrenberg, Margaret. *Women in Prehistory.* London: British Museum Publications, 1989.

Fedigan, Linda Marie. *Primate Paradigms: Sex Roles and Social Bonds.* Montreal: Eden Press, 1982.

Fisher, Helen. E. *The Sex Contract: The Evolution of Human Behavior.* New York: Morrow, 1982.

Fleagle, R. F., and Kay Simons. "Sexual dimorphism in early anthropoids." *Nature,* 287 (1980): pp. 328-330.

Forsyth, Adrian. *A Natural History of Sex.* New York: Charles Scribner's Sons, 1986.

Frayser, Susan G. "Varieties of sexual experience: An anthropological perspective on human sexuality." New Haven, CT: Human Relations Area Files, 1985.

Gallup, G. G. "Permanent breast enlargement in human females: A sociobiological analysis." *Journal of Human Evolution,* II (1982): pp. 597-601.

Goodall, Jane. *In the Shadow of Man.* Boston: Houghton Mifflin, 1971.

Halliday, T. *Sexual Strategy,* Oxford: Oxford University. Press, 1980.

Hamilton, M. E. "Revising evolutionary narratives; A consideration of alternative assumptions about sexual selection and competition for mates." *American Anthropologist,* 3 (1984): pp. 651-662.

Haraway, Donna. *Simians, Cyborgs, and Women.* London: Free Association Books, 1991.

Harlow, Harry F., and Stephen J. Suomi "Nature of love-simplified." *American Psychologist,* 25 (1970): pp. 161-168.

Harrison, Richard, and William Montagna. *Man.* New York: Appleton-Century-Crofts, 1969.

Hrdy, Sarah. *The Woman That Never Evolved.* Cambridge: Harvard University Press, 1981.

Jurmain, Robert, and Harry Nelson. *Introduction of Physical Anthropology.* New York: West, 1994.

Katch, Victor L., Barbara Campaigne, Patty Freedson, Stanley Sady, Frank L. Katch, and Albert R. Benke. "Contribution of breast volume and weight to body fat distribution in females." *American Journal of Physical Anthropology,* 53 (1980): pp. 93-100.

Leibowitz, Lila. "Desmond Morris is wrong about breasts, buttocks & body hair." *Psychology Today,* 3(9) (1970): pp. 16, 18, 22.

Low, Bobbi S. "Sexual selection and human ornamentation." *Evolutionary Biology and Human Social Behavior: An Anthropological Perspective.* Eds. Napolean, A. Chagnon, and William Irons. North Scituate, MA: Duxbury, 1979, pp. 462-487.

Low, Bobbi S., "Fat and deception: Response to Caro and Sellen's (1990) comments on Low, Alexander, and Noonan (1987)." *Ethology and Sociobiology,* 11(10) (1990): pp. 67-74.

Low, Bobbi S., R. D. Alexander, and K. M. Noonan, "Human hips, breasts, and buttocks: Is fat deceptive?" *Ethology and Sociobiology,* 8 (1987): pp. 249-257.

Margulis, Lynn and Dorion Sagan. *Mystery Dance: On the Evolution of Human Sexuality.* New York: Summit Books, 1991.

Mascia-Lees, Frances E., John H. Relethford, and Tom Sorger. "Evolutionary perspectives on permanent breast enlargement in human females." *American Anthropologist,* 88 (1986): pp. 423-428.

Mayr, Ernest. "Sexual Selection and Natural Selection." Ed. Barnard Campbell. *Sexual Selection and the Descent of Man, 1871-1971.* Chicago: Aldine, 1972.

Montagna, W. "The evolution of human skin." *Journal of Human Evolution,* 14 (1985): pp. 3-22.

Morgan, Elaine. *The Descent of Woman.* New York: Stein and Day, 1972.

Morris, Desmond. *The Naked Ape: A Zoologist's Study of the Human Animal.* New York: McGraw-Hill, 1967.

Relethford, John. *The Human Species.* Mountain View, CA: Mayfield, 1991.

Savage-Rumbaugh, Sue, and Beverly Wilkerson. "Socio-sexual behavior in Pan paniscus and Pan troglodytes: A comparative study." *Journal of Human Evolution,* 7 (1978): pp. 327-344.

Sherfey, Mary Jane. "A theory of female sexuality." *Sisterhood is Powerful,* Ed. Robin Morgan. New York: Vintage Books, 1970, pp. 220-230.

Smith, Noel W. "Psychology and evolution of breasts." *Human Evolution,* 1(3) (1986): pp. 285-286.

Smith, Robert. "Human sperm Competition." *Sperm Competition and the Evolution of Animal Mating Systems,* Ed. Robert Smith. Orlando, FL: Academic Press, 1984, pp. 601-659.

Wickler, Wolfgang. "Socio-sexual signals and intra-specific imitation among primates," *Primate Ethology,* Ed. D. Morris. London: Widenfeld and Nicolson, 1967.

Wickler, Wolfgang. *The Sexual Code.* Garden City, NY: Doubleday, 1972.

Chapter 10

Berger, John. *Ways of Seeing.* New York: Penguin, 1973.

Blok, Josine. *The Early Amazons: Modern and Ancient Perspectives on a Persistent Myth.* Leiden: E.J. Brill, 1995.

Budte, E. A. Wallis. *From Fetish to God in Ancient Egypt.* London: Oxford University Press, 1934.

Bynum, Caroline Walker, Steve Harrell, and Paula Richman, Eds. *Gender and Religion: On the Complexity of Symbols.* Boston: Beacon, 1986.

Bynum, Caroline Walker. *Fragmentation and Redemption: Essays on Gender and the Human Body in Medieval Religion.* New York: Zone Books, 1991

Campbell, John Francis. *Popular Tales of the West Highlands.* London: A. Gardner, pp. 1890-1893.

Campbell, Joseph. *The Masks of God, Occidental Mythology.* New York: The Viking Press, 1968.

Campbell, Joseph. *The Hero With a Thousand Faces.* Bollinger Series XVII. Princeton: Princeton University Press, 1973.

Campion, Timothy. *Prehistoric Europe.* New York: Academic Press, 1984.

Child, Francis James, Ed. *The English and Scottish Popular Ballads.* Boston: Houghton, Mifflin and Company, 1894.

Corrington, Gail Paterson. "The milk of salvation: Redemption by the mother in late antiquity and early Christianity." *Harvard Theological Review,* 82(4) (1989): pp. 393-420.

Crossley, Holland. *The Norse Myths.* New York: Pantheon Books, 1980.

Davidson, H. R. Ellis. *Gods and Myths of Northern Europe.* New York: Penguin Books, 1964.

Dotty, William G. *Mythography: The Study of Myths and Rituals.* University, AL: University of Alabama Press, 1986.

Everything You Always Wanted to Know About Sex but Were Afraid to Ask. Director, Woody, Allen, 1972.

Giedion, S. *The Eternal Present Volume I: The Beginnings of Art.* New York: Bollingen Foundation, 1962.

Gimbutas, Marija. *The Gods and Goddesses of Old Europe: 7000 to 3500 BC Myths, Legends, and Cult.* Berkeley: University of California Press, 1974.

Gimbutas, Marija. *The Language of the Goddess.* San Francisco: Harper and Row, 1989.

Gimbutas, Marija. *The Civilization of the Goddess.* San Francisco: Harper/San Francisco, 1991.

Harva, Uno, Finno-Ugric. *Siberian Mythology.* New York: Cooper Square Publishers, 1964.

Johnson, Buffie. *Lady of the Beasts: Ancient Images of the Goddess and Her Sacred Animals.* San Francisco: Harper and Row, 1981.

Keuls, Eva. *The Reign of the Phallus: Sexual Politics in Ancient Athens.* New York: Harper and Row, 1985.

Kleinbaum, Abby Wettan. *The War Against the Amazons.* New York: McGraw-Hill, 1983.

Lederer, Wolfgang. *The Fear of Women.* New York: Harcourt, Brace, Javanovich, 1968.

Leroi-Gourhan, Andre. *The Dawn of European Art: An Introduction to Paleolithic Cave Painting.* Trans. Sara Champion. Cambridge: Cambridge University Press, 1980.

Levy, G. Rachel. *The Gate of the Horn: A Story of the Religious Conceptions of the Stone Age, and Their Influence upon European Thought.* London: Faber, 1948.

LiDonnici, Lynn. "The images of artemis ephesia and greco-roman worship: A reconsideration." *Harvard Theological Review,* 85 (4) (1992): pp. 389-415.

Marshark, Alexander. *The Roots of Civilization: The Cognitive Beginnings of Man's First Art, Symbol, and Notation.* New York: McGraw-Hill, 1972.

Miles, Margaret. "The virgin's one bare breast: Female nudity and religious meaning in Tuscan early Renaissance culture." *The Female Body in Western Culture,* Ed. Susan Suleiman. Cambridge: Harvard University Press, 1986, pp. 193-208.

Moon, Beverly, Ed. Archive for Research in Archetypal Symbolism. *An Encyclopedia of Archtypal Symbolism.* Boston: Sambala, 1991.

Neumann, Erich. *The Great Mother.* Trans. Ralph Manheim. Princeton, NJ: Princeton University Press, 1963.

Sanday, Peggy Reeves. *Female Power and Male Dominance.* Cambridge: MA. Cambridge University Press, 1981.

Schultz, Bernice Engle. "The Amazons in ancient Greece." *Psychoanalytic Quarterly,* 11 (1942): pp. 512-554.

Sjöö, Monica, and Barbara Mor. *The Great Cosmic Mother.* San Francisco: Harper and Row, 1987.

Tran, Tam Tinh. "Isis lactans: Corpus des monuments Greco-Romains d'Isis Allaitant" *EPRO 37,* (1973): pp. 1-21.

Warner, Marina. *Alone of All Her Sex: The Myth and the Cult of the Virgin Mary.* New York, Vintage Books, 1983.

Warner, Marina. *Monuments & Maidens: The Allegory of the Female Form.* New York: Atheneum, 1985.

Witt, R. E. *Isis in the Greco-Roman World.* Ithaca, NY: Cornell University Press, 1971.

Chapter 11

Akre, James. Infant Nutrition Unit, World Health Organization. Personal communication. July 21, 1997.

Baldwin, Elizabeth. "Breastfeeding and the law." *La Leche League.* 2 p. Online. Internet. April 15, 1997.

Baldwin, Elizabeth. "A current summary of breast-feeding legislation in the United States." *La Leche League.* 4 p. Online. Internet. April 15, 1997.

Baldwin, Elizabeth, JD. Personal interview. April 18, 1997.

Dettwyler, Katherine. Associate Professor of Anthropology, Texas A&M University. Personal interview. April 30, 1997.

Dettwyler, Katherine. *Dancing Skeletons: Life and Death in West Africa.* Prospect Heights, IL: Waveland, 1994.

Dettwyler, Katherine A., and Patricia Stuart-Macadam, Eds. *Breast-feeding: Biocultural Perspectives.* Hawthoren, NY: Aldine de Gruyter, 1995.

Hochswender, Woody. "Tempest in a B-cup." *Esquire,* (December, 1993): pp. 119-120.

Rohter, Larry. "Florida approves public breast-feeding." *The New York Times,* March 4, 1993: A8.

Sosnow, Kayla. "Legal system battles threat of bare-breasted woman." *Iguana,* (January, 1997): pp. 20-24.

Sosnow, Kayla. Top Free advocate. Personal Interview. June 6, 1997.

Index

Order Your Own Copy of
This Important Book for Your Personal Library!

BREASTS
The Women's Perspective on an American Obsession

_____ in hardbound at $39.95 (ISBN: 0-7890-0422-4)

_____ in softbound at $17.95 (ISBN: 1-56023-927-1)

COST OF BOOKS_____

OUTSIDE USA/CANADA/
MEXICO: ADD 20%_____

POSTAGE & HANDLING_____
_(US: $3.00 for first book & $1.25
for each additional book)
Outside US: $4.75 for first book
& $1.75 for each additional book)_

SUBTOTAL_____

IN CANADA: ADD 7% GST_____

STATE TAX_____
_(NY, OH & MN residents, please
add appropriate local sales tax)_

FINAL TOTAL_____
_(If paying in Canadian funds,
convert using the current
exchange rate. UNESCO
coupons welcome.)_

☐ **BILL ME LATER:** ($5 service charge will be added)
(Bill-me option is good on US/Canada/Mexico orders only;
not good to jobbers, wholesalers, or subscription agencies.)

☐ Check here if billing address is different from
shipping address and attach purchase order and
billing address information.

Signature_____

☐ **PAYMENT ENCLOSED: $**_____

☐ **PLEASE CHARGE TO MY CREDIT CARD.**

☐ Visa   ☐ MasterCard   ☐ AmEx   ☐ Discover

Account # _____

Exp. Date _____

Signature _____

Prices in US dollars and subject to change without notice.

NAME _____

INSTITUTION _____

ADDRESS _____

CITY _____

STATE/ZIP _____

COUNTRY _____ COUNTY (NY residents only) _____

TEL _____ FAX _____

E-MAIL_____
May we use your e-mail address for confirmations and other types of information? ☐ Yes   ☐ No

Order From Your Local Bookstore or Directly From
The Haworth Press, Inc.
10 Alice Street, Binghamton, New York 13904-1580 • USA
TELEPHONE: 1-800-HAWORTH (1-800-429-6784) / Outside US/Canada: (607) 722-5857
FAX: 1-800-895-0582 / Outside US/Canada: (607) 772-6362
E-mail: getinfo@haworth.com
PLEASE PHOTOCOPY THIS FORM FOR YOUR PERSONAL USE.

BOF96

DEMCO